مجالس شهر رمضان

sittings
DURING THE BLESSED MONTH OF
RAMAḌĀN

SHAYKH MUHAMMAD BIN SĀLIH
AL-UTHAYMĪN

© **Riwâyah Publishing**, A Product of **RiMarket.Net**, The World's Provider of Arabic Books

No part of this book may be reproduced in any form without written permission from **RiMarket.Net**, except if it is being copied for the purpose of spreading authentic knowledge and not to sell. In such a case, we encourage everyone to convey the statements of Allâh, His Messenger (ﷺ), and the explanations of the Trustworthy People of Islâmic Legislative Knowledge. For surely the success is with Allâh.

First Edition: رَجَب Rajab 1434/May 2013
ISBN Number: 978-0-9846600-4-9
Cover Design by: Usûl Design/usuldesign@gmail.com
Translation: Abûl Uthaymîn Nûh bin 'Abdullâh Al-Ghânî
Formatting & Editing: Abû Nûh bin Shamsuddîn
Riwâyah Publishing Address:
924 Bergen Avenue, 322 PMB
Jersey City, New Jersey, USA 07306
Website: www.rimarket.net
Text us at. 973.332.3345
E. admin@rimarket.net

May Allâh, the Most High, reward everyone who assisted in this humble effort. We ask Allâh by His Beautiful Names and Lofty Attributes to allow this book to be knowledge that the people will benefit from until the Day of Judgment.

Printed in the United States of America

فِهْرِس

The Author's Introduction	5
The First Sitting	6
The Second Sitting	14
The Third Sitting	22
The Fourth Sitting: The Ruling of Standing in Prayer during the Evenings of Ramadân	31
The Fifth Sitting: The Virtues of Reciting the Qur'ân and Its Types	42
The Sixth Sitting: The Categories of People Pertaining to Fasting	53
The Seventh Sitting	62
The Eighth Sitting: The Remaining Categories of People Pertaining to Fasting and the Ruling of Making up the Fast	71
The Ninth Sitting: The Wisdoms of Fasting	81
The Tenth Sitting: The Etiquettes of the Compulsory Fast	88
The Eleventh Sitting: The Recommended Etiquettes of Fasting	99
The Twelfth Sitting: The Second Category of Recitation of the Qur'an	109
The Thirteenth Sitting: The Etiquettes of Reciting the Qur'ân	118
The Fourteenth Sitting:	135
The Fifteenth Sitting: The Conditions that Must be Fulfilled in order for something to actually break the fast & The things that are permissible for the fasting person to do	144
The Sixteenth Sitting: Regarding Alms giving	153
The Seventeenth Sitting: Those Entitled to Receive the Zakât	163
The Eighteenth Sitting: The Battle of Badr	174
The Nineteenth Sitting: The Battle of the Meccan Conquest	182
The Twentieth Sitting: The Means of True Victory	190
The Twenty First Sitting: The Virtues of Last Ten Days of Ramadân	201
The Twenty Second Sitting: Striving Hard in the Last Ten Days and in the Night of Qadar	210

The Twenty Third Sitting: The Description of the Paradise (May Allâh Make Us Amongst from its Dwellers)..220

The Twenty Fourth Sitting: The Description of the People of Paradise (May Allâh make us among them, with His Bounty and Kindness)............................235

The Twenty Fifth Sitting: The Description of the Hell-Fire (May Allâh Protect Us From It)..247

The Twenty Sixth Sitting: Things that lead to the Hellfire..................................264

The Twenty Seventh Sitting: The Second Category of Things which Lead an Individual to Enter the Hell-Fire (Temporarily)..278

The Twenty Eighth Sitting: The Zakât of Fitr..289

The Twenty Ninth Sitting: Repentance..300

The Thirtieth Sitting: Pertaining to the End of Ramadân..................................310

مُقَدِّمَة

The Author's Introduction

In the name of Allâh, the Most Merciful, the One Who Bestows His Mercy upon others, all Praise is due to Allâh. We thank Him, we seek His aid, we ask for His forgiveness, and we repent to Him. We seek refuge with Allâh from the evil of our own souls and from the evil of our shortcomings. Whomsoever Allâh (ﷻ) has guided none can lead astray; and whosoever Allâh (ﷻ) has misguided no one can bring him back to the (straight) path. I further bear witness that none has the right to be worshiped except Allâh alone. (He is) without a partner. And I testify that Muhammad is His slave and His Messenger. May Allâh (ﷻ) shower His Mercy and Blessings on him, his family members, his Companions, and whoever follows their footsteps till the Day of Judgment.

To proceed: [that which is between your hands oh reader] are sittings for the Blessed Month of Ramadân that contain many [legislative] rulings concerning fasting, the night prayers, almsgiving, and some other suitable issues for this Blessed Month of Ramadân. I compiled these issues to address them in the day sessions or the night sessions. I have selected speeches of these sessions from the book (entitled) <u>Pleasing the Eyes of Those who can See with the Summarization of the Book of Insight</u> and I have adjusted what is needed to be adjusted from that book. I have mentioned in this book many rules and etiquettes relating to this Blessed Month because of the people's need for these rulings. And I have named this book <u>Sittings During the Blessed Month of Ramadân</u>.

This book was printed several times, and then I later decided to comment on it in a summarized manner and then emanate its narrations. (I decided) to add what I thought was needed to be added, and to delete whatever was unnecessary, which is very seldom. I ask Allâh (ﷻ) to make our deeds sincerely for Him Alone and to make [this work] beneficial for the people. Verily He is the Most Generous, the Most Bounteous.

رَمَضَان Sittings During the Blessed Month of Ramaḍān

المَجلِسُ الأوَّلُ
The First Sitting

All praise is due to Allâh, the One who created and originated. He created water and soil. He originated everything and spread them (about). The crawling of the black ant in the darkness of the night is not hidden from His Sight. The smallest atom in the heaven(s) or the earth is not hidden from His knowledge.

﴿ لَهُۥ مَا فِى ٱلسَّمَٰوَٰتِ وَمَا فِى ٱلۡأَرۡضِ وَمَا بَيۡنَهُمَا وَمَا تَحۡتَ ٱلثَّرَىٰ ۝ وَإِن تَجۡهَرۡ بِٱلۡقَوۡلِ فَإِنَّهُۥ يَعۡلَمُ ٱلسِّرَّ وَأَخۡفَىٰ ۝ ٱللَّهُ لَآ إِلَٰهَ إِلَّا هُوَ ۖ لَهُ ٱلۡأَسۡمَآءُ ٱلۡحُسۡنَىٰ ۝ ﴾

"To Him belongs all that is in the heavens, all that is on the earth, all that is between them, and all that is under the soil. If you speak aloud, then verily, He [Allâh] knows the secret and that which is yet more hidden. None deserves to be worshipped but He, to Him belongs the Most Beautiful of Names" [Taha:6-8]

He created Ādam, tested him, chose him, accepted his repentance, and (then) guided him (aright). He sent Nûh, who built the Ark by Allâh's command, and sailed. He saved Al-Khalîl, and that is Ibrâhîm, from the burning fire, and its heat turned cool and peaceful for him. So take a lesson from what happened. Then He gave Mûsa nine clear signs, but Pharaoh still persisted in his arrogance and did not pay heed to them. He strengthened 'Isâ with miracles that amazed the creatures. He sent down the Book to Muhammad (ﷺ), in it are clear signs and guidance.

I thank Him for His bounties that reach us constantly, and I send peace and salutations upon His Messenger Muhammad (ﷺ) who was sent from the Mother of the cities [Mecca]. (Likewise, may the peace and blessings) be upon his companion, Abû Bakr, (ﷺ) who was with him in the cave, upon 'Umar who had an inspiring opinion that was fortified by his Lord, upon 'Uthmân, the husband of (the Prophet's) two daughters. (Indeed) this is not a fabricated story. And (I send peace and salutations) upon the son of (the Prophet's) uncle (i.e. the Prophet's cousin 'Ali ﷺ), the ocean of knowledge, the brave lion, and upon the rest of his companions whose virtues spread throughout the world. May the peace and blessings of Allâh be upon all of them.

O people! Verily we are shaded by a blessed month and a tremendous season in which Allâh (ﷻ) ennobles the reward and gives generously. (He) opens the doors of good for those who desire good: it is the month of goodness and blessings. It is the month of scholarship and gifts:

﴿ شَهْرُ رَمَضَانَ ٱلَّذِىٓ أُنزِلَ فِيهِ ٱلْقُرْءَانُ هُدًى لِّلنَّاسِ وَبَيِّنَٰتٍ مِّنَ ٱلْهُدَىٰ وَٱلْفُرْقَانِ ﴾ (١٨٥)

"The Month of Ramadân in which was revealed the Qur'ân, a guidance for mankind and clear proofs for the guidance and the Criterion (between right and wrong)."[Al-Baqarah: 185]

It is a month that is surrounded with mercy, forgiveness, and salvation from the Hell-Fire. Its beginning is mercy, its middle is forgiveness, and its end is a salvation from the Hell-Fire. There are famous prophetic narrations highlighting the virtues of Ramadân, and there are numerous reports pertaining to the virtues of this month. It is reported in the two authentic books of Al-Imâm Al-Bukhârî and Muslim from the narrations of Abû Hurayrah (ﷺ) that the Prophet (ﷺ) said:

إِذَا جَاءَ رمضانُ فُتِّحَتْ أبوابُ الجَنَّةِ، وغُلِّقَتْ أبوابُ النار، وصُفِّدتِ الشَّياطينُ

"When Ramadân arrives, the doors of the heavens are opened, the doors of the Hell-Fire are closed, and the devils are shackled."
[Collected by Al-Bukhârî and Muslim]

The doors of Paradise will be opened only because of the multiplicity of the righteous deeds that are performed in this blessed month, likewise (as a means) of encouraging the slaves to increase in their good deeds. The doors of the Hell-fire will be closed because during this month, sins will be so far away from the believers. The devils will be chained so that they will not have the opportunity to do what they used to do (outside of) the month of Ramadân.

Al-Imâm Ahmad reported (in his Musnad) from Abû Hurayrah (ﷺ) that the Messenger of Allâh (ﷺ) said:

أُعْطِيَتْ أُمَّتِي خَمْسَ خِصَالٍ في رمضانَ لَمْ تُعْطَهُنَّ أُمَّةٌ من الأُمَمِ قَبْلَها؛ خُلُوفُ فَمِ الصائمِ أطيبُ عند الله من ريح المسْك، وتستغفرُ لهم الملائكةُ حتى يُفطروا، ويُزيِّنُ اللهُ كلَّ يومٍ جنتَهُ ويقول: يُوشِكُ عبادي الصالحون أن يُلْقوا عنهم المؤونة والأذى ويصيروا إليك، وتُصفَّدُ فيه مَرَدَةُ الشياطينِ فلا يخلُصون إلى ما كانوا يخلُصون إليه في غيرِهِ، ويُغْفَرُ لهم في آخر ليلة، قِيلَ يا رسول الله أهِيَ ليلةُ القَدْرِ؟ قال: لاَ ولكنَّ العاملَ إنما يُوَفَّى أجْرَهُ إذا قضى عَمَلَه

"My Ummah has been given five qualities in Ramadân that were not given to the nations before them: the 'Khulûf (i.e. the breath)' from the one who fasts, with Allâh, is better than the fragrance of musk. (Secondly) the Angels seek 'istighfâr (i.e forgiveness) for the (believers) until they break their fast. (Thirdly,) Allâh (ﷻ) beautifies His Paradise every day and says: My pious slaves are about to throw the burden and the harm off them and turn to you (i.e. Paradise). (Fourthly) the devils will be chained so that they will not have the opportunity to do what they used to do (outside of) Ramadân. (Lastly) their sins will be forgiven at every last hour of the night. It is said: O messenger of Allâh do you mean the Night of Qadar? He said: no but every laborer receives the fruit of his labor upon the completion of his work."[Ahmad Shâkir graded its chain to be weak, Al-Albânî said its chain is very weak in Daî'f At-Targhîb. However some parts of the hadîth has corroborating text, as mentioned by Al-Uthaymîn in his Majmû']

The First Quality: The bad breath that comes from the mouth of the one who fasts is, with Allâh, like the fragrance of the musk. The word "khulûf with the vowel "a" or u" after the letter "khâ" refers to the bad breath that generates from the mouth of the one who fasts due to the emptiness of his stomach from food. This smell is disliked by the people, but with Allâh it is like the smell of musk. This is because it comes from (one being) obedient to Allâh and (from) worshiping Him (through fasting). And everything that occurs due to the worship of Allâh and His obedience, Allâh (ﷻ) replaces it with what is better. [Have you not pondered over the] martyr who is killed (fighting) in the way of Allâh, fighting to make the word of Allâh victorious. He will come on the Day of Judgment, blood flowing from his injuries, its color will be as red as the color of blood, but its smell will be like the scent of musk.

Likewise in Hajj, Allâh (ﷻ) vies the Angels in glory with the people of 'Arafah. And He will say to his Angels:

انْظُرُوا إلى عبادِي هؤلاء جاؤوني شُعْثاً غُبْراً

"Look at these slaves of mine, they came to me shaggy matted and dusty" [Reported by Ahmad and Ibn Hibbân. Al-Albânî graded it to be authentic in Sahîh At-Targhîb and Sahîh Al-Jâmi'. Al-Uthaymîn graded it authentic due to corroborating narrations]

Being shaggy matted and dusty in this occasion is beloved to Allâh because it occurs due to the (believers being) obedient to Allâh and adhering to His commands by abstaining from the prohibitions of the Ihrâm (i.e. when one enters into devotion of performing Hajj or 'Umrah) and leaving the luxurious life.

The Second Quality: The Angels ask forgiveness for them until they break their fast. The Angels are honorable slaves of Allâh, they do not disobey Allâh regarding what He has commanded them with and they do what they are commanded to do. Therefore, they deserve the honor of their supplication being accepted by their Lord, because He is the one who commanded them with that. Allâh (ﷻ) asks them to seek forgiveness for those who fast from this Ummah as a way of honoring them, and proving their dignity and the virtue of their fasting. The word "istigfâr" means to seek "magfirah", which is concealment of the sin in this world and (being pardoned from) the sin in the Hereafter. This is one of the highest demands and ultimate goals. For verily every son of Ādam is a sinner, they wrong themselves. As a result they are in constant need of Allâh's forgiveness.

The Third Quality: Allâh beautifies His Paradise every day and He will say: "**My righteous slaves will soon throw their burdens and the harm which they are experiencing and turn to you.**" So Allâh (ﷻ) beautifies His Paradise everyday to have it ready for His pious slaves, and to urge them upon doing good deeds that will help them acquire that Paradise. As He, the Glorified, states: "**My pious slaves shall soon throw the burden and harm off them,**" meaning the burden of this worldly life and its hardships. And (they) will turn towards doing the righteous deeds in which is their happiness in this world, in the Hereafter, and (a means for them) reaching the home of peace and dignity.

The Fourth Quality: The rebellious devils will be tied down with chains and collars so they will not be able to reach the righteous slaves, in order to misguide them from the truth or prevent them from doing good deeds. This is from Allâh's support of His pious slaves, by detaining their enemy (Iblîs) who invites his party to be from the dwellers of the Hell-Fire.

This is the reason why you find that in this month of Ramadân, more than any other month, many pious people increase in their (worship) and try to stay away from doing evil.

The Fifth Quality: Allâh (ﷻ) forgives the Muslims on the last night of this month: and that is if they carry out what is upon them to do in this blessed month of fasting, night-prayer, and so on. He (ﷻ), out of His Bounty, will give them their reward in full at the completion of their deeds. Because the laborer gets the compensation of his work after he completes it.

Allâh, the Glorified, has bestowed on His slaves the virtue of obtaining this reward from three aspects:

The First Aspect: He has legislated for them some righteous deeds that lead to their sins being forgiven and their ranks being raised. Had it not been because He [Allâh] has legislated these acts of worship on them they would not have worshiped Allâh with them. That is because worship can only be derived from the revelations of Allâh revealed to His Messengers. For this reason, Allâh denounced those who legislate besides Him, and He (even) considered that as a form of associating partners with Him. As He, the Most High, stated:

﴿ أَمْ لَهُمْ شُرَكَٰٓؤُاْ شَرَعُواْ لَهُم مِّنَ ٱلدِّينِ مَا لَمْ يَأْذَنۢ بِهِ ٱللَّهُ وَلَوْلَا كَلِمَةُ ٱلْفَصْلِ لَقُضِيَ بَيْنَهُمْ وَإِنَّ ٱلظَّٰلِمِينَ لَهُمْ عَذَابٌ أَلِيمٌ ﴿٢١﴾ ﴾

"Or have they partners (with Allâh – false gods) who have instituted for them a religion which Allâh has not ordained? And had it not been for a decisive Word (gone forth already), the matter would have been judged between them. And verily, for the Thâlimûn (polytheists and wrong doers) there is a painful torment". [Ash-Shûrâ: 21]

The Second Aspect: He granted them the success to do the righteous deeds. For verily, many people have deserted these (noble acts of worship). Had it not been for Allâh's Help and Him (granting them) success, they would not have carried out these (righteous deeds). Therefore to Allâh belongs all bounty and favor. Allâh (ﷻ) states:

﴿ يَمُنُّونَ عَلَيْكَ أَنْ أَسْلَمُوا قُل لَّا تَمُنُّوا عَلَيَّ إِسْلَامَكُم بَلِ اللَّهُ يَمُنُّ عَلَيْكُمْ أَنْ هَدَاكُمْ لِلْإِيمَانِ إِن كُنتُمْ صَادِقِينَ ﴿١٧﴾ ﴾

"They regard as favor to you (O Muhammad [ﷺ]) that they have embraced Islâm. Say: "Count not your Islâm as a favor to me. Nay, but Allâh has conferred a favor upon you that He has guided you to the Faith if you indeed are true" [Al-Hujurât: 17]

The Third Aspect: Out of His bounty, He multiples the reward. Every good deed will be multiplied by ten, to seven hundred, and (even) more than that. Therefore the bounty and favor is from Allâh, and the reward is from Him as well. Thus all praise belongs to Allâh, Lord of the worlds.

O my brothers, reaching the month of Ramadân is indeed a great blessing from Allâh, (which He bestowed) upon the one who reached it and gave it its due right by turning towards Allâh with repentance from (ones) sins and by being obedient to Allâh. (Likewise Ramadân is a blessing for the one who) was previously negligent of Allâh and then (became one who) remembers his

Lord. (Ramadân is also a blessing) for the one who was far away from Allâh and then drew closer to Him.

> **O he who committing sins did not suffice him in Rajab**
> **Until he disobeyed his Lord in Sha'bân**
> **The month of fasting has arrived to you after them**
> **So do not turn it into a month of disobedience as well**
> **Recite the Qur'ân and glorify the praises of your Lord**
> **For verily it is the month of Qur'ân and glorification**
> **How many have you known who fasted with you in the past?**
> **From among your family members, neighbors and brothers**
> **Death has perished them and spared you after them**
> **How close is the farness from the approaching one!**
> [From Ibn Rajab's Latâif Al-Mâ'rif page 282]

O Allâh we ask You to awaken us from the recumbence of negligence and grant us success to increase in righteousness before passing away. (O Allâh) sustain us [by allowing us to] take advantage of our time at times of respite. And forgive us, and our parents and all the Muslims with Your Mercy; You are the Most Merciful. And May the peace and blessings of Allâh be upon our Prophet Muhammad (), upon his family, and his companions in general.

المَجْلِسُ الثَّانِي
The Second Sitting

All praise belongs to Allâh, the Most Kind, the Most Merciful, Owner of Bounty, the Self-Sufficient, the Owner of a Powerful Sovereign, the Patient, the Most Bounteous, the Most Gracious, the Most Beneficent, He is the First, there is nothing before Him. [He is] the Last, there is nothing after Him. [He is] the Most High; there is nothing above Him. [He is] the Most Near, nothing is nearer than Him. His Knowledge encompasses what is happening and what has already occurred. He elevates and humiliates whom He wills. He withholds and gives; and He does what He wants [all based on] His Wisdom. Every day He is (engaged) in some affair. He stabilized the earth with mountains. He sends down rain from the heavy clouds to revive the land. He decreed death on whomever lives on [the earth] in order to recompense the evil doers according to what they did and compensate [the righteous ones] with a fine [reward]. I praise Him upon His beautiful and perfect attributes, and I thank Him for His out flowing bounties. And it is with being grateful to Him that His gifts and bounties increase.

I bear witness that there is no deity that has the right to be worshiped but Allâh Alone, without a partner, the King who rewards everyone according to what they do. I also bear witness that Muhammad is His slave and His Messenger, the one who was sent to both mankind and jinn. May the peace and blessings of Allâh be upon him, his family members, his Companions and whoever follows their footsteps till the Day of Judgment.

O My Brothers! Know that fasting is one of the best acts of worship, and greatest acts of obedience. There are many reports and prophetic narrations that mention the virtues of fasting. From among the virtues of fasting is that Allâh (ﷻ) has prescribed it on every nation, as He (ﷻ) states:

Sittings During the Blessed Month of Ramaḍān رَمَضَان

$$\text{﴿ يَٰٓأَيُّهَا ٱلَّذِينَ ءَامَنُواْ كُتِبَ عَلَيۡكُمُ ٱلصِّيَامُ كَمَا كُتِبَ عَلَى ٱلَّذِينَ مِن قَبۡلِكُمۡ لَعَلَّكُمۡ تَتَّقُونَ ﴾ (١٨٣)}$$

"O you who believe! Observing (the Fast) is prescribed for you as it was prescribed for those before you, that you may become Al-Muttaqûn (the pious)" [Al-Baqarah: 183]

[The fact that Allâh obligated] fasting upon every nation, indicates the great reward that is found (by observing it).

From among the virtues of fasting during [the month of] Ramadân is that it is a reason for our sins to be forgiven and for our shortcomings to be expiated. As it is reported in Al-Bukhârî and Muslim, that the Prophet (ﷺ) said:

مَنْ صَامَ رمضان إيماناً واحْتِساباً غُفِرَ لَهُ ما تقدَّم مِن ذنبه

"Whoever fasts the month of Ramadân sincerely to Allâh while seeking the reward of it will have his previous sins forgiven." [Collected by Al-Bukhârî and Muslim]

Meaning: [the fasting person] must be pleased with the obligation of fasting during the month of Ramadân while seeking the reward of his fast with his Lord, without having any dislike in his heart with its obligation or any doubt in its reward. If this happened then Allâh will forgive his previous sins.

It is also mentioned in <u>Saḥîḥ Muslim</u> from the narrations of Abû Hurayrah (ﷺ) who said that the Prophet (ﷺ) said:

الصَّلواتُ الخَمْسُ والجمعةُ إلى الجمعةِ ورمضانُ إلى رمضانَ مُكفِّراتٌ ما بينهُنَّ إذا اجْتُنبت الْكَبائرِ

"Performing the five daily prayers, establishing the Friday congregational prayer constantly, and fasting from one Ramadân to another Ramadân expiates what is between them as long as the major sins are abstained from." [Collected by Muslim]

From among the virtues of fasting is that [the] reward is unspecified. Rather Allâh (ﷻ) gives [those who observe the fast] their reward in full without reckoning. It is also reported in Sahîh Al-Bukhârî and Muslim from the narrations of Abû Hurayrah (ﷺ) that the Messenger of Allâh (ﷺ) said:

قال الله تعالى: كُلُّ عَمَلِ ابنِ آدمَ لَهُ إلاَّ الصومَ فإنَّهُ لي وأنا أجزي بهِ. والصِّيامُ جُنَّةٌ فإذا كان يومُ صومِ أحدِكم فلاَ يرفُثْ ولا يصْخَبْ فإنْ سابَّهُ أحدٌ أو قاتله فَلْيقلْ إني صائمٌ، والَّذي نَفْسُ محمدٍ بيدهِ لَخُلُوفُ فمِ الصَّائمِ أطيبُ عند اللهِ مِن ريحِ المسكِ، للصائمِ فَرْحَتانِ يَفْرَحُهما؛ إذَا أفْطَرَ فرحَ بفطرهِ، وإذَا لَقِيَ ربَّهُ فرحَ بصومِهِ

"Allâh (ﷻ) said: 'Every act of the son of Ādam is his except for fasting; for indeed it is for Me and I will give the reward of it.' Fasting is a salvation from the Hell-Fire. Therefore if one of you is fasting he should not be obscene in his language nor indulge in unnecessary argument. If someone insults him or tries to pick a fight with him, he should say to that individual: 'I am fasting.'"

"I swear by Him in whose Hand is Muhammad's soul, the bad breath from the mouth of the individual who fasts is, with Allâh, better than the fragrance of the musk. The one who fasts has two occasions of happiness, the first one is his happiness when he breaks his fast, and the second happiness is when he receives his reward with his Lord." [Collected by Al-Bukhârî and Muslim]

In another narration of Al-Imâm Muslim there is the wording:

كُلُّ عملِ ابنِ آدمَ لَهُ يُضَاعَفُ الحَسَنَةُ بعَشرِ أمثالِها إلى سَبْعِمائةِ ضِعْفٍ، قَالَ اللهُ تعالى إلاَّ الصَومَ فإنه لِي وأنَا أجْزِي به يَدَعُ شهْوَتَه وطعامه من أجْلِي

"Every act of the son of Ādam is His, every good deed will be multiplied for him ten to seven hundred times, except fasting, for verily it is Mine and I give the reward for it. The slave restrains his sexual desire(s) and food for My Sake"

<u>This Great Hadîth indicates the virtues of fasting from many aspects:</u>

The First Aspect: Allâh (ﷻ) has chosen fasting for Himself besides the other acts of worship, and this is only because of the nobility of fasting with Allâh, and because of His love for this worship. Likewise (fasting) proves the sincerity of the slave with His Lord (ﷻ). That is because fasting is a secret act of worship between the slave and his Lord. None can witness it except Allâh. Sometimes the one who fasts may be in seclusion far away from the people and can do what is forbidden for the one who fasts to do, but he will refrain himself from it out of fear of Allâh and his hope in His reward. He knows that he has a Lord that can see him in his seclusion. Thereupon, Allâh (ﷻ) thanked him for his sincerity and chose to reward the one who fasts for his fasting besides the rest of the acts of worship. That is why Allâh (ﷻ) said: **"He leaves his sexual desire(s) and his food for *My* sake."** The benefit of this virtue appears as well on the Day of Judgment as Ibn 'Uyaynah, may Allâh have mercy on him, said: **"On the Day of Judgment, Allâh will reckon His slave and will pay his grievance from his deeds until when all his deeds are gone except fasting, Allâh will pay his grievance for him and grant him paradise with his fasting."** [Reported in <u>At-Targhîb wa At-Tarhîb</u>]

The Second Aspect: Allâh (ﷻ) said regarding fasting: *"I give the reward of fasting"*. He has attributed the reward of fasting to Himself, that is because good deeds are multiplied by numbers, one good deed is multiplied by ten to seven hundred and more, but as for fasting, Allâh (ﷻ) has attributed its reward to Himself without the consideration of a number. Allâh, the Most High is the Most Generous, the Most Bounteous, and of course the greatness of gifts is based on the greatness of the giver. Therefore the reward of fasting will be very great without a limit.

Fasting is to exercise patience upon the obedience of Allâh, being patient with Allâh's set limits, and being patient upon the harms that are written on you of hunger, thirst, and weakness in one's body and soul. The three types of patience are all found in the one who fasts. Therefore the one who fasts qualifies to be (considered) amongst the patient. Allâh (ﷻ) said:

﴿ إِنَّمَا يُوَفَّى ٱلصَّٰبِرُونَ أَجْرَهُم بِغَيْرِ حِسَابٍ ۝ ﴾

"Verily, the patient will have their reward without measure." [Az-Zumar: 10]

The Third Aspect: Fasting is a protection and a veil that shields you from idle-talk and ill-words. That is why the Prophet (ﷺ) said:

فَإِذَا كَانَ يَوْمُ صَوْمِ أَحَدِكُمْ فَلَا يَرْفُثْ وَلَا يَصْخَبْ

"When one of you is fasting he should not say bad words or argue" [Collected by Al-Bukhârî]

Likewise, fasting protects a person from the Hell-Fire, as it is narrated by Al-Imâm Ahmad in his Musnad with a sound chain of narration from the narrations of Jâbir (ﷺ): *"Fasting is a* protection; with it a slave is protected from the Hell-Fire"[Al-Albânî graded it to be Hasan in Sahîh Al-Jâmi']

The Fourth Aspect: The bad breath from the one who fasts is better than the smell of musk with Allâh, because it is from the traces of fasting. Due to that it is beloved to Allâh (ﷻ) more than the smell of musk. If this indicates anything, it indicates the magnitude of fasting with Allâh. Even the thing that is disliked by the people and is disgusting to them, with Allâh it is beloved because it derives from the (slaves) obedience to Allâh by way of fasting.

The Fifth Aspect: the one who fasts will have two happy occasions: the first is when he breaks his fast, and the second is when he meets his Lord. As for his happiness (at the time of) breaking his fast, (this includes) him being happy with what Allâh (ﷻ) blessed him with by allowing him to carry out the worship of fasting which is one of the best of the good deeds. There are many people who were deprived of this opportunity, so they did not fast.

Likewise the one who fasts becomes happy with what Allâh (ﷻ) makes lawful for him after breaking his fasts of food, drink, and intimacy which were (all) previously forbidden to him at the time of his fast.

As for his happiness when meeting his Lord; that is when he sees the reward of his fasting with Allâh (ﷻ) available and complete at the time when he is in desperate need of (this reward).

This is when it will be said: **"Where are those who fast (in the worldly life)?" Let them enter Paradise from the door of Ar-Rayyân, which no one enters other than them."** [Collected by Al-Bukhârî]

رَمَضَان Sittings During the Blessed Month of Ramaḍān

This narration also directs the one who fasts not to retaliate on those who insult them or pick a fight with them and not to weaken himself in the presence of the one who does that by keeping silent. Rather he should advise him and let him know that he is fasting, (as a way of letting) him know that the nobility of fasting is what prevents him from taking revenge and not because he is weak. (At that point) the insults and fighting will stop:

﴿ وَلَا تَسْتَوِى ٱلْحَسَنَةُ وَلَا ٱلسَّيِّئَةُ ٱدْفَعْ بِٱلَّتِى هِىَ أَحْسَنُ فَإِذَا ٱلَّذِى بَيْنَكَ وَبَيْنَهُۥ عَدَٰوَةٌ كَأَنَّهُۥ وَلِىٌّ حَمِيمٌ ۝ وَمَا يُلَقَّىٰهَآ إِلَّا ٱلَّذِينَ صَبَرُواْ وَمَا يُلَقَّىٰهَآ إِلَّا ذُو حَظٍّ عَظِيمٍ ۝ ﴾

"The good deed and the evil deed cannot be equal. Repel (the evil) with one which is better (i.e. Allâh orders the faithful believers to be patient at the time of anger, and to excuse those who treat them badly) then verily he, between whom and you there was enmity, (will become) as though he was a close friend But none is granted it (the above quality) except those who are patient – and none is granted it except the owner of the great portion (of happiness in the Hereafter, i.e., Paradise, and of a high moral character) in this world. [Fussilat: 34-35]

From among the virtues of fasting is that it intercedes for those who fast on the Day of Judgment. As it is narrated on the authority of 'Abdullâh bin 'Amr (ﷺ) that the Messenger of Allâh (ﷺ) said:

الصِّيَامُ وَالْقُرْآنُ يَشْفَعَانِ لِلْعَبْدِ يَوْمَ الْقِيَامَةِ، يَقُولُ الصِّيَامُ: أَيْ رَبِّ مَنَعْتُهُ الطَّعَامَ وَالشَّهْوَةَ فَشَفِّعْنِي فِيهِ، وَيَقُولُ الْقُرْآنُ مَنَعْتُهُ النَّوْمَ بِاللَّيْلِ فَشَفِّعْنِي فِيهِ، قَالَ فَيُشَفَّعَانِ

"The Qur'ân and fasting will intercede for the slave on the Day of Judgment. Fasting will say: 'O my Lord I prevented him from his food and his desire(s) therefore accept my intercession for him. The Qur'ân will say: 'I prevented him from his sleep in the night, therefore accept my intercession for him.' He said: 'then intercession will be granted for them (Fasting and Qur'ân).'"
[Ahmad Shâkir graded this narration to be authentic in his checking of Musnad of Ahmad, Al-Albânî graded it to be Hasan Sahîh in Sahîh At-Targhîb. **Note:** Muqbil declared it to be weak in Ash-Shafâ'h.]

O my brothers! Know that the virtues of fasting cannot be attained until the slave establishes the etiquettes of fasting. Therefore, strive hard in perfecting your fast and in preserving its boundaries. Turn to your Lord with repentance from your sins and your remissness in that.

O Allâh preserve our fast, and let it intercede for us. (O Allâh) forgive us, our parents, and all the Muslims. O Allâh! Send your peace and salutation upon our Messenger Muhammad (), his family members, and his companions.

المَجْلِسُ الثَّالِثُ
The Third Sitting

All praise is due to Allâh, the One Who there is no withholder of what He has given, there is no giver of what He has withheld. Obedience to Him is the best gain of the laborers and fearing Him is the highest kinship for the pious. He prepared the hearts of His (pious believers) with faith, and He eases for them the difficulties (that are obstacles in the way of being obedient to Him). As a result they do not find any hardship in the path of His service. He predestined wretchedness on the wretched due to their deviation from the path; thus they fell in to perdition. They turned away from Him and disobeyed Him. Consequently He burnt them in a blazing fire. We thank Him for what He has given us from His bounty.

I bear witness that there is no deity that has the right to be worshiped but He alone. He crushed the disbelievers and defeated them. I bear witness that Muhammad is His slave and His Messenger, the one who was chosen by His Lord. May Allâh (ﷺ) shower His blessings on him, his companion Abû Bakr, the one who exceeded (the people) in virtues and rank, 'Umar, the one who the devil ran away from, 'Uthmân, the owner of two lights, the pious, the bashful, and on 'Alî, his cousin. (May Allâh shower His blessings) on the rest of (the Prophet's) companions, those who have achieved the highest status in the religion, and on those who follow their footsteps in a good manner as long as the sun rises and sets.

O My Brothers in Al-Islâm! Verily fasting during the month of Ramadân is one of the pillars of Al-Islâm and (one of) its great structures. Allâh (ﷺ) states:

Sittings During the Blessed Month of Ramaḍān رَمَضَان

$$\text{﴿ يَٰٓأَيُّهَا ٱلَّذِينَ ءَامَنُواْ كُتِبَ عَلَيۡكُمُ ٱلصِّيَامُ كَمَا كُتِبَ عَلَى ٱلَّذِينَ مِن قَبۡلِكُمۡ لَعَلَّكُمۡ تَتَّقُونَ ۝ أَيَّامٗا مَّعۡدُودَٰتٖۚ فَمَن كَانَ مِنكُم مَّرِيضًا أَوۡ عَلَىٰ سَفَرٖ فَعِدَّةٞ مِّنۡ أَيَّامٍ أُخَرَۚ وَعَلَى ٱلَّذِينَ يُطِيقُونَهُۥ فِدۡيَةٞ طَعَامُ مِسۡكِينٖۖ فَمَن تَطَوَّعَ خَيۡرٗا فَهُوَ خَيۡرٞ لَّهُۥۚ وَأَن تَصُومُواْ خَيۡرٞ لَّكُمۡ إِن كُنتُمۡ تَعۡلَمُونَ ۝ شَهۡرُ رَمَضَانَ ٱلَّذِيٓ أُنزِلَ فِيهِ ٱلۡقُرۡءَانُ هُدٗى لِّلنَّاسِ وَبَيِّنَٰتٖ مِّنَ ٱلۡهُدَىٰ وَٱلۡفُرۡقَانِۚ فَمَن شَهِدَ مِنكُمُ ٱلشَّهۡرَ فَلۡيَصُمۡهُۖ وَمَن كَانَ مَرِيضًا أَوۡ عَلَىٰ سَفَرٖ فَعِدَّةٞ مِّنۡ أَيَّامٍ أُخَرَۗ يُرِيدُ ٱللَّهُ بِكُمُ ٱلۡيُسۡرَ وَلَا يُرِيدُ بِكُمُ ٱلۡعُسۡرَ وَلِتُكۡمِلُواْ ٱلۡعِدَّةَ وَلِتُكَبِّرُواْ ٱللَّهَ عَلَىٰ مَا هَدَىٰكُمۡ وَلَعَلَّكُمۡ تَشۡكُرُونَ ۝ ﴾}$$

"O you who have believed, decreed upon you is fasting as it was decreed upon those before you that you may become righteous [Fasting for] a limited number of days. So whoever among you is ill or on a journey [during them] - then an equal number of days [are to be made up]. And upon those who are able [to fast, but with hardship] - a ransom [as substitute] of feeding a poor person [each day]. And whoever volunteers excess - it is better for him. But to fast is best for you, if you only knew. "The month of Ramaḍân [is that] in which was revealed the Qur'ân, a guidance for the people and clear proofs of guidance and criterion. So whoever sights [the new moon of] the month, let him fast it; and whoever is ill or on a journey - then an equal number of other days. Allâh intends for you ease and does not intend for you hardship and [wants] for you to complete the period and to glorify Allâh for that [to] which He has guided you; and perhaps you will be grateful" [Al-Baqarah: 183-185]

رَمَضَان Sittings During the Blessed Month of Ramaḍān

Also the Prophet (ﷺ) said:

بُنِيَ الإِسْلامُ عَلَى خَمْسٍ: شَهَادَةِ أَنْ لا إِلهَ إِلاَّ الله وأنَّ محمداً رسولُ الله، وإقامِ الصلاةِ، وإيتاءِ الزكاةِ، وحَجِّ الْبَيْتِ، وَصومِ رمضانَ

ولمسلم: وصومِ رمضانَ وَحَجِّ البيتِ

"Al-Islâm is built on five (matters): 'Testifying that none has the right to be worshiped but Allâh and that Muhammad is the Messenger of Allâh, establishing the prayer, almsgiving, performing pilgrimage to the sacred house of Allâh, and fasting [during the month of] Ramadân" [Collected by Al-Bukhârî]

In the reporting of Al-Imâm Muslim is the wording: "…Fasting Ramadân, and performing the Pilgrimage to the Sacred House of Allâh." [Collected by Muslim]

All the Muslims have agreed, without any doubt, that fasting is a legislated obligation upon every Muslim, and that it is among the things which are known in our religion by necessity. Therefore whoever rejects the obligation of fasting has indeed disbelieved. He will be asked to repent (by the authorized Muslim ruler). If he repents then he is safe, otherwise he will be killed as a disbeliever, an apostate. He is not washed or shrouded, and prayer is not performed over him. Mercy must not be asked for his soul, and his body must not be buried in the Muslim graveyard. Rather he must be buried far away from the people so that the people will not be harmed by his bad smell, and in order that his family will not be harmed by looking at (his dead corpse).

Fasting during the month of Ramadân was legislated in the second year of the Hijrah. Thus the Prophet (ﷺ) fasted for nine years before his death. The obligation of fasting took place in two stages:

The First Stage: The option of either fasting or feeding, while fasting was more virtuous than feeding.

The Second Stage: (Allâh) obligating upon every individual [to fast] without it being optional. It is mentioned in Sahîh Al-Bukhârî and Muslim from the narrations of Salamah bin Al-Akwa' (ﷺ) that he said: **"When this verse was revealed:**

$$﴿ وَعَلَى ٱلَّذِينَ يُطِيقُونَهُۥ فِدْيَةٌ طَعَامُ مِسْكِينٍ ﴾$$

'And upon those who are able [to fast, but with hardship] - a ransom [as substitute] of feeding a poor person [each day].' [Al-Baqarah: 184]

Some people would feed instead of fasting, until the verse that comes after it was revealed (abrogating the rule of the previous)." That is Allâh's statement:

$$﴿ فَمَن شَهِدَ مِنكُمُ ٱلشَّهْرَ فَلْيَصُمْهُ وَمَن كَانَ مَرِيضًا أَوْ عَلَىٰ سَفَرٍ فَعِدَّةٌ مِّنْ أَيَّامٍ أُخَرَ ﴾$$

"So whoever sights [the new moon of] the month, let him fast it; and whoever is ill or on a journey - then an equal number of other days." [Al-Baqarah: 185]

So Allâh (ﷺ) then made fasting obligatory upon every one, no longer optional.

[As for the time of the fast] it is not obligatory until after the sighting of the new moon is confirmed. Therefore we should not fast before the entering of the month, due to the Prophet's statement (ﷺ):

رَمَضَان Sittings During the Blessed Month of Ramaḍān

لَا يَتَقَدَّمَنَّ أَحَدُكم رمضانَ بصومِ يومٍ أَو يومينِ إِلَّا أَنْ يكونَ رجلٌ كان يصومُ صَوْمَهُ فَلْيَصُمْ ذَلِكَ الْيَوْمَ

"None of you should precede the month of Ramadân with a day of fasting or two, except an individual whose custom of fasting falls on that day (i.e supererogatory fasting), then he should fast that day." [Collected by Al-Bukhârî]

The entering of the Month of Ramadân is determined by one of two things:

The First: Sighting of the new moon, based on Allâh's statement:

﴿ فَمَن شَهِدَ مِنكُمُ ٱلشَّهْرَ فَلْيَصُمْهُ ﴾

"So whoever sights [the new moon of] the month, let him fast it." [Al-Baqarah:185]

The Prophet's Statement (ﷺ):

إِذَا رَأَيْتُمُ الهلالَ فصوموا

"Fast if you see the new moon" [Collected by Al-Bukhârî and Muslim]

It is not a condition that each and every one must see the moon. Rather, if a trustworthy person saw (the new moon), it is then obligatory for everyone to observe the fast.

The one who sighted the moon must fit [the following] conditions: 1. Puberty 2. Sanity 3. Al-Islâm 4. His information must be trusted based on his trustworthiness and his insight. But as for the one who did not reach puberty, his sighting will not be accepted, and if the sighting of the young ones is not accepted then the witness of the insane is worthier of being rejected. Likewise the sighting of the disbeliever will not be accepted due to the statement of the Prophet (ﷺ) which is narrated by Ibn Abbâs (رضي الله عنه) who said: **"A Bedouin came to the Prophet (ﷺ) and said: 'Verily I sighted the moon.' Then the Prophet (ﷺ) said to him: 'Do you testify that none has the right to be worshiped but Allâh?' He said: 'yes.' Then the Prophet said: 'Do you testify that Muhammad is the Messenger of Allâh?' He said: 'yes.' Then the Prophet (ﷺ) said: 'O Bilâl announce to the people to fast tomorrow.'"** [Graded to be weak by Al-Albânî in <u>Da'îf Abû Dâwûd</u>. Al-Uthaymîn declared it weak due to a disconnected chain. However it has a corroborating text with an authentic chain as mentioned by Al-Albânî in his comments on <u>At-Ta'lîqât Ar-Radiyah</u>]

Also the individual whose information is not trusted, because of the fact that he is known for lying, being hasty in making judgments, or he has weak eyesight: the entering of the month cannot be confirmed with the sighting of such an individual due to doubts in his truthfulness.

The sighting of one trustworthy Muslim is a sufficient testimony due to the statement of Ibn 'Umar (رضي الله عنه) who said:

تَرَاءَى الناسُ الهلالَ فأخْبَرتُ النبي صلى الله عليه وسلّم أنّي رأيتُهُ فصامَ وأمَرَ الناسَ بصيامِهِ

"People were trying to sight the moon for the month of Ramadân, and I saw it then informed the Prophet (ﷺ) that I have seen the moon. So the Prophet (ﷺ) fasted and commanded the people to fast." [Abû Dâwûd narrated this hadîth and said it is according to the conditions of Muslim. It has been graded authentic by Al-Albânî]

رَمَضَان Sittings During the Blessed Month of Ramaḍān

It is obligatory upon the one who sights the moon with certainty to inform those in authority. Likewise (is the case for the one who) sighted the moon of Shawwâl, and Dhûl-Hijjah, because the obligation of fasting, breaking the fast, and performing the pilgrimage are based on the sighting of the moon in these months. If an obligation cannot be fulfilled except by way of another thing, then that thing becomes obligatory as well. If the individual saw it while being far away from the people and he cannot inform those in authority, then he should go ahead and fast (by himself). Afterwards he should try, to the best of his ability, to pass the information to those in authority.

If an announcement is made on the radio by the authorities or other than them from the trust worthy Muslims, then it is obligatory upon whoever the information reached to fast or break his fast in Ramadân or other than Ramadân; because the announcement from the (Muslim Authorities) is a legislated proof that must be followed. This is the reason why the Prophet (ﷺ) commanded Bilâl to announce to the people the entering of the month in order for them to fast when the Prophet (ﷺ) was certain with the entering of the month. (He) made it obligatory upon them to fast upon hearing this announcement.

If there is a legal confirmation of the sighting of the moon, then the mansions of the moon will not be considered. That is because the Messenger of Allâh (ﷺ) has related the ruling of fasting upon sighting the moon and not its mansions. As he (ﷺ) said: **"Fast if you see the moon and break your fast if you see it"** [Collected by Al-Bukhârî and Muslim].

The Prophet (ﷺ) also said: **"If two trustworthy Muslims testified that they have seen the moon, then you should fast according to their sighting, likewise break your fast according to their sighting"** [Narrated by Ahmad. Graded to be authentic Al-Albânî in <u>Irwâ Al-Ghalîl</u>]

The Second Way of deciding the beginning of the month is the completion of thirty days of the previous month. That is because it is impossible for the lunation to exceed thirty days or decrease to less than twenty nine days. Sometimes it happened to be three or four subsequent months, all completing with thirty days and sometimes it happens to be twenty nine days in three subsequent months. But most of the time it happens that a month or two completes with thirty and the next with twenty nine. Therefore whenever the month completes thirty days, then the next day is automatically considered the beginning of the new month even if the moon is not yet sighted. This is based on the Prophet's statement (ﷺ):

صوموا لرؤيته وأفطروا لرؤيته فإن غمي عليكم الشهر فعدوا ثلاثين

"Fast upon sighting the moon and break your fast upon sighting the moon and if the clouds block your view (from seeing the moon) then complete the thirty days of the month."[Collected by Muslim]

According to Al-Bukhârî's narration:

صوموا لرؤيتِهِ وأفطِروا لرؤيتِهِ ، فإنْ غبِّيَ عليكم فأكملوا عدةَ شعبانَ ثلاثينَ

"And if [you experience difficulty in sighting the moon] due to cloudy [skies] then complete thirty days of Sha'bân" [Collected by Al-Bukhârî]

In the narration of 'Âishah (رضي الله عنها) it says:

كان رسول الله صلى الله عليه وسلم يتحفظ من شعبان ما لا يتحفظ من غيره ثم يصوم لرؤية رمضان فإن غم عليه عد ثلاثين يوما ثم صام

"The Prophet (ﷺ) used to fast in the month of Sha'bân more than in the other months. Then he would fast the month of Ramadân upon seeing the crescent, but if he could not sight the crescent he would wait till the thirty days of Sha'bân [completed] and then fast the first day of Ramadân" [Collected by Abû Dâwûd, Ibn Khuzaymah, and Ad-Dâraqutnî. Al-Albânî graded it to be authentic in Sahîh Abû Dâwûd]

With these narrations, the impermissibility of fasting the month of Ramadân before sighting its crescent or completing the thirty days of Sha'bân is clearly (established). Likewise the impermissibility of fasting on the thirtieth day of Sha'bân whether the sky is clear or cloudy (is also established by way of these texts), based on 'Ammâr bin Yâsir's statement (ﷺ):

مَنْ صَامَ اليومَ الَّذي يشكُّ فيه فقد عصى أبا القاسمِ صلى الله عليه وسلّم

"Whoever fasts on the day of doubt has indeed disobeyed Abâl-Qâsim (i.e. The Prophet Muhammad ﷺ)." [Collected by Abû Dâwûd, At-Tirmidhî, and An-Nasâ'î. Al-Bukhârî mentioned it (in his Sahîh) with a disconnected chain. Al-Albânî graded it to be authentic in Irwâ Al-Ghalîl]

O Allah grant us success to follow the guidance, and keep us away from the causes of destruction and wretchedness. Make this month a month of good and blessing for us. (O Allah) help us to be obedient to You in this month, and keep us away from the means of being disobedient to You. With Your Mercy, forgive us and our parents and all the Muslims, for verily You are the Most Merciful. And may Allah (ﷻ) shower His blessings and Mercy on our Messenger Muhammad, (ﷺ) his family members, his companions, and those who follow their way in a good manner till the Day of Judgment.

المَجْلِسُ الرَّابِعُ
The Fourth Sitting
The Ruling of Standing in Prayer during the Evenings of Ramadân

All praise be to Allâh the One who, with His bounty, assists the feet of those who tread His path, saves the perishing souls from being perished with His mercy, and eases the path of guidance for the believers. I praise Him upon every sweet and bitter condition of my life, and bear witness that there is no deity that has the right to be worshiped but Him alone, without a partner, Owner of Might and Power. All souls humble to Him willingly or unwillingly and all souls depend on Him.

I bear witness that Muhammad is His slave and Messenger, the one who executed the commands of his Lord secretly and openly. (May the peace and blessings of Allâh be upon him), upon his companion Abû Bakr who is attacked by the falsifying sect (i.e the Shiites and their likes), upon 'Umar the one who was able to control his soul, upon 'Uthmân the one who spent abundant wealth (in the way of Allâh), upon 'Alî, the one who drove the enemies away in a severe clash of abundant hosts, upon the rest of his companions, and those who follow their footsteps in a proper manner till the Day of Judgment.

O My Brothers! Indeed Allâh (ﷻ) has legislated for His slaves different kinds of worship so that they can take a portion from each kind, and in order that they will not get bored by worshipping Him with the same kind of worship, leading them to stop worshiping Him, thus being from the wretched. (Allâh) made some (acts of worship) obligatory upon the slaves and some He made supererogatory, by which the slaves can attain extra closeness to their Lord and (reach) perfection in (their) worship.

From amongst the kinds of worship which Allâh has legislated upon us is the Salâh. He (ﷻ) has prescribed upon us five daily prayers which we perform, but we get the reward of fifty prayers on our scales. Allâh (ﷻ) urged the slaves to increase in the supererogatory prayers in order to complete their obligations and increase in their closeness to their Lord.

From among the supererogatory prayers are **the Rawâtib**, the prayers which we perform (before or) after the obligatory prayers: two units before the Fajr prayer, four units before the midday prayer, two units after it, two units after the sunset prayer, and another two units after the evening prayer.

Also from among the supererogatory prayers is the **night prayer** which Allâh (ﷻ) praises those who perform it in various occasions in His Book. As He, the Most High, said:

$$﴿ وَٱلَّذِينَ يَبِيتُونَ لِرَبِّهِمْ سُجَّدًا وَقِيَٰمًا ﴿٦٤﴾ ﴾$$

"And those who spend the night in prostration and standing before their Lord." [Al-Furqân: 64]

(Also Allâh's statement):

$$﴿ تَتَجَافَىٰ جُنُوبُهُمْ عَنِ ٱلْمَضَاجِعِ يَدْعُونَ رَبَّهُمْ خَوْفًا وَطَمَعًا وَمِمَّا رَزَقْنَٰهُمْ يُنفِقُونَ ﴿١٦﴾ فَلَا تَعْلَمُ نَفْسٌ مَّآ أُخْفِىَ لَهُم مِّن قُرَّةِ أَعْيُنٍ جَزَآءًۢ بِمَا كَانُوا۟ يَعْمَلُونَ ﴿١٧﴾ ﴾$$

"Their sides keep away from their beds; and they call on their Lord in fear and hope, and spend out of what We have bestowed on them. And no soul knows what joy of the eyes is kept hidden for them, as a reward for the good they used to do." [As-Sajdah: 16, 17]

The Prophet (ﷺ) said regarding the night prayer:

أفضل الصلاة بعد الفريضة صلاة الليل

يا أيها النَّاسُ أفشُوا السَّلامَ وأطعِمُوا الطعامَ وصِلوا الأرحامَ وصَلُّوا بالليلِ والنَّاسُ نيامٌ تدخُلوا الجنَّةَ بسلامٍ

"The best prayer after the compulsory prayer is the night prayer" In another narration he (ﷺ) said: "O people! Spread the greetings of peace, feed the poor, keep the family ties, and pray in the night while the people are sleeping. If you do so, you will enter paradise with peace." [Authenticated by Al-Albânî]

And from the night prayer is the **witr prayer**. The least of the witr is one unit and the most is eleven units. Therefore it is okay to pray one unit for Witr. The proof of that is the statement of the Prophet (ﷺ):

ومَنْ أحبَّ أن يُوتِرَ بواحدةٍ فليفعلْ

"Whoever wants to pray one rak'ah for witr then do so." [Graded authentic by Al-Albânî in Saḥîḥ An-Nasâî and Saḥîḥ Abû Dâwûd]

If he wills he can complete all the units with one salâm, as it is narrated by At-Tahâwî that **"Umar bin Al-Khattâb prayed three units with one salâm."** [Ibn Hajr said its chain is strong in Fath Al-Bârî]

If he wills, he can pray and salâm (i.e conclude his prayer) after every two units and then pray one other unit, thus concluding his prayer. This is also reported in Al-Bukhârî from the narration of 'Abdullâh bin 'Umar (ﷺ).

And if he wills he can pray five units with one salaam (at the end) with one sitting for the tashahud. As it is also reported that the Prophet (ﷺ) said:

$$\text{فمن أحبَّ أن يوترَ بخمسٍ فليفعَل}$$

"Whoever wants to pray five units for Witr let him do so." [Graded authentic by Al-Albânî in Sahîh An-Nasâî and Sahîh Abû Dâwûd]

It is also narrated by 'Âishah (ﷺ):

$$\text{كان رسولُ اللهِ – صلَّى اللهُ عليهِ وسلَّمَ – يصلِّي من الليلِ ثلاثَ عشرةَ ركعةً يوترُ من ذلكَ بخمسٍ لا يجلسُ إلَّا في آخرِهنَّ متَّفقٌ عليه}$$

"The Prophet (ﷺ) used to pray thirteen units in a night, praying five units for Witr, and sit only in the last unit." [Collected by Al-Bukhârî and Muslim]

It is also reported that he would pray Witr with seven units and would connect them like he did with the five units, as it is narrated on the authority of Umm Salamah (ﷺ):

$$\text{ان رسولُ اللهِ صلَّى اللهُ عليهِ وسلَّمَ يوترُ بسبعٍ وبخمسٍ ، لا يفصلُ بينهنَّ بسلامٍ ولا كلامٍ}$$

"The Prophet (ﷺ) used to pray Witr with five units or seven, connecting between them without separating between them with salâm or speech" [Al-Albânî graded it authentic in Sahîh Ibn Mâjah and Sahîh An-Nasâî]

Likewise the Prophet (ﷺ) prayed witr with nine units. He would sit in the eighth unit and say the tashahhud without saying the salâm (i.e. he would not conclude his prayer) and then he would rise up and add the ninth unit, then salâm out and make supplication. This is also narrated by 'Âishah (رضي الله عنها):

كان يصلي تسع ركعات لا يجلس فيها إلا في الثامنة فيذكر الله ويحمده ويدعوه ثم ينهض ولا يسلم، ثم يقوم فيصلي التاسعة ثم يقعد فيذكر الله ويحمده ويدعوه ثم يسلم تسليما يسمعنا

"He used to pray witr with nine units. He would not sit in it except on the eighth unit. He would then remember Allâh, praise Him, invoke Him, and then rise up without saying the salâm (to conclude the prayer) and add the ninth unit. Then he would sit down, remember Allâh, praise Him, and invoke Him. Then he would say the salâm in a manner in which we could hear his salâm". [Collected by Muslim]

Sometimes he would pray eleven units separating between every two units with a salâm, and then pray one unit to complete the eleventh unit. This is also narrated by 'Âishah (رضي الله عنها):

كانَ النَّبيُّ صلَّى اللهُ عليهِ وسلَّمَ يصلِّي ما بينَ أن يفرُغَ من صلاةِ العشاءِ إلى الفجرِ إحدى عشرةَ ركعةً يسلِّمُ في كلِّ اثنتينِ ويوترُ بواحدةٍ

"The Prophet (ﷺ) used to pray eleven units between the evening prayer and morning prayer, concluding the prayer after every two units, and he would offer witr with one unit." [Graded authentic by Al-Albânî in Sahîh Ibn Mâjah]

If (a person wills) he can pray four units and then conclude the prayer with the salâm and then rise up and pray another four, then conclude the prayer with a salâm, and then rise up and pray another three. As this is also narrated by 'Āîshah (رَضِيَ اللهُ عَنْهَا):

يصلي أربعا فلا تسأل عن حسنهن وطولهن ثم يصلي أربعا فلا تسأل عن حسنهن وطولهن ثم يصلي ثلاثا

"The Prophet (ﷺ) used to pray four long and beautiful units, and then pray another four long and beautiful units and then pray another three" [Collected by Al-Bukhârî and Muslim]

The Scholars of the Hanbalî and Shafiî schools of Islâmic jurisprudence said it is permissible to connect the eleven units with one taslîm and one tashahhud, and that it is also permissible to sit at the tenth and eleventh raka'h.

The virtue of praying in the night of Ramadân is greater than praying in any other month. This is based on the Prophet's statement (ﷺ):

من قام رمضان إيمانا واحتسابا ، غفر له ما تقدم من ذنبه

"Whoever stands (in the night of) Ramadân with faith, desiring its reward, his previous sins will be forgiven." [Collected by Al-Bukhârî and Muslim]

(As for the term) **"with faith"** in the hadîth, it is to have faith in Allâh and in the reward which He prepared for those who stand in the evening. (While) the phrase **"desiring"** refers to seeking Allâh's reward, without showing off, without seeking to be heard by the people, and without any worldly purposes. Standing at night during Ramadân, as it is mentioned in the hadîth, includes standing in the beginning and the end of the night. Therefore, the tarâwîh prayer is also considered night prayer. For that reason we must show eagerness and care for it, seeking the reward for it from Allâh (ﷻ). And these are only a few nights that every reasonable thinking believer will take advantage of before they pass by. These prayers are called tarâwîh "which means relaxation" because (the Muslims) used to prolong their units and then take a short break after every four units. The Prophet (ﷺ) was the first person who started the tarâwîh prayer in the Masjid in a congregation. He then stopped, fearing that it will be made obligatory on his Ummah.

It is narrated by 'Âîshah (رضي الله عنها):

صلَّى في المسجدِ ذاتَ ليلةٍ . فصلَّى بصلاتِه ناسٌ . ثم صلَّى من القابلةِ . فكثُر الناسُ . ثم اجتمعوا من الليلةِ الثالثةِ أو الرابعةِ . فلم يخرجْ إليهم رسولُ الله صلَّى الله عليه وسلَّمَ . فلما أصبح قال " قد رأيتُ الذي صنعتُم . فلم يمنعْني من الخروج إليكم إلا أني خشيتُ أن تُفرضَ عليكم " . قال : وذلك في رمضانَ .

"The Prophet (ﷺ) once prayed in the Masjid in the night, and the people prayed behind him. Then the next day when he prayed more people came and prayed with him. So on the third or the fourth day the people gathered in the Masjid waiting for the Prophet (ﷺ) to come and lead them in the prayer, but he did not come out. When he reached the morning he said to the people: 'I saw what you did, but I refused to come out for the fear that it will be obligated on you.' And this was in the month of Ramadân." [Collected by Al-Bukhârî and Muslim]

It is also narrated by Abû Dharr (ﷺ):

صمنا مع النبيِّ صلَّى اللهُ عليهِ وسلَّمَ فلم يقمْ بنا حتى بقِيَ سبعٌ من الشهرِ ، فقام بنا حتى ذهب ثلثُ الليلِ ، ثم لم يقمْ بنا في السادسةِ ثم قام بنا في الخامسةِ حتى ذهب شطرُ الليلِ أي : نصفُه ، فقلنا : يا رسولَ اللهِ لو نَفَّلْتَنَا بقيةَ ليلتِنا هذه ؟ فقال صلَّى اللهُ عليهِ وسلَّمَ : إنه مَن قام مع الإمامِ حتى ينصرفَ كُتِبَ له قيامُ ليلةٍ

"We fasted with the Prophet (ﷺ) and he did not stand in the night with us until the last seven nights of the month. He stood and led us in the prayer till one third of the night was over, then he skipped the sixth night and prayed with us in the seventh night till half of the night was over. So we said to him: 'O Messenger of Allâh, would you pray with us the rest of the night?' The Prophet (ﷺ) replied: 'Whoever stands with the Imâm till the Imâm leaves, it will be written for him the reward of standing the whole night in prayer.'" [Graded authentic by Al-Albânî and Muqbil]

The pious predecessors have differed about the number of units for tarâwîh along with its witr. Some of them said it is forty one units, others said it is thirty nine, while others said it is twenty three, twenty one, or thirteen. Some said it is eleven, and others said different than the above mentioned. However, the strongest position is the statement of those who said it is thirteen or eleven, which is supported by the narration of 'Âishah (رضي الله عنها). When she was asked about the Prophet's (ﷺ) prayer she said:

ما كان يزيد في رمضان ولا غيره على إحدى عشرة ركعة

"He used to not exceed eleven units in his night prayer whether in the month of Ramadân or other than the month of Ramadân." [Collected by Al-Bukhârî]

It is also narrated by As-Sâib bin Yazîd (ﷺ):

أَمَرَ عُمَرُ أُبَيَّ بْنَ كَعْبٍ، وَتَمِيمًا الدَّارِيَّ أَنْ يَقُومَا لِلناسِ فِي رمضانَ بِإِحْدَى عَشْرَةَ رَكعةً

"'Umar bin Khattâb commanded Ubayy bin Ka'b and Tamîm Ad-Dârî to lead the people with eleven units." [Al-Albânî graded its chain to be authentic in his checking of Mishkât Al-Masâbîh]

The pious predecessors used to prolong (this prayer) as it is mentioned in the narration of As-Sâ'ib bin Yazîd who said: **"The Imâm would recite more than a hundred verses of the Qur'ân in one standing to the point that we would lean on sticks."** [A part of the previously mentioned hadîth]

This is contrary to what the people do today in their tarâwîh prayer. (They) pray with very excessive speed, void of calmness and tranquility, which is one of the pillars of prayer. Without (tranquility) the prayer will not be accepted. Likewise (nowadays the people) make it hard upon the elderly, the sick, and the weak who pray behind them. As a result they transgressed on themselves and on others. The scholars mentioned that it is disliked for the Imâm to rush his prayer in a manner that does not allow others to implement the Sunnan of the Prophet (ﷺ). Then how about the one who prays so quickly that the congregants (behind him) are not able to implement some of the pillars of salâh?! May Allâh (ﷺ) grant us security.

It is not befitting for a man to abandon the tarâwîh prayer or to leave the congregational prayer before the Imâm finishes. Rather he should pray witr with the Imâm in order for him to obtain the reward of the one who prays the whole night.

It *is* permissible for women to attend the tarâwîh prayer in the Masjid as long as they are safe from temptation and the people are safe from their temptation. This is based on the Prophet's (ﷺ) statement: **"Do not stop the female slaves of Allâh from coming to the Masjid"** [Collected by Al-Bukhârî & Muslim]

Also this was the custom of the pious predecessors. But (the Muslim women) must come to the Masjid fully covered in their veils, without displaying their charms, without being perfumed, and without raising their voices. This is based on Allâh's statement:

$$\{ \text{وَلَا يُبْدِينَ زِينَتَهُنَّ إِلَّا مَا ظَهَرَ مِنْهَا} \}$$

"And do not display their charms except that which is apparent." [An-Nûr: 31]

"That which is apparent" is what they cannot hide: their garment, their veil etc. This is because when the Prophet (ﷺ) commanded the women to go out for the 'Eîd prayer, Umm 'Atiyah said: **"'O Messenger of Allâh some of us do not have a garment to wear.' The Prophet (ﷺ) said: 'Let her sister give her a garment to wear.'"** [Collected by Al-Bukhârî and Muslim]

The Sunnah concerning the women is to stay far behind the men, beginning their rows from the back, contrary to the rows of the men which start from the front. The proof for this is the Prophet's statement (ﷺ):

$$\text{خَيْرُ صُفُوفِ الرِّجَالِ أَوَّلُهَا وَشَرُّهَا آخِرُهَا ، وَخَيْرُ صُفُوفِ النِّسَاءِ آخِرُهَا وَشَرُّهَا أَوَّلُهَا}$$

"The best rows for the men are the front rows and the worst are the back rows. The best rows for the women are the last rows and the worst are the ones in the front" [Collected by Muslim]

Sittings During the Blessed Month of Ramaḍān

The (women) should leave the Masjid immediately after the Imâm concludes the prayer. They should not delay except for a valid excuse. This is what the pious predecessors used to do as it is mentioned in the narration of Umm Salamah (bint Abî Umayah) (رضي الله عنها):

كان رسولُ اللهِ صلَّى اللهُ عليه وسلَّم إذا سلَّمَ، قام النساءُ حين يَقضي تسليمَه، ويَمكُثُ هو في مَقامِه يسيرًا قبل أن يقومَ . قال : نرَى – واللهُ أعلمُ – أن ذلك كان لكي ينصَرِفَ النساءُ، قبل أن يُدرِكَهنَّ أحدٌ من الرجالِ .

"The Women during the time of the Prophet (ﷺ) used to leave the Masjid immediately after the Prophet (ﷺ) said the salâm, and the Prophet (ﷺ) would remain at his position for a while before leaving." She said "Allâh knows best, but I think the Prophet did that in order to allow time for the women to depart before the men reach them." [Collected by Al-Bukhârî]

O Allâh grant us the success of that which You have granted the people of success, and with Your Mercy forgive us, our parents, and every Muslim. May Allâh (ﷺ) send His Peace and Blessings upon our Prophet, his family members, and all his Companions.

المَجْلِسُ الخَامِسُ
The Fifth Sitting
The Virtues of Reciting the Qur'ân and Its Types

All praise belongs to Allâh, the Inviter to His door, the Granter of success to whom He wills towards attaining His reward. He bestowed His favor on us by revealing His Book that contains clear and unclear verses. As for those who in their hearts is some crookedness, they follow the unclear verses. As for those who are firmly grounded in knowledge, they say:

﴿ءَامَنَّا بِهِۦ كُلٌّ مِّنْ عِندِ رَبِّنَا﴾

"We believe in them, all of it [i.e. the clear and the unclear verses] are from our Lord." [Āli Imrân: 7]

I thank Him for showing us the guidance and making its means accessible for us. I further bear witness that none has the right to be worshiped except Allâh (ﷻ). He is alone without a partner, a testimony through which I hope to attain salvation from His punishment. I further bear witness that Muhammad (ﷺ) is His slave and Messenger, the most complete individual in his actions. May peace be upon him, his best companion Abû Bakr, upon 'Umar through whom Allâh (ﷻ) elevated this religion and through whom this world became upright, upon 'Uthmân the martyr of his home and his niche, upon 'Alî who is famous for his knowledge of problem solving and clarification of ambiguous issues, upon his family, all his Companions, and those who follow their footsteps till the Day of Judgment.

O My Brothers! Allâh (ﷻ) mentioned in His Glorious Book:

$$\text{﴿ إِنَّ ٱلَّذِينَ يَتْلُونَ كِتَٰبَ ٱللَّهِ وَأَقَامُوا۟ ٱلصَّلَوٰةَ وَأَنفَقُوا۟ مِمَّا رَزَقْنَٰهُمْ سِرًّا وَعَلَانِيَةً يَرْجُونَ تِجَٰرَةً لَّن تَبُورَ ۝ لِيُوَفِّيَهُمْ أُجُورَهُمْ وَيَزِيدَهُم مِّن فَضْلِهِۦٓ إِنَّهُۥ غَفُورٌ شَكُورٌ ۝ ﴾}$$

"Verily those who recite the Book of Allâh, established the prayer, and spent out of what We have provided them, secretly and openly, hoping for a trade-gain that will never perish, that Allâh (ﷻ) may complete their reward for them and increase them of His Bounty, verily He is Oft Forgiving Thankful." (i.e. He appreciates the deeds of His slaves)." [Fâtir 29-30]

Reciting the Book of Allâh is of two types.

The First Type of Recitation: The practical recitation. That is by affirming its chronicles, abiding by its rules, implementing the commands, and abstaining from its prohibitions. We shall talk on this subject matter in details in the next Sitting if Allâh wills.

The Second type of Recitation: The verbal recitation. That is the literal recitation. There are many textual proofs which mention the virtue of reciting the entire Qur'ân, or some specific chapters, or (single) verses from it.

It is narrated by 'Uthmân bin 'Affân (ﷺ) that the Prophet (ﷺ) said:

$$\text{خَيْرُكُمْ مَنْ تَعَلَّمَ القُرْآنَ وعلمه}$$

"The best of you are those who learn the Qur'ân and teach it to others" [Collected by Al-Bukhârî]

Likewise on the authority of 'Âîshah (ﷺ): the Messenger of Allâh (ﷺ) said:

الماهرُ بالقرآن مع السَّفرةِ الكرامِ البررة، والذي يقرأ القرآنَ ويتتعتعُ فيه وهو عليه شاقٌ له أجرانِ

"The one who skillfully recites the Qur'ân will be with the Ambassador Angels, the honorable, and the obedient. While the one who recites the Qur'ân with difficulty will have two rewards." [Collected by Al-Bukhârî and Muslim]

He receives double reward: one for his recitation and the second for his struggle to recite.

It is also narrated by Abû Mûsâ Al-Ash'arî (ﷺ) that the Messenger of Allâh (ﷺ) said: "The example of the believer who recites the Qur'ân is like a citron, its smell is good and its taste is good. The example of a believer who does not recite the Qur'ân is like a dry date, it has no smell but its taste is good. The example of the hypocrite who recites the Qur'ân is like a scent fruit, the smell is good but the taste is bad. And the hypocrite who does not recite the Qur'an is like colocynth, it has no smell and it tastes bitter." [Collected Al-Bukhârî and Muslim]

It is also narrated by Abû Umâmah (ﷺ) that the Messenger of Allâh (ﷺ) said:

اقرءوا القُرآنَ فإنه يأتي يومَ القيامةِ شفيعاً لأصحابه

"Read the Qur'an, for verily it will intercede for its reciters on the Day of Standing." [Collected by Muslim]

It is also narrated by 'Uqbah bin 'Âmir (ﷺ) that the Messenger of Allâh (ﷺ) said: "Would one of you go to the Masjid and learn a verse or two from the Book of Allâh or recite them? This will be better for him than possessing two camels. And reciting three verses is better than having three camels. And reciting four verses is better for him than having four camels and your reward is based on the number of verses that you recited."[Collected by Muslim]

It is also narrated by Abû Hurayrah (ﷇ) that the Prophet (ﷺ) said:

$$\text{ما اجْتَمَعَ قومٌ في بيتٍ مِنْ بيوتِ اللهِ يَتْلُونَ كتابَ اللهِ ويَتدارسونَهُ بَيْنَهُمْ إلاَّ نَزَلَتْ عليهِمُ السكينةُ، وغَشِيَتْهُمُ الرحمةُ، وحفَّتهمُ الملائكةُ، وَذَكَرَهُمُ اللهُ فيمَنْ عنده}$$

"No people will gather in one of the houses of Allâh, reciting the Book of Allâh, studying it amongst themselves, except that tranquility will descend upon them, they will be overwhelmed with mercy, encircled by the Angels, and Allâh (ﷻ) will mention them to those who are with Him"[Graded authentic by Al-Albânî in Sahîh Al-Jâmi']

Likewise the Prophet (ﷺ) said:

$$\text{تعاهَدوا القرآنَ ، فوالذي نفسي بيدِهِ ، لهو أشَدُّ تفصِّيًا منَ الإبلِ مِن عُقُلِها}$$

"Read the Qur'ân constantly, for verily I swear by Him in whose Hand is my soul, it is slipperier than the camel from its loop." [Collected by Al-Bukhârî]

The Prophet (ﷺ) also said:

$$\text{لا يقُلْ أحَدُكم: نَسِيَتُ آية كَيْتَ وكيْتَ بل هو نُسِّيَ}$$

"One of you should not say I forgot such and such a verse, rather he was made to forget it." [Collected by Muslim]

That is because his statement **"I forgot it"** may indicate his negligence with the Book of Allâh (ﷻ).

It is also narrated by 'Abdullâh bin Mas'ud (ﺭ) that the Prophet (ﷺ) said:

من قرأ حرفاً من كتاب الله فله به حسنة والحسنة بعشر أمثالها، لا أقول الم حرف ولكن ألف حرف ولام حرف وميم حرف

"Whoever recites a letter from the Book of Allâh (ﷻ), will have a reward for that and the reward will be multiplied ten times. I am not saying (alif lâm mîm) is a letter, rather alif is a letter, lâm is a letter, and mîm is a letter." [Graded authentic by Al-Albânî in Sahîh At-Tirmidhî]

It is also narrated by 'Abdullâh bin Mas'ûd (ﺭ) that the Prophet (ﷺ) said: **"Indeed this Qur'ân is the Feast of Allâh, therefore welcome His Feast to the best of your ability. This Qur'ân is the firm-rope of Allâh, the clear light, the beneficial cure, it is a protection for whoever holds fast to it and a salvation for whoever follows it. There is no deviation in it so as to be blamed. There is no crookedness in it that needs to be straightened out. Its miracles remain forever, and frequent repetition of its verses does not create boredom. Recite it for verily Allâh will reward you for reciting it. With each letter you have ten reward, I do not intend that "Alif Lâm Mîm is a single letter, rather alif by itself is a letter, Lâm by itself is a letter, and Mîm by itself is a letter."** [Graded weak by Al-Albânî in Daî'f At-Targhîb and Ad-Daî'fah]

O my brothers! These are the virtues and rewards of reciting the Qur'ân for whoever seeks the reward of Allâh and His pleasure. Easy deeds for big rewards: a golden opportunity which none will let go but the loser. And the loser is the one who is in need of the profit at a time when he cannot attain it. These virtues include all the chapters of the Qur'ân. However there are some narrations which mention the virtue of certain specific chapters of the Qur'ân such as Al-Fâtihah. There is a narration in Sahîh Al-Bukhârî from the narrations of Abû Sa'îd bin Mu'alla (ؓ) that the Prophet (ﷺ) said to him:

$$ \text{لَأُعَلِّمَنَّكَ أَعْظَمَ سورةٍ في القرآنِ ﴿ٱلْحَمْدُ لِلَّهِ رَبِّ ٱلْعَٰلَمِينَ ۝﴾ هي السَّبْعُ المَثَانِي والقرآنُ العظيمُ الذي أُوتِيتُه} $$

"I will teach you the greatest chapter in the Qur'ân:

$$ \text{﴿ٱلْحَمْدُ لِلَّهِ رَبِّ ٱلْعَٰلَمِينَ ۝﴾} $$

'All praise is due to Allâh, The Lord of the worlds' (i.e. Surah Al-Fâtihah). It is the seven oft-repeated verses and the great Qur'ân that is given to me."

Due to this chapter's virtue, it is considered as one of the pillars of the prayer. Whoever prays without reciting Al-Fâtihah, his prayer is invalid. This is based on the Prophet's (ﷺ) statement found in Al-Bukhârî and Muslim:

$$ \text{لا صلاةَ لمن لم يقرأْ بفاتحةِ الكتابِ} $$

"There is no prayer for whoever did not recite Al-Fâtihah" [Collected by Al-Bukhârî and Muslim]

It is also narrated by Muslim from the narration of Abû Hurayrah (ؓ) that the Prophet (ﷺ) said:

من صلَّى صلاةً لم يقرأ فيها بأمِّ القرآنِ فهيَ خداجٌ ثلاثًا ، غيرُ تمامٍ فقيلَ لأبي هريرةَ : إنَّا نكونُ وراءَ الإمامِ . فقالَ : اقرأ بها في نفسكِ

"'Whoever prays without reciting Al-Fâtihah, his prayer is incomplete.' He repeated it three times. So it was said to Abû Hurayrah: 'What if we pray behind the Imâm?' He said: 'recite it to yourself.'" [Collected by Muslim]

Another example of these specified chapters (which have distinct virtues) is Al-Baqarah and Āli Imrân. The Prophet (ﷺ) said:

اقرؤوا الزهراوين البقرةُ وآل عمران فإنهما يأتيان يومَ القيامةِ كأنَّهُمَا غَمامتانِ أو غَيَايتانِ أو كأنَّهما فِرْقَانِ مِنْ طيرِ صوافَّ تُحاجَّانِ عن أصحابهما اقرؤوا سُورَةَ البقرةِ فإنَّ أخْذَها بَرَكَةٌ وتَرْكَها حسرةٌ لا يستطيعها البَطَلَةُ

"Read the Zahrawayn: meaning Al-Baqarah and Alî Imrân. For verily they will come on the Day of Judgment like two big clouds or two flocks of birds defending the one who used to recite them. Read Al-Baqarah for verily holding on to it is a blessing and leaving it is a loss which the magicians cannot overcome." [Collected by Muslim.]

It is also narrated by Muslim from the narration of Abû Hurayrah (ﷺ) that the Messenger of Allâh (ﷺ) said:

إنَّ البيتَ الَّذي تُقرأُ فيه سورةُ البقرةِ لا يَدْخله الشَّيطانُ

"The devil does not enter the home in which Al-Baqarah is recited." [Collected by Muslim]

This is also because Ayatul Kursî is in Al-Baqarah. It is reported that the Prophet (ﷺ) said: **"Whoever recites it at night will be in Allâh's protection. The devil cannot approach him until he reaches the morning."** [Collected by Al-Bukhârî]

It is also narrated by Ibn Abbâs (ﷺ) that Angel Jibrîl (ﷺ) said while he was with the Prophet (ﷺ): **"This is a door that is open from the sky and it has never been opened."** He said: "then an Angel descended from that door and came to the Prophet (ﷺ) and said:

أَبْشِرْ بِنُورَيْنِ قَدْ أُوتِيتَهُما لَمْ يُؤْتَهُمَا نَبِيٌّ قَبْلَكَ فَاتِحَةُ الكِتَابِ وخَواتِيمُ سُورَةِ البَقَرَةِ لَنْ تَقْرَأَ بِحَرْفٍ مِنْهُما إِلاَّ أُوتِيتَهُ

"Rejoice with the two lights that are given to you that were not given to the Prophets before you: the Opening chapter and the last verses of Al-Baqarah. You will not recite a letter from them except that you are given it." [Collected by Muslim]

From the Specific Qur'ânic Chapters that have distinct virtue:

﴿ قُلْ هُوَ ٱللَّهُ أَحَدٌ ۝ ﴾

In Al-Bukhârî on the authority of Abî Sa'îd Al-Khudarî, he reported that the Prophet (ﷺ) said about (this chapter): **"By the One in whose Hand is my soul, indeed it is equal to a third of the Qur'ân."** [Collected by Al-Bukhârî]

The fact that it equals a third of the Qur'ân in virtue, does not mean that it replaces it. For this reason, if a person were to recite this chapter three times in the prayer, it would not replace Al-Fâtihah. That fact that something is equal to another thing in reward, does not necessitate that it replaces it as well.

In Al-Bukhârî and Muslim on the authority of Abî Ayyûb Al-Ansârî (ﷺ), he reports that the Prophet (ﷺ) said: **"Whoever says: (There is no deity that deserves to be worshipped but Allâh alone, without any partners, to Him belongs the Dominion, to Him Belongs the Praise) ten times, it is as if he freed four souls from the children of Ismâî'l."**

In another narration reported by At-Tabarânî (it states): "It will be for him, like ten freed slaves from the children of Ismâî'l." [Collected by Al-Bukhârî and At-Tabarânî in <u>Al-Kabîr</u>]

And with that, if a person had to free four people as an expiation for a particular sin, and then he said this aforementioned invocation, it would not replace the obligation for him to free these slaves, although (freeing these slaves) and the (aforementioned supplication) are equal in reward.

Other examples of the specified chapters (which have distinct virtues): "Al-Falaq and An-Nâs." The proof for this is the narration of 'Uqbah bin 'Âmir (ﷺ). He reported that the Prophet (ﷺ) said: **"Have you not seen the verses that are revealed tonight, the likes of them were never seen: Al-Falaq and An-Nâs."** [Collected by Muslim]

In the narration of An-Nasâ'î it says that the Prophet (ﷺ) commanded 'Uqbah to recite them and then said: **"No one can ask with their likes or seek refuge with their likes."** [Al-Albânî graded it to be Hasan Sahîh in <u>Sahîh An-Nasâî'</u>]

Therefore strive hard O my brothers in the recitation of the Blessed Qur'ân especially in this month in which the Qur'ân was revealed. Reciting the Qur'ân in the month of Ramadân has a special virtue. Jibrîl (ﷺ) used to review the Qur'ân with the Prophet (ﷺ) one time every year. But in the year in which the Prophet (ﷺ) died, Jibrîl came and reviewed the entire Qur'ân with him twice in order to stabilize the Qur'ân in his heart. The pious predecessors used to recite the Qur'ân frequently during the month of Ramadân, in and outside the prayer. **Az-Zuhri** (ﷺ) used to say when ever Ramadân arrived:

إنما هو قراءة القرآن و إطعام الطعام

"(This month is the month) of reciting the Qur'ân and feeding the poor." [Reported by Ibn Abdul Barr in At-Tamhîd, with a weak chain]

Likewise **Mâlik**, may Allâh have mercy on him, used to leave off the Books of Hadîth and the circles of knowledge and turn to the recitation of the Qur'ân. [Likewise this is not authentically reported from Al-Imâm Mâlik]

Qatâdah used to complete the Book of Allâh every seven nights, and in Ramadân he would complete the whole Qur'an every three nights. In the last ten days of Ramadân he used to complete the whole Qur'an every night.

Ibrâhîm Al-Nakha'î used to complete the entire Qur'ân every three days in the month of Ramadân. In the last ten days of Ramadân he would complete it every two nights.

And **Al-Aswad** used to recite the entire Qur'ân every two nights throughout the year.

Therefore imitate these pious people[1], and follow their footsteps. If you do so, you will join with the obedient and purified ones. Take advantage of the day and night hours (doing that) which will bring you closer to your Lord, (ﷺ) the Oft Forgiving. Our

---

[1] Review the biographies of these scholars in such book as Hilyatu al-Awliyah by Abu Nu'aym, Siyar 'Alâm An-Nubalâ by Adh-Dhahabî, and Sifatu As-Safwa by Ibn Jawzî.

lives quickly come to an end and time flies like the period of an hour of a day.

O Allāh help us to recite Your Book in a manner that pleases You, and guide us to the safe path with Your Book. And take us from the darkness of blasphemy to the light of Islam with Your Book; let it be a proof for us and not against us, O Lord of the worlds. O Allāh raise our ranks with it, save us from lowliness, expiate our sins with it, and forgive us, our parents, and the rest of the Muslims with your Mercy. For verily You are the Most Merciful.

May Allāh shower His mercy on our Prophet Muhammad (ﷺ), His family members, and all his Companions.

المَجْلِسُ السَّادِسُ
The Sixth Sitting
The Categories of People Pertaining to Fasting

All praise and thanks are due to Allâh, the One Who perfected, with His wisdom, what He has created and built. With His wisdom and mercy He placed the legislation in order that it will be a way of life for us. He commanded us to be obedient to Him not because He is in need of our obedience. Rather, (obeying Allâh) is for our own benefit. He forgives all sins for those who repent to Him and seek closeness to Him. And He gives generously to those who are kind (and perform good deeds).

﴿ وَٱلَّذِينَ جَٰهَدُوا۟ فِينَا لَنَهْدِيَنَّهُمْ سُبُلَنَا وَإِنَّ ٱللَّهَ لَمَعَ ٱلْمُحْسِنِينَ ۝ ﴾

"Those who strived in Our cause We will guide them to our path, and indeed Allâh is with the doers of good." [Al-Ankabût: 69]

I thank Him for His bounties openly and secretly. Furthermore, I testify that none has the right to be worshipped but Him alone, without a partner, a testimony that I hope will grant me success to (obtain) the Abode of Bliss. Also, I testify that Muhammad is His slave and Messenger, whom He raised up above the seven heavens and brought closer to Him, peace be upon him and upon his companion Abû Bakr, the one who carried out the acts of worship and is pleased with the responsibility, the one who is honored by his Lord in His saying:

"When he said to his Companion: 'be not sad, verily Allâh is with us.'" [At-Tawbah: 40]

And upon 'Umar, the one who proclaimed his Islâm with dignity and integrity, upon 'Uthmân, the one who was pleased with his Lord's Decree, when the people sanctioned him to kill him, and upon 'Ali the one who is close to the Prophet (ﷺ) in kinship, and has indeed achieved his goals. (May the peace and blessings of Allâh be) upon the rest of (the Prophet's) family, Companions, and whoever follows their footstep till the Day of Judgment.

O My Brothers! In the third sitting we spoke about the legislation of fasting. We mentioned that it went through two stages before the (final) ruling was stabilized. There are ten categories of people with regard to the ruling of fasting:

The First Category: The sane resident Muslim who reached puberty, has the ability to fast, and is free from any obstacles preventing him from fasting. If an individual meets these conditions then fasting during the month of Ramadân will become obligatory upon him to perform it at its time according to the proofs from the Book of Allâh, the Sunnah of His Messenger (ﷺ), and the consensus of the scholars. Allâh (ﷻ) said:

﴿ شَهْرُ رَمَضَانَ ٱلَّذِىٓ أُنزِلَ فِيهِ ٱلْقُرْءَانُ هُدًى لِّلنَّاسِ وَبَيِّنَٰتٍ مِّنَ ٱلْهُدَىٰ وَٱلْفُرْقَانِ فَمَن شَهِدَ مِنكُمُ ٱلشَّهْرَ فَلْيَصُمْهُ وَمَن كَانَ مَرِيضًا أَوْ عَلَىٰ سَفَرٍ فَعِدَّةٌ مِّنْ أَيَّامٍ أُخَرَ يُرِيدُ ٱللَّهُ بِكُمُ ٱلْيُسْرَ وَلَا يُرِيدُ بِكُمُ ٱلْعُسْرَ وَلِتُكْمِلُوا۟ ٱلْعِدَّةَ وَلِتُكَبِّرُوا۟ ٱللَّهَ عَلَىٰ مَا هَدَىٰكُمْ وَلَعَلَّكُمْ تَشْكُرُونَ ۝١٨٥ ﴾

"The month of Ramadân in which was revealed the Qur'ân, a guidance for mankind and clear proofs for the guidance and the criterion (between right and wrong). So whoever of you sights (the crescent on the first night of) the month of Ramadân (i.e. is present at his home), he must observe the fast of that month, and whoever is ill or on a journey, the same number [of days which one did not observe the fast must be made up] from other days. Allâh intends for you ease, and He does not want to make things difficult for you. (He wants that you complete the same number (of days), and that you magnify Allâh [i.e. to say Takbîr (Allâhu-Akbar; Allâh is the Most Great) on seeing the crescent of the months of Ramadan and Shawwal] for having guided you, so that you may be grateful to Him." [Al-Baqarah: 185]

The Prophet (ﷺ) said: "**If you have sighted the crescent, then fast**" [Collected by Al-Bukhârî and Muslim]

Likewise the consensus of the Muslims agreed upon the obligation of fasting during its time for whoever meets these conditions.

But as for the disbeliever, it is not obligatory upon him to fast, because his worship is invalid. If he became Muslim during the month of Ramadân he will not be required to make up the days he has missed. (This is based on) Allâh's statement:

﴿ قُل لِّلَّذِينَ كَفَرُوٓاْ إِن يَنتَهُواْ يُغۡفَرۡ لَهُم مَّا قَدۡ سَلَفَ ﴾

"Say to those who disbelieve if they desist (from their disbelief) their previous sins will be forgiven." [Al-Anfâl: 38]

If (a disbeliever) he became Muslim after the rising of the dawn in the month of Ramadân it will become a must on him to fast the rest of the day until the setting of the sun, because he has now become a responsible person. However it is not obligatory on him to make up the hours he did not fast in them, because he was not a Muslim then.

The Second Category: The prepubescent child is not obliged to fast until he reaches puberty. This is based on the Prophet's statement (ﷺ):

رُفِعَ القَلَمُ عن ثلاثةٍ: عن النائم حتى يستيقظَ وعن الصغير حتى يكبُرَ وعن المجنونِ حتى يفيقَ

"The pen is lifted off of three (people): the one who is asleep until he wakes up, the child until he reaches puberty, and the insane until he recovers" [Collected by Ahmad, Abû Dâwûd and An-Nasâ'î. Al-Albânî graded it to be authentic].

However it is recommended for his guardian to command him to fast in order to train him upon obedience to his Lord before he reaches puberty, (in attempt to) follow the examples of the pious predecessors (ﷺ). The Prophet's Companions (ﷺ) used to make their children fast. They would bring them to the Masjid along with some toys that were made of fur. When the children complained about being hungry and started to cry they would give them the toys in order to keep them busy.

Many parents these days ignore this issue, not commanding their children to fast. As a matter of fact, some of them even stop their children from fasting in spite of their desire to do so, thinking that he (i.e. the parent) is being merciful to them. But in reality, being merciful to them is by (helping them become) accustom to establishing the religious symbols of Allâh (ﷺ) and its valuable teachings. Therefore, stopping (the children) from fasting or being neglectful in cultivating them upon the religious symbols of Al-Islâm is a form of oppression by the guardian against the wards. However, if (the children were to observe the) fast and are harmed (as a result of) fasting, then in this case (the parent) should stop them from fasting.

A boy becomes pubescent with one of these three signs:

The First Sign: having a wet dream. The proof for this is (Allâh's Statement):

﴿ وَإِذَا بَلَغَ ٱلۡأَطۡفَٰلُ مِنكُمُ ٱلۡحُلُمَ فَلۡيَسۡتَـٔۡذِنُواْ كَمَا ٱسۡتَـٔۡذَنَ ٱلَّذِينَ مِن قَبۡلِهِمۡۚ كَذَٰلِكَ يُبَيِّنُ ٱللَّهُ لَكُمۡ ءَايَٰتِهِۦۗ وَٱللَّهُ عَلِيمٌ حَكِيمٌ ۝ ﴾

"And when the children among you reaches the wet dream (i.e. becomes pubescent) then let them (also) ask for permission, as those senior to them (in age)." [An-Nûr]

The Prophet (ﷺ) said: "The Friday ritual washing is obligatory upon every (pubescent)." [Collected by Al-Bukhârî]

The Second Sign: Growing pubic hair. This is based on the statement of 'Atiyyah Al-Qurathî (ﷺ) that he reported: "We came to the Prophet (ﷺ) on the day of the battle of Banu Quraydha to see who is qualified to join the battle and they allowed only those who have had a wet dream or grew pubic hair." [This is an authentic hadîth narrated by Ahmad and An-Nasâ'î]

The Third Sign: Reaching the age of fifteen. The proof for this is what is narrated by 'Abdullâh bin Umar (ﷺ): "I was brought to the Prophet (ﷺ) on the day of Uhud when I was fourteen, but the Prophet did not permit me to fight." In the narration of Al-Bayhaqî he said: "He did not consider me a pubescent. And I was brought to him again on the day of the Battle of the Ditch when I was fifteen and he let me join the army." (In the narration of Al-Bayhaqî and Ibn Mâjah) is the addition: "And he considered me a

pubescent." [Narrated by At-Tirmidhî, An-Nasâî, Abû Dâwûd, Ibn Mâjah and others]

Nâfi' said: "I came to 'Umar bin Abdul Azîz when he was the caliphate and mentioned this hadîth to him." So he said: **"This is the age between childhood and adulthood. So he informed his laborers to give every fifteen year old child his share."** [Collected by Al-Bukhârî]

The same signs of puberty are applied to the female with the addition of **the monthly period**. Therefore whenever a woman sees blood, she has reached puberty. Her pen of accountability will start running even if it is before the age of ten.

If someone became pubescent during the day of Ramadân while he is fasting, he should continue to fast the rest of the day and there is nothing on him. (However) if he reaches puberty in the day of Ramadân while not fasting, he should fast immediately after he found out that he reached puberty and he does not have to make up the day because the obligation of fasting on that day came in before he reached the age of accountability.

The Third Category: The insane person, the one who has lost his mind. Fasting is not obligatory upon him due to the aforementioned hadîth: **"the pen is lifted off of three …"** From among the three is the insane person, until he comes back to his senses.

His fasting is invalid because he does not have an intellect to comprehend his worship or to intend it. And worship is not accepted except with an intention. The proof for this is the Prophet's statement (ﷺ):

إنما الأعمالُ بالنيَّاتِ وإنما لكلِّ امرأ ما نَوى..

"Actions are only considered based on their intentions, and a person will only have what he intends" [Collected by Al-Bukhârî]

If his insanity comes and go, then in this case it is obligatory upon him to fast in the days in which he is sane. If he became insane in the daytime of Ramadân, his fasting is still valid just as if he fainted due to sickness or other than that. That is because he intended to fast at a time in which he was sane. Thus his intention was sound and valid. There is no proof indicating the invalidation of the fast of such a person. Especially if he knows that it happens to him on some specific occasions. Based on this, it is not obligatory on him to make up the day in which he became insane, similar to the case of the child who reaches puberty in the day of Ramadân or the disbeliever who embraced Al-Islâm.

The Fourth Category: Is **reaching the age of senility** "mental infirmity." For these individuals neither fasting nor feeding is obligatory upon them, because they do not have the ability to distinguish between things. In this case they resemble the child who did not reach the age of discernment. But if they lose their sanity sometimes and recover at another, then in this case fasting will be obligatory on them at the time in which they recover and not the time in which they lose their sanity. The same ruling is applied to their prayer.

The Fifth Category: The one who is in a state of **perpetual disability** and is not able to fast. For example, a fragile old man, or the one who is suffering from a terminal sickness; like the individual who is suffering from cancer. For these individuals fasting is not obligatory upon them because they do not have the ability to fast. As He (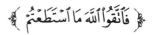) states:

﴿ فَٱتَّقُوا۟ ٱللَّهَ مَا ٱسْتَطَعْتُمْ ﴾

"Fear Allâh to the best of your ability" [At-Taghâbun 16]

Likewise His statement, the Most High:

$$\lambda\ \text{يُكَلِّفُ اللَّهُ نَفْسًا إِلَّا وُسْعَهَا}$$

"Allâh does not place a burden upon a soul greater than it can bear" [Al-Baqarah: 286]

However it is a must for them to replace (the daily) fast with feeding a poor person for everyday (which they missed). This is because Allâh (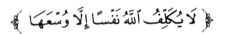) has made feeding a replacement for fasting and gave the believers the option of either fasting or feeding when fasting was first legislated. Therefore, if you are unable to fast you should ransom your day of fasting by feeding a poor person.

Also you are given the choice of either giving each poor person a **mudd**[2] of raw grains, which is one-fourth of a prophetic sâ', which weighs approximately the amount of 510 grams of pure barley or you can cook the food and invite poor people according to the number of days that you have not fasted.

Al-Bukhârî may Allâh be merciful to him said: **"The old person, who cannot fast, must feed the poor. For verily, Anas bin Mâlik continued to feed a poor person each day for a year or two when he grew old and was not able to fast. He fed them bread and meat."** [Collected by Al-Bukhârî]

---

[2] A **mudd** is equal to the volume of a .75L/750ml container. If one were to fill this size container up with rice, dates, beans, soup, lentils, etc although the weight may vary, it would be the amount that a person is obliged to give a poor person for each day which he was not able to observe the fast.

Likewise Al-Bukhârî narrated that Ibn Abbâs said: **"The old man or woman who is unable to fast must feed a poor person for each day they have not performed the fast."** [Collected by Al-Bukhârî]

O my brothers! This legislation is wisdom and mercy from Allâh (ﷻ) which He has mercifully bestowed upon His slaves. It is based on ease, sympathy, perfection, and wisdom. Allâh the Most High has obligated this legislation upon every responsible Muslim according to what is suitable for him, in order that every individual will carry out his responsibility with an open heart, internal tranquility in carrying out his obligations, and while being pleased with Allâh as his Lord, Al-Islâm as his religion, and Muhammad as his Prophet. Therefore, be grateful to Allâh, O believers, for having this correct religion, and be grateful to Him for His bounties upon you, by guiding you to this religion while many people have gone astray from this right path. And continue to ask Allâh (ﷻ) to keep you firm upon this religion until death (reaches you).

O Allâh we bear witness to You that You are Allâh and none has the right to be worshiped but You alone, the Only One, the Self-Sufficient who begets not and is not begotten and there is nothing comparable to Him.

You are the Owner of Might and Bounty. You are the Most Bounteous. You are the Decorator of the heavens and the earth. You are the Ever-Living, the Self-Sufficient. We are asking You to grant us success (to obtain) Your love and pleasure, and to make us amongst those who are pleased with You as their Lord, with Al-Islâm as their religion, and with Muhammad as their Prophet. We ask You to keep us firm upon that until death, to forgive us our sins and shortcomings, and to bestow upon us Your mercy. For verily You are the Giver. May peace be upon our Prophet Muhammad (ﷺ), his family members, his companions, and whoever follows their footsteps until the Day of Judgment.

المَجْلِسُ السَّابِعُ
The Seventh Sitting

All praise and thanks are due to Allâh, the One who is High above all partners, free from all kinds of deficiency and rivals, glorified from having a wife or children. The One who raised the seven strong heavens, which stand without any pillar holding them, the One who made the earth as a carpet and stabilized it with firm mountains, the Knower of the secrets of the hearts and the One Who decreed what has been and what will be of misguidance and guidance. It is in the ocean of His kindness that the boats of the slaves sail, and it is in the realm of His generosity that the horses of the ascetics itinerate. With Him is the need of the needy, and the goals of the aimers. He sees, with His eyes, the striving of those who strive in His cause, and He sees the creeping of the black ant in the darkness of the night. He knows the whisper of the heart within the depth of its creed. He is Generous to those who ask Him and He gives them ample provision. He has given abundantly to those strivers who are sincere in their intentions.

I praise Him with a praise that is innumerable. And I am grateful to Him for His bounties upon me. Whenever He is thanked He gives more. I bear witness that none has the right to be worshiped but Allâh alone without a partner, and I also bear witness that to Him belongs the sovereignty and He is the Most Merciful to the slaves.

Likewise I testify that Muhammad (ﷺ) is His Messenger and His slave. He was sent to all the creatures and to every country. Peace be upon him, his companion Abû Bakr, the one who sacrificed his soul and his wealth and was generous, 'Umar the one who supported the religion in an excellent manner, upon 'Uthmân, the one who prepared the Muslim army with his wealth at the time when the Muslims were facing financial difficulties, this indeed is enough of an honor for him on the Day of Judgment, and likewise upon 'Alî, the one who is known for his courage, his braveness, upon his family members, the rest of his companions, and those who follow their footsteps till the Day of Judgment.

Dear brothers! In our last session we mentioned five out of the ten categories of people pertaining to fasting during the month of Ramadân. In this session, inshâ Allâh, we will mention some of the remaining categories.

The Sixth Category: The Traveler. The one who's traveling is not for the purpose of breaking his fast. If he travels for the purpose of breaking his fast then in this case it will be impermissible for him to break his fast and it will be obligatory on him to fast. However if his traveling is for a valid reason then in this case he is given the choice of either fasting or breaking his fast, regardless of how long his journey takes, and whether his journey is casual or continual: such as the pilots or taxi drivers. This is because of the generality of the statement of Allâh:

﴿ وَمَن كَانَ مَرِيضًا أَوْ عَلَىٰ سَفَرٍ فَعِدَّةٌ مِّنْ أَيَّامٍ أُخَرَ يُرِيدُ ٱللَّهُ بِكُمُ ٱلْيُسْرَ وَلَا يُرِيدُ بِكُمُ ٱلْعُسْرَ ﴾

"And whoever amongst you is sick or on a journey then he should make up the days that he did not fast in the other days, Allâh desires ease for you and not hardship" [Al-Baqarah: 185]

Another proof is what is mentioned in Al-Bukhârî and Muslim from the narration of Anas bin Mâlik (ﷺ) who said:

كُنَّا نُسَافِرُ مَعَ النَّبِيِّ صلى الله عليه وسلم فَلَمْ يَعِبِ الصَّائِمُ عَلَى المُفْطِرِ وَلَا المُفْطِرُ عَلَى الصَّائِمِ. وفي صحيح مسلم عن أبي سعيدٍ الخدريِّ

رضي الله عنه قال: يَرَوْنَ أَنَّ مَنْ وَجَدَ قُوَّةً فصَامَ فإنَّ ذلك حَسَنٌ، ويرونَ أنَّ منْ وَجَدَ ضَعْفاً فَأفْطَرَ فإنَّ ذلك حَسَنٌ

"We were with the Messenger of Allâh (ﷺ) on a journey in which some of us fasted and others did not, but the Prophet (ﷺ) did not criticize those who were fasting because of their fasting and those who did not fast for not fasting" and in the narration of Muslim it is narrated by Abû Sa'îd Al-Khudrî (ﷺ) who said: "(During traveling) they used to consider it better to fast for those who had the ability to fast and they used to consider it better not to fast for those who were weak and were not able to fast." [Collected by Al-Bukhârî and Muslim]

In the Sunan of Abû Dâwûd it is reported on the authority of Hamza bin 'Amr Al-Aslamî (ﷺ) that he said: "**O Messenger of Allâh! I am an owner of a ride that I treat and travel on constantly, and perhaps this month may come across me while I am on a journey, but I find it to be much easier on me to fast while traveling than to make up my fast. That is because I am a youth and I am strong, so would it better for me to fast while traveling or to break my fast and make up the days I missed?** Then the Prophet (ﷺ) said to me: "O Hamza! You can choose either one." [Graded to be weak by Al-Albânî in <u>Da'îf Abû Dâwûd</u>. In its chain are weak and unknown narrators, See Irwâ Al-Ghalîl as well 4/61]

If a taxi driver finds it difficult to fast during Ramadân due to intense heat, he should break his fast and fast when the climate cools down, when he finds it easy on him to fast.

What is better for the traveler is to choose what is easier on him between fasting and breaking his fast. If he finds it equal between fasting and breaking his fast, then in this case it is better for him to fast because that is quicker for him in discharging himself from his responsibility. Also he will find it easy to fast because he is fasting with the people. Likewise this is the action of the Prophet (ﷺ), as it is narrated in <u>Saḥîḥ Muslim</u> from the narration of Abû Dardâ (ؓ) who said:

خَرَجنا مع النبي صلى الله عليه وسلّم في رمضانَ في حرٍّ شديدٍ، حتى إنْ كان أحَدُنا ليضع يَدَه على رأسِهِ من شدةِ الحرِّ، وما فينا صائمٌ إلاَّ رسول الله صلى الله عليه وسلّم وعبدُالله بنُ رواحة

"We went out on a journey with the Prophet (ﷺ) in severe heat, to the point that one of us would place his hand on his head to avoid the heat of the sun, and this was in the month of Ramadân. None of us were fasting except the Prophet (ﷺ) and 'Abdullâh bin Rawâha". [Collected by Muslim]

Likewise the Prophet (ﷺ) broke his fast on a journey when he saw that it was hard upon his Companions to fast. As it is narrated by Jâbir bin 'Abdullâh (ؓ) who said:

أنَّ النبي صلى الله عليه وسلّم خرج إلى مكةَ عامَ الفتحِ فصامَ حتى بَلَغَ كُرَاعَ الْغَميمَ، فصامَ الناسُ معه فقيل له: إنَّ الناسَ قد شقَّ عليهم الصيامُ، وإنَّهم ينظُرونَ فيما فَعَلت، فَدعَا بقَدَحٍ مِن ماءٍ بعد العصر فشَرِبَ والناسُ ينظرون إليه، رواه مسلم.

"The Prophet (ﷺ) traveled with his Companions on the day of the Meccan Conquest in Ramadân. When his Companions saw him fasting they also fasted until when they arrived at a place called "Kurâ' Al-Ghamîm" the people came and complained to him saying: 'Verily the people are facing hard time with the fasting and waiting to see what you will do.' So the Prophet (ﷺ) asked for a cup of water and drank it following the 'Asr prayer while the people were looking." [Collected by Muslim]

It is also reported on the authority of Abû Sa'îd Al-Khudrî (﷠) that he said: "The Prophet (ﷺ) stood at a river from the rainfall while the people were fasting on an extremely hot day. They were walking and the Prophet (ﷺ) was riding on his mule. So the Prophet (ﷺ) said to them: 'Drink O people,' but they refused to drink. So he said to them: 'My condition is different from yours, I am on a ride but you are walking, my condition is easier than yours.' But they still refused to drink. So, the Prophet (ﷺ) got down from his mule and drank and the people also drank even though the Prophet (ﷺ) did not want to break his fast." [Authenticated by Al-Albânî in <u>As-Silsilah As-Sahîhah</u>]

Therefore, if it is hard upon you to fast then you must break your fast, because in the aforementioned hadîth of Jâbir, it was said to the Prophet (ﷺ) **"some people persist to fast after you have commanded them to break their fast."** The Prophet (ﷺ) said:

أولَئِكَ العُصاةُ، أولئك العصاة رواه مسلم.

"They are the disobedient ones, they are the disobedient." [Collected by Muslim]

It is also narrated in the authentic books of Al-Bukhârî and Muslim from the narration of Jâbir bin 'Abdullâh that:

أنَّ النبي صلى الله عليه وسلّم كان في سفرٍ، فرأى زحاماً ورجلاً قد ظُلِّلَ عليه، فقال: «ما هذا؟» قالوا: صائمٌ، فقال: «ليس من البرِّ الصيامُ في السفر».

"The Prophet (ﷺ) was on a journey and he saw a man in a crowd shaded by the people, so he said: 'What is the matter with this man?' And they said 'he is fasting.' Then the Prophet (ﷺ) said: 'Fasting while traveling is not an act of obedience.'" [Collected by Al-Bukhârî and Muslim]

Likewise if you begin your day traveling and then find it difficult to complete it, you can break your fast as long as you left your city. That is because the Prophet (ﷺ) and his companions fasted until when they arrived at Kurâ' Al-Ghamîm, he broke his fast and the people broke their fast as well. Kurâ' Al-Ghamîm is the name of a black mountain located at the sides of Al-Hurrah, extending from there to the valleys of Ghamîm between Usfan and Marriz-zahran.

If the traveler arrives at his hometown in the day light of Ramadân without fasting then he has to make up the day because he did not begin his day fasting. The obligatory fasting is only considered valid if it begins from the rising of the dawn. However, (we ask) is it obligatory on him to fast the rest of the day?

There are differences of opinions regarding this issue. Some of the scholars said: It is a must on him to fast the rest of the day out of respect for the sacredness of that day and then make up that day later. This is the famous opinion of Al-Imâm Ahmad bin Hanbal, may Allâh have mercy on him. While other scholars said: It is not obligatory upon him to fast the rest of the day because it is not going to benefit him since he has to make up the day anyway.

The inviolability of that day has already been violated in the beginning of the day openly and secretly. 'Abdullâh bin Mas'ûd (ﷺ) said: **"Whoever ate in the beginning of the day should eat at the end of the day."**

Meaning "whoever it is permissible for him to eat in the beginning of the day for a valid excuse can eat at the end of the day" This is the school of thought of Mâlik, Ash-Shâfiî' and another opinion of Ahmad. However (it is important to note that) he should not eat or drink in public, because the people may not know the reason why he is drinking or eating and they will have a negative thought towards him as a result or other people may even imitate him.

The Seventh: The sick person whose sickness is hoped to be cured. For this individual there are three states:

<u>The First State</u>: If he is able to fast without any difficulties or harm then in this case it is obligatory on him to fast. That is because he does not have a valid excuse which allows him to break his fast.

<u>Second State</u>: If he is able to fast but with some difficulties, without the fear of harm himself by fasting, then he should break his fast. This is based on Allâh's statement:

﴿ وَمَن كَانَ مَرِيضًا أَوْ عَلَىٰ سَفَرٍ فَعِدَّةٌ مِّنْ أَيَّامٍ أُخَرَ ﴾ ۱۸۵

"And whoever is sick or on a journey then he should make up the days that he missed in the days other than the month of Ramadan" [Al-Baqarah: 185]

It is disliked for him to fast along with difficulty because by doing this he is leaving the ease which Allâh has given him and instead chooses to torture himself. The Prophet (ﷺ) said:

إن الله تبارك و تعالى يحب أن تؤتى رخصه ، كما يكره أن تؤتى معصيته

"Allâh (ﷻ) loves that His concessions should be taken just as He dislikes to be sinned against." [Collected by Ahmad and Ibn Hibbân and Ibn Khuzaymah. Graded Authentic by Al-Albânî]

<u>Third State</u>: If fasting actually harms him, then it is **impermissible** for him to fast based on Allâh's statement:

Sittings During the Blessed Month of Ramaḍān رَمَضَان

$$\{ \text{وَلَا تَقْتُلُوٓا۟ أَنفُسَكُمْ ۚ إِنَّ ٱللَّهَ كَانَ بِكُمْ رَحِيمًا} \}$$

"Do not kill yourselves; verily Allâh is merciful towards you" [An-Nisâ: 29]

And His statement, the Most High:

$$\{ \text{تُلْقُوا۟ بِأَيْدِيكُمْ إِلَى ٱلتَّهْلُكَةِ} \}$$

"Do not throw your hands in to destruction" [Al-Baqarah: 195]

Also because of the Prophet's (ﷺ) statement:

إِنَّ لِنَفْسِكَ عَلَيْكَ حَقًّا

"Verily your body has a right over you" [Collected by Al-Bukhârî]

From among the rights which your body has over you is that you should not harm yourself, (but rather take) Allâh's legislative concessions. (This is) based on the Prophet's statement:

لا ضَرَرَ ولا ضِرارَ

"There is neither harm nor reciprocating harm" [Collected by Ibn Mâjah. Al-Albânî graded it to be authentic in Sahîh Ibn Majah]

If (a sick person) is fasting Ramadân and then finds it difficult upon himself to complete his fast, in this case it is permissible for him to break his fast due to the existence of an excuse. And if he broke his fast and then feels that he has the ability to fast the rest of the day would his fasting be considered valid? The answer is no; because he broke his fast in the beginning of the day, and the obligatory fast will not be considered valid except if it is commenced from the rising of the dawn. But, is it obligatory upon him to fast the rest of the day? The scholars have different opinions regarding it, and we have already explained this when talking about the traveler who arrived at his hometown without fasting.

Also if the doctors affirmed that fasting may harm (this sick person) or may delay his treatment then in this case it is permissible for him to break his fast in order to preserve his health and avoid the delay of his treatment. If there is hope for his treatment then he should wait until when he is treated then he can make up his fast. But if his sickness is perpetual, in this case his condition is like the condition of the fifth category. He must ransom his day with feeding a poor man or woman.

O Allāh grant as success towards doing things that please You, and keep us far away from things that lead to being disobedient to You and sinning against You. Forgive us, our parents, and all the Muslims with Your mercy. For verily You are the Most Merciful.

And may Allāh shower His blessings on our Messenger Muhammad (), his family members, and all his Companions.

المَجْلِسُ الثَّامِنُ
The Eighth Sitting
The Remaining Categories of People Pertaining to Fasting and the Ruling of Making up the Fast

All praise and thanks are due to Allâh (ﷻ) the One, the Great, the Omnipotent, the Able, the Most Powerful, the One who subdues, the Most High above all thoughts and visions, He has designated every creature with deficiency and need, and has shown the traces of His ability through the alternation of the day and night. He hears the whimpering of the sick person as he complains (about) the harm which he is suffering from, and He sees the crawling of the black ant on a black stone in a dark night in the dark cave, and He knows the secrets of the hearts. His Attributes are similar to His Essence (i.e. they are unique, and there is nothing like them), those who resemble Him to His creatures have disbelieved. We affirm that which He affirms for Himself, from attributes and qualities, based on what is mentioned in the Qur'an and the Sunnah.

﴿ أَفَمَنْ أَسَّسَ بُنْيَـٰنَهُۥ عَلَىٰ تَقْوَىٰ مِنَ ٱللَّهِ وَرِضْوَٰنٍ خَيْرٌ أَم مَّنْ أَسَّسَ بُنْيَـٰنَهُۥ عَلَىٰ شَفَا جُرُفٍ هَارٍ ﴾

"Is it then he, who laid the foundation of his building on piety to Allâh and His Good Pleasure, better, or he who laid the foundation of his building on an undetermined brink of a precipice ready to crumble down" [At-Tawbah: 109]

I praise Him (ﷻ) upon good and harm, and I also bear witness that none has the right to be worshipped but Allâh Alone having no partner, having exclusive possession of creation and management of affairs.

$$\{ \text{وَرَبُّكَ يَخْلُقُ مَا يَشَاءُ وَيَخْتَارُ} \}$$

"Your Lord creates what He wills and chooses." [Al-Qasas: 68]

I bear witness that Muhammad is His slave and His Messenger, peace be upon him, upon Abû Bakr, his companion in the cave, upon 'Umar the suppresser of the disbelievers, upon 'Uthmân the obtainer of martyrdom in his home, upon 'Alî the one who stood praying at night, upon (the Prophet's) family, and the rest of his companions especially the Muhâjirûn and the Ansâr.

O My Brothers! We have already spoken about seven of the categories, and here is the remaining ten:

The Eighth category: The Menstruating Woman, It is not permissible for her to fast. If she fasts her fast is invalid. This is due to the Prophet's (ﷺ) statement:

ما رأيت مِنْ ناقصاتِ عَقْلٍ ودينٍ أذْهَبَ للبِّ الرَّجل الحازم مِنْ إحداكُنَّ، قُلنَ: وما نقصانُ عقلِنا ودينِنا يا رسولَ اللهِ؟ قال: أليسَ شهادةُ المرأةِ مثلَ نصْفِ شهادةِ الرَّجلِ؟ قُلنَ: بلى. قال: فذلك نقصانُ عَقْلِها، أليس إذا حاضتْ لم تُصلِّ ولَم تُصم؟ قلن: بلى. قال: فذلك مِنْ نقصانِ دِيْنِها، متفق عليه.

"'I have not seen anyone more deficient in intellect and religion than you. A cautious sensible man could be led astray by some of you." The women asked, 'O Messenger of Allâh! What is deficient in our intelligence and religion?' He said, 'Is not the witness of two women equal to that of one man?' They replied in the affirmative. He said, 'This is the deficiency in her intelligence. Isn't it true that a woman can neither pray nor fast during her menses?' The women replied in the affirmative. He said, 'This is the deficiency in her religion …..'" [Collected by Al-Bukhârî and Muslim]

The menstrual bleeding is a natural bleeding that comes out of a woman during specific days.

If she fasts and then sees blood (later), even if it is a minute before the setting of the sun, her fast for that day is invalid and she has to make it up, unless if it is a supererogatory fast. In that case her making up the day will be voluntary and not obligatory.

If she is purified from her bleeding in the day time of Ramadân, her fasting in the remaining hours of that day is invalid because of the existence of an obstacle that prevented her from fasting in the beginning of the day. But (one may ask) is it obligatory on her to fast the remaining hours of that day even though it is invalid? The scholars differed regarding this. And we have already mentioned the (various positions concerning this during our discussion) about the traveler after his arrival to his home land.

If she is purified during the night from her bleeding then fasting will become obligatory upon her, even if it is a minute before dawn, because there is no obstacle that stops her from fasting. And her fast will be considered valid even if she did not perform the ritual purification until after the rising of the dawn similar to the "junub", [i.e. the one who is in a state of major ritual impurity due to sexual intercourse or ejaculation] his fast is valid even if he did not perform the ritual washing until after dawn. The proof for this is the statement of ʿĀîshah (رَضِيَ اللهُ عَنْهَا):

كان النبيُّ صلَّى اللهُ عليه وسلَّم يُدرِكُه الفجرُ جُنُبًا في رمضانَ من غيرِ حُلُمٍ، فيغتَسِلُ ويصومُ

"The Prophet (ﷺ) used to reach the morning in a state of major ritual impurity due to sexual intercourse. He would perform the full body wash and then observe the fast." [Collected by Al-Bukhârî and Muslim]

The postpartum bleeding is similar to the menstrual bleeding; the same rulings are applied: (the woman experiencing postpartum bleeding) must make up the number of days that she has missed. This is due to Allâh's statement:

$$\text{﴿ فَعِدَّةٌ مِّنْ أَيَّامٍ ﴾}$$

"They should make up the number of days that they have missed in other than the month of Ramadân" [Al-Baqarah: 184]

When 'Âishah (رضي الله عنها) was asked why is it that women make up their fast and not their prayer? She said: "(We used to be in that state) and we were commanded to make up the days of fasting which we missed, but we were not commanded to make up the prayers." [Collected by Muslim]

The Ninth Category: A nursling mother or a pregnant woman who fears harm for herself or her baby due to fasting. For these women it is permissible for them to break their fast and make it up later. This is based on the hadîth of Anas bin Mâlik Al-Ka'bî (ﷺ) who reported that the Prophet (ﷺ) said:

$$\text{إن الله وضع عن المسافر شطرَ الصلاة وعن المسافر والحامل والمرضع الصومَ أو الصيام}$$

"Indeed Allâh has given the traveler the authorization of shortening the prayer; and has given the traveler, the pregnant woman, and the nursling mother the legislative concession to

break their fast." [Reported by the five scholars of hadîth and this is the narration of Ibn Mâjah, which Al-Albânî graded to be Hasan Sahîh]

She must make up the days which she missed whenever she has the ability to do so and feels safe and secure, similar to the situation of the sick.

The Tenth Category: The one who is in need of breaking his fast due to someone else's necessity: for example to save the drowning person or the one caught in a fire. If it is the case that the only way one can save (a person who is in dire need) is by strengthening himself with food and drink, then it is permissible for him to break his fast. As a matter of fact breaking his fast (in such as case) becomes obligatory. That is because saving the innocent soul from destruction is obligatory. However (the rescuer) must make up that day. (Other examples include) the individual who needs to break his fast in order to have some strength to fight in the cause of Allâh. In this case he should break his fast and make it up later, whether he is on a journey or in his homeland which is under siege by the enemy. That is because by doing this, he is defending the Muslims and making the word of Allâh superior.

It is mentioned in <u>Sahîh Muslim</u> from the narration of Abû Sa'îd Al-Khudrî (رضي الله عنه) who said:

سافَرْنا مع رسول الله صلى الله عليه وسلّم إلى مكةَ ونحنُ صيامٌ فنَزلْنا منزلاً فقال رسولُ الله صلى الله عليه وسلّم: «إنكم قد دَنَوْتم مِنْ عدوِّكم والْفِطرُ أقوى لكم» فكانتْ رخصةً فمِنّا مَنْ صامَ ومنا مَنْ أفْطر، ثم نزلنا منزلاً آخرَ فقال رسولُ الله صلى الله عليه وسلّم: «إنكم مُصبِّحو عدوِّكم والفِطر أقوى لكم فأفْطِروا وكانتْ عزْمةً فأفْطَرنا».

"We travelled with the Prophet (ﷺ) to battle the enemy while we were fasting until when we reached a certain distance the Prophet (ﷺ) said: 'Verily you are approaching your enemy and breaking your fast will keep you more energetic.' So it was an optional concession for us to break our fast. Some of us broke our fasting and others continued to fast until we travelled further and settled at another place. Then the Prophet (ﷺ) said: 'Verily you will be meeting your enemies in the morning and breaking your fasting is more energetic for you therefore break your fast.' It then became obligatory upon us to break our fasting." [Collected by Muslim]

From this narration we understand that having the energy to fight against the enemy is by itself an excuse to break the fast besides traveling, because the Prophet (ﷺ) has made it the reason for commanding them to break their fast (and not the fact that they were travelling).

All of the abovementioned people (who are allowed to break their fast), are also allowed to eat in public. And they should not be prevented from eating in public as long as their excuse is apparent to the people, like the sick person or the old man who is not able to fast. But if the persons excuse is not apparent to the people, such as the menstruating woman or the one who is rescuing (someone), then in this case it is disliked for them to eat in public in order to avoid negative thoughts and accusations, likewise to avoid having the ignorant person be deceived into thinking that it is permissible to break their fast in the day light of Ramadân without any excuse.

Everyone who is obligated to make up days of fasting, from those who have been previously mentioned, must make up the exact number of days which they missed, based on Allâh's statement:

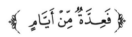

"Make up the number of days you have missed in other days" [Al-Baqarah: 184]

If a person missed the entire month of Ramadân, then he must make up the entire month according to the number of days in that month, either twenty nine or thirty.

It is preferable to hasten towards making up your fast as soon as the excuse vanishes, that is because it is quicker in hastening towards good and freeing yourself from the obligation.

However, it is permissible to delay it until when it is left between you and the next Ramadân the number of days that you have missed, based on Allâh's statement:

$$\text{﴿ فَعِدَّةٌ مِّنْ أَيَّامٍ ﴾}$$

"Make up the number of days you have missed in other days" [Al-Baqarah: 184]

And from the complete ease (of the religion) is the permissibility of delaying making up the missed days. For example if you have ten days of fasting to make up, it is permissible for you to delay it until there is only ten days until the next Ramadân.

It is not permissible to delay the making up of the missing days until the next Ramadân arrives without a valid excuse, due to 'Âishah's statement (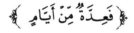): **"There used to be some days of fasting for me to make up and I would not have the chance to make them up until Sha'bân."** [Collected by Al-Bukhârî]

Also, delaying the fasting until the next Ramadân arrives may lead to the number of days piling up. A person may not be able to make up the days or he may die before he is able to make them up. Also, fasting is an act of worship that is repeatedly performed.

رَمَضَان Sittings During the Blessed Month of Ramaḍān

Therefore it is not permissible to delay it until the entering of the next fast, similar to the prayer. But if his (legislative) excuse remains until his death, then he is not going to be held accountable for that. Allâh has obligated on him to make up the days that he has missed in other days. If he died before having the ability to fast, this is like the one who dies before reaching the month of Ramaḍân. For this individual fasting is not obligatory. However, if he has the ability to make up the missing days but was neglectful until he dies, then his close family member should fast on his behalf, due to the Prophet's (ﷺ) statement:

مَنْ ماتَ وعليه صيامٌ صامَ عنه وليُّه

"Whoever dies with the debt of fasting, his guardian should fast on his behalf" [Collected by al-Bukhârî and Muslim]

His guardian means anyone who inherits him or his kin. And it is permissible for a group of people, totaling the number of days he missed, to collectively fast a single day.

Al-Bukhârî said: Hasan said: **"It is permissible for thirty people to fast on his behalf in one day."** [Al-Hâfith said in <u>Fath Al-Bârî</u>: 'Ad-Daraqutnî connected this narration in the "Book of Slaughtering."]

If he does not have a family member or he has a family member who is not willing to fast on his behalf, then in this case, they have to feed a poor person the number of days missed using the wealth which he left behind. For each poor man 510 grams of barley (or 750ml of dates, rice, cereal, soup, cheese etc.)

O my brothers! These are the categories of people with regard to fasting. Allâh has legislated for each category that which is suitable for his condition. Therefore know the wisdom of your Lord in this legislation, and be grateful for His bounties upon you in that He has granted you ease and leniency. And ask Him to keep you firm upon this path until death.

O Allāh forgive us the sins that pose as a barrier between us and Your remembrance. And pardon us for our remissness in being obedient and grateful to You. Keep us firm upon the path to You. Grant us light by which we can be guided to You. O Allāh, grant us the sweetness of holding firmly to Your worship, and take us to the path of those whom You are pleased with. O Allāh give us protection from humiliation, and keep us awake from our negligence, and inspire us to be guided. Beautify, with Your Bounty, our intentions. O Allāh resurrect us along with the pious, join us with your righteous slaves, and may peace and blessings of Allāh be upon our Prophet Muhammad (ﷺ) his family members, and his companions.

المَجْلِسُ التَّاسِعُ
The Ninth Sitting
The Wisdoms of Fasting

Praise be to Allâh, the Arranger of the Nights and Days, the Rotator of months and years, the King, the Holy, the One who is free from all deficiency, the Owner of exclusive possession of greatness, eternity and perpetuity. He is free from incompleteness and from resembling His creatures. He sees what is inside the veins and bones, and He hears secret conversations and hidden dialogues. He is the Deity of mercy and Owner of abundant bounties. He is the Lord of Might, severe in His Punishment. He decreed the affairs and made them run in the best order. He laid down the legislations with wisdom. It is with His power that the wind blows and the clouds move. The alternation of the day and night happen with His wisdom and mercy.

I praise Him for His great attributes and out flowing bounties. I thank Him, the thanks of the one who asks for more, and I bear witness that none has the right to be worshiped but Allâh alone, the One who is beyond all thoughts and imaginations. I further bear witness that Muhammad is His slave and His Messenger. May Allâh bestow peace and blessings upon him, Abû Bakr, the first to embrace Islam, 'Umar the one who the devil was afraid of, 'Uthmân, the one who prepared the army of hardship with his wealth, upon 'Alî, the ocean of knowledge and the brave lion, upon the rest of his family members, his companions, and those who follow their footstep till the Day of Judgment. To proceed:

O Slaves of Allâh! Know, may Allâh have mercy on you, that Allâh, the Glorified, has the complete authority and perfect wisdom in what He has created and legislated. He is the Wise in His creation and His legislation. He has not created His slaves in vain, and has not left them aimlessly, (without a purpose). He has not legislated the legislations in vain. Rather He created (the human being) for a great matter, and He clarified for them the straight path. He legislated upon them the legislations in order for them to increase in their faith, and (so that they may) complete their acts of worship. There is no act of worship that Allâh legislates except that there is a perfect wisdom behind it; it is known by those who know it and unknown to those who do not know it. Just because we are ignorant of some of the wisdom behind certain legislations does not mean that there is no wisdom within it. Rather it proves our inability of discovering the wisdom behind it and our deficiency in knowledge. This is based on Allâh's statement:

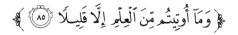

"You are not given anything from the knowledge but a little" [Al-Isrâ: 85]

Allâh has indeed legislated the legislations and arranged the transactions between the slaves as a trial and a test for His slaves, in order to distinguish between the one who is sincere and truthful in worshipping Allâh from the one who worships his desires. Therefore whoever acknowledges these legislations with an open heart and a tranquil soul is indeed a worshiper of his Lord, pleased with His legislations, and has chosen to obey his Lord, instead of his own (personal) desires. As for the one who did not turn to the worship of his Lord and only adheres to the legislation which suits his desires, such an individual worships his desires, dislikes Allâh's legislation, and turns away from being obedient to his Lord. This individual made his heart to be followed instead of making it that which follows. He has also made the legislation of Allâh to follow his desires despite the deficiency of his knowledge and wisdom. Allâh, the Most High said:

$$\text{﴿ وَلَوِ اتَّبَعَ الْحَقُّ أَهْوَاءَهُمْ لَفَسَدَتِ السَّمَاوَاتُ وَالْأَرْضُ وَمَن فِيهِنَّ ۚ بَلْ أَتَيْنَاهُم بِذِكْرِهِمْ فَهُمْ عَن ذِكْرِهِم مُّعْرِضُونَ ﴿٧١﴾ ﴾}$$

"And if the truth had been in accordance with their desires, verily, the heavens and the earth, and whosoever is therein would have been corrupted! Nay, We have brought them their reminder, but they turn away from their reminder" [Al-Mu'minûn: 71]

From Allâh's wisdom is that He has legislated upon us different kinds of worship, in order for us to accept them with pleasure, and as a purification for the believers. From amongst the slaves, there are some who are pleased with a certain acts of worship and thus they stick to it and may not be pleased with other kind of worship. As a result they neglect (that which they are not comfortable with).

(Allâh) made some acts of worship relate to our limbs, such as the prayer. While other acts of worship relate to our wealth such as almsgiving. Other acts of worship combine between the two such as the pilgrimage and Jihâd. (There are some) acts of worship which relate to holding the soul from its desire and lusts such as fasting. When the slave established these acts of worship and completed them in a manner required from him without disliking or neglecting them, rather while working diligently, becoming fatigued, sacrificing what is precious to him for the sake of his Lord, restraining his soul from what it desires out of obedience to his Lord, and adhering to Allâh's commandments while being pleased with His legislation, this indeed indicates the completeness of (this person's) servitude to his Lord and his total submission to Allâh's Will. It also indicates his love and veneration for his Lord. As a result he deserves to be described as a slave of (Allâh), the Lord of all the worlds.

After the abovementioned clarifications, we must know that fasting has various wisdoms which makes it worthy of being one of the obligations and pillars of this religion.

From among the wisdoms behind the legislation of fasting is that it is an act of worshipping the Most High, in which the slave seeks closeness to his Lord by deserting things which are beloved to him such as food, drinks, and intercourse. By doing this, the truthfulness of his faith becomes apparent, along with his total servitude, strong love (for his Lord), and (the extent of his) hope in Allâh. This is because the human being will not leave something that he loves except for something that he loves more. When the believer knows that the pleasure of his Lord is in fasting, by abstaining from things that he loves and desires, he gave preference to the pleasure of his Lord over his own pleasure. He left things that he loves despite his love for it. And this is because the relaxation of his heart and its tranquility are found only in leaving those things for the sake of the Almighty. For this reason many believers, if they were imprisoned and tortured in order to break their fast for a single day without a legislated excuse, they would not do so. This wisdom is the greatest of all the wisdoms behind fasting.

From among the wisdoms behind the legislation of fasting is that it is a means of attaining piety. As He, the Most High, said:

﴿ يَٰٓأَيُّهَا ٱلَّذِينَ ءَامَنُوا۟ كُتِبَ عَلَيْكُمُ ٱلصِّيَامُ كَمَا كُتِبَ عَلَى ٱلَّذِينَ مِن قَبْلِكُمْ لَعَلَّكُمْ تَتَّقُونَ ۝ ﴾

"O you who believe, Fasting is prescribed on you as it was prescribed on those before you so that you may attain piety" [Al-Baqarah: 183]

The fasting person is commanded with doing acts of obedience and abstaining from sins. As the Prophet (ﷺ) said:

مَنْ لَمْ يَدَعْ قَوْلَ الزُّورِ وَالعَمَلَ بِهِ وَالجَهْلَ فَلَيْسَ لِلَّهِ حَاجَةٌ فِي أَنْ يَدَعَ طَعَامَهُ وَشَرَابَهُ

" Whoever does not leave the statements of slander or doing an act of slander and ignorance then Allâh is not in need of his abstinence of food and drink" [Collected by Al-Bukhârî]

Likewise the one who fasts, whenever he intends to commit sin and then remembers that he is fasting, he stops himself from falling in to it. This is the reason why the Prophet (ﷺ) commanded the one who is observing the fast to say to the one who insults him or tries to pick a fight with him: "**Verily I am a fasting person**" in order to remind him that the fasting man is prohibited from cursing and insulting, and to remind himself that he is fasting, so as to avoid taking revenge by cursing and insulting.

From among the wisdoms behind fasting is that the heart becomes occupied with contemplation and with the remembrance of Allâh. This is because engaging in fulfilling our desires necessitates negligence of the heart, and is cause for the heart becoming hard and blinded from the truth. This is the reason why the Prophet (ﷺ) guided us to lessen our eating and drinking as he (ﷺ) said:

مَا مَلَأَ ابْنُ آدَمَ وِعَاءً شَرًّا مِنْ بَطْنٍ، بِحَسْبِ ابْنِ آدَمَ لُقَيْمَاتٌ يُقِمْنَ صُلْبَهُ، فَإِنْ كَانَ لَا مَحَالَةَ فَثُلُثٌ لِطَعَامِهِ وَثُلُثٌ لِشَرَابِهِ وَثُلُثٌ لِنَفْسِهِ

"The son of Ādam never fills up a vessel that is worse than the belly, few mouthfuls of food that keeps up the backbone of the son of Ādam is sufficient for him, and if he needs to eat more than these few mouthfuls then he should give one third for his food, one third for water, and one third for his breath" [Collected by Ahmad, An-Nasâ'î, Ibn Mâjah. Graded authentic by Al-Albânî in Sahîh Ibn Mâjah]

Also it is narrated in Sahîh Muslim that Handhalah Al-Usayidî, one of the scribes of the Prophet (ﷺ), said to the Prophet (ﷺ): "Verily Handhalah has become a hypocrite. So the Prophet (ﷺ) said to him: 'What is this that you are saying?' He said: 'O Messenger of Allâh we would be with you and you would remind us of the Hell-Fire and of Paradise to the point that we would feel like we can see them with our eyes. But once we leave from being with you and we begin to mix with our wives, children, and families we forget (most of these reminders).'" [Collected by Muslim]

Also Abû Sulaymân Al-Dâranî said: "**Verily once the souls starves and feels thirsty, the heart becomes pure, clean and soft, but when it is full, the heart turns blind.**"[3]

From the wisdom of fasting is that the rich will recognize Allâh's bounties upon them; for indeed Allâh blessed them with food, drink, and marriage, bounties that many creatures have been deprived of. As a result the rich person will be grateful to Allâh for these bounties, thanking Him upon this ease, remembering, with that, his poor brother who probably sleeps empty-bellied. Consequently, he will be generous towards this poor man with a charity by which he will clothe his nakedness and nourish his hunger. The Prophet (ﷺ) was the most generous person, but he

---

[3] **Abû Sulaymân Ad-Dâranî:** He is Abdur Rahmân bin Ahmad bin Ahmad bin 'Atiyah. Ad-Dhahabî described him with his statement: "The Great Imâm, the pious scholar of his generation." He died in the year 215 of the Islâmic Calendar. Review Siyar 'Alâm An-Nubalâ.

used to be more generous in the month of Ramadân when Jibrîl would come and study the Qur'ân with him.

From the wisdoms behind fasting is training oneself to be disciplined and to exhibit self-control. (Teaching oneself to) have the strength of holding its bridle, in order to be able to guide one's soul and control it to (do) that in which lies its happiness and benefit. Verily the soul, by its nature, inclines to evil except the ones that are protected by our Lord through His mercy. So if a man let's go of his soul's bridle without controlling it, it will drag him to destruction. But if the individual takes control of his soul, he will be able to lead it to the highest rank and utmost goals.

From the wisdoms of fasting is that it breaks down the soul and puts restriction to its pride until it submits to the truth and is humble to the creation. For verily, satisfaction from food, drink, and intimacy with women all lead to self-deceit, pride, and arrogance, which ultimately results in belittling the creation and rejecting the truth. That is because when the soul needs these things it becomes busy in trying to obtain them, but once a person obtains them, he feels like he has succeeded in his (mission). This produces within him the blameworthy pride which leads to his destruction. (Surely) the safe one is he who is saved by Allâh.

From the wisdom behind fasting: The blood vessels become narrow due to hunger and thirst. As a result the passage of the devil becomes narrow as well. This is because the devil travels in the son of Ādam through the blood vessels as it is authenticated in <u>Sahîh Al-Bukhârî</u> and <u>Sahîh Muslim</u>. Therefore, with fasting the devilish insinuation and the booster of the desires and anger calms down. This is the reason why the Prophet (ﷺ) said:

يا مَعْشَرَ الشباب مَن استطاع منكم الْبَاءَةَ فليتزوج فإنَّه أغَضُّ للبَصر وأحْصَنُ لِلفَرْجِ، ومَن لم يستطعْ فعليه بالصومِ فإنه له وِجاءُ

"O group of youth! Whoever amongst you who has the ability to marry, he should get married, because it is the best way of lowering the gaze and preserving the chastity. But whoever cannot afford to do so then he should fast, for verily it weakens ones desires." [Collected by Al-Bukhârî and Muslim]

Likewise from the wisdom of fasting: The healthiness that results from fasting due to minimizing our food and drink (intact), which allows our digestive system to relax for a certain period of time, and diminishes the moistness and the harmful waste materials in our body and other than that. Therefore how great and perfect is our Lord's wisdom! And how beneficial are His legislations to the creation!

O Allāh, give us understanding of your religion. Inspire us with secretes of Your legislations. Rectify our religious and worldly affairs; forgive us, our parents, and the rest of the Muslims with Your mercy. Indeed You are the Most Merciful. And may peace and blessings be upon our Prophet Muhammad (ﷺ), his family, and all his companions.

المَجْلِسُ العَاشِرُ
The Tenth Sitting
The Etiquettes of the Compulsory Fast

Praise be to Allâh, the One who has guided the slaves to perfect etiquettes, opened for them the doors of the treasure of His mercy and His generosity. He illuminated the insight of the believers. As a result they comprehended the realities and sought the reward by doing good deeds; and He has blinded the insight of those who turn away from His obedience. As a result it has set a barrier between them and His light. He guided the first with His mercy and bounty, and misguided the second with his justice and wisdom. This indeed is a reminder for men of understanding.

I also bear witness that none has the right to be worshipped but Allâh alone without a partner. To Him belong the Kingdom; and He is the Almighty, the All-giver. I also bear witness that Muhammad is His slave and His Messenger, the one who is sent with the most precious acts of worship and perfect etiquettes. Peace be upon him, his family members, his companions, and whoever follows their footsteps in the best manner till the Day of Resurrection.

O My Brothers! Know that there are many etiquettes which the fasting person must implement in order for his fast to be complete.

These etiquettes are of two kinds: The obligatory etiquettes: the fasting person *must* adhere to these etiquettes and safeguard them. **The highly recommended etiquettes**: the fasting person *should* adhere to these etiquettes and safeguard them.

From among the obligatory etiquettes are as follows: the fasting person must carry out all acts of worship that Allâh obligated on him. From among the most important acts of worship is the five daily prayers which is one of the most important pillars of Al-Islâm after the two declarations of faith. Therefore it is obligatory to preserve the prayer, carrying it out along with its pillars and conditions. This means that the fasting person must pray these prayers in the congregation inside the Masjid at their fixed times, along with their pillars, conditions, and obligations. For verily (praying in a proper manner) is from the piety which is one of the wisdoms behind the legislation of fasting. Neglecting the prayer contradicts piety and necessitates punishment. Allâh, the Most High, said:

$$﴿ فَخَلَفَ مِنۢ بَعْدِهِمْ خَلْفٌ أَضَاعُوا۟ ٱلصَّلَوٰةَ وَٱتَّبَعُوا۟ ٱلشَّهَوَٰتِ ۖ فَسَوْفَ يَلْقَوْنَ غَيًّا ۝ ﴾$$

"Then, there has succeeded them a posterity who have given up As-Salât (the prayers) [i.e. made their *Salat* (prayers) to be lost, either by not offering them or by not offering them perfectly or by not offering them in their proper fixed times, etc.] and have followed lusts. So they will be thrown in Hell" [Maryam: 59]

Some people neglect praying in congregation, despite the fact that it is obligatory upon them. (In the Qur'ân) Allâh has commanded us to prayer in congregation. As He, the Most High, said:

$$﴿ وَإِذَا كُنتَ فِيهِمْ فَأَقَمْتَ لَهُمُ ٱلصَّلَوٰةَ فَلْتَقُمْ طَآئِفَةٌ مِّنْهُم مَّعَكَ وَلْيَأْخُذُوٓا۟ أَسْلِحَتَهُمْ فَإِذَا سَجَدُوا۟ فَلْيَكُونُوا۟ مِن وَرَآئِكُمْ وَلْتَأْتِ طَآئِفَةٌ أُخْرَىٰ لَمْ يُصَلُّوا۟ فَلْيُصَلُّوا۟ مَعَكَ وَلْيَأْخُذُوا۟ حِذْرَهُمْ وَأَسْلِحَتَهُمْ ﴾$$

"When you (O Messenger Muhammad ﷺ) are among them, and lead them in the Salât, let one party of them stand up [in Salat (prayer)] with you taking their arms with them; when they finish their prostrations, let them take their positions in the rear and let the other party come up which has not yet prayed, and let them pray with you taking all the precautions and bearing arms." [An-Nisâ: 102]

Allâh has commanded us, in this verse, to establish the prayer in congregation even at times of war and fear, which means that it is more required from us (to perform prayer in congregation) at times of peace and harmony.

It is also narrated by Abû Hurayrah (ﷺ) that he said: "A blind man came to the Prophet (ﷺ) and said to him: 'O Messenger of Allâh! I do not have a guide who will guide me to the Masjid.' Then the Prophet (ﷺ) gave him the authorization of praying in his house. When (the blind man) turned his back, the Prophet (ﷺ) called him and asked him: 'Do you hear the call for prayer?' He said: 'yes.' Then the Prophet (ﷺ) said to him: 'Then answer the call." [Collected by Muslim]

The Prophet (ﷺ) did not authorize for him to (leave off) the congregation even though he was a blind man without a guide.

The one who abandons the congregational prayer and is neglectful of its obligation is indeed a great loser who has deprived himself of abundant good and multiple good deeds. That is because the reward of praying in the congregation is multiplied. As it is mentioned in Sahîh Al-Bukhârî and Sahîh Muslim from the narration of Ibn 'Umar (ﷺ) that the Prophet (ﷺ) said: "Observing the prayer in the congregation surpasses establishing it individually by twenty seven ranks" [Collected by Al-Bukhârî and Muslim]

Likewise he will miss the social interest of observing the prayer in the Masjid some of which is: sewing love and unity in the hearts of the believers towards one another, teaching the ignorant, helping the needy, and other than that.

By abandoning the group prayer you are putting yourself at risk of being punished and you are at risk of resembling the hypocrites. It is mentioned in (Sahîh Al-Bukhârî and Sahîh Muslim) from the narration of Abû Hurayrah (ﷺ) who said that the Prophet (ﷺ) said:

أَثْقَلُ الصَّلَوَاتِ على المنافقين صلاةُ العشاءِ وصلاةُ الفجرِ، ولو يَعْلَمون ما فيهما لأَتَوْهُما ولوْ حَبْواً. ولقد هممْتُ أنْ آمُرَ بالصلاةِ فتقامَ، ثم آمرَ رجلاً فيصلِّي بالناس، ثم أنطلق معي برجالٍ معهم حِزَمٌ من حطبٍ إلى قومٍ لا يشهدون الصلاةَ فأحرق عليهم بيوتَهم بالنار

"The most difficult prayers upon the hypocrites are the night prayer and the dawn prayer. If only they knew the reward of establishing them in the congregation they would come to observe them even if they are to crawl to them. I indeed wanted to command the prayer to be established and then command someone to lead the prayer, and then proceed with a group of men who will carry with them wood to the houses of those who do not observe the prayer in the congregation in order to put their houses on fire." [Collected by Al-Bukhârî and Muslim]

It is also mentioned in Sahîh Muslim from the narration of Ibn Mas'ûd (ﷺ): "'Whoever is pleased to meet with his Lord tomorrow upon Al-Islâm then he should preserve these prayers where they are being called. For verily your Lord has prescribed for your Messenger paths of guidance and these prayers are indeed from these paths of guidance.' Then he said: 'Indeed I have seen us "he meant the Companions" and none fails to attend it except a hypocrite who is known with hypocrisy. Indeed two men would carry a disabled person between them and would walk him to the row." [Collected by Muslim]

From among the errors which some of the fasting people fall into: they exaggerate in their remissness of the prayer, sleeping until the prayer time is out. This is one of the major sins and from the worse kind of negligence of the prayer. Some of the scholars said: "The one who delays the prayer till its time is out, without a valid excuse, his prayer will not be accepted even if he prayed it hundred times." This is due to the Prophet's (ﷺ) statement:

مَنْ عَمِلَ عَمَلاً لَيْسَ عَلَيْهِ أَمْرُنا فهو رَدٌّ

"Whoever does an action which is not according to this affair of ours, it is rejected." [Collected by Al-Bukhârî and Muslim]

(Intentionally) praying outside the prescribed time is not from the affair of the Prophet (ﷺ). Therefore it will be rejected.

From the Obligatory Etiquettes: the fasting person must stay away from all statements and actions that Allâh and His Messenger have made impermissible.

So he must avoid **lying** which is to narrate what is contrary to the reality. The worst lie is to fabricate a lie against Allâh and His Messenger. Such as saying Allâh and His Messenger (ﷺ) have made permissible that which is actually impermissible and vice-verse.

Allâh the Most High said:

﴿ وَلَا تَقُولُوا لِمَا تَصِفُ أَلْسِنَتُكُمُ ٱلْكَذِبَ هَٰذَا حَلَٰلٌ وَهَٰذَا حَرَامٌ لِّتَفْتَرُوا۟ عَلَى ٱللَّهِ ٱلْكَذِبَ إِنَّ ٱلَّذِينَ يَفْتَرُونَ عَلَى ٱللَّهِ ٱلْكَذِبَ لَا يُفْلِحُونَ ﴿١١٦﴾﴾

"And say not concerning that which your tongues put forth falsely: 'This is lawful and this is forbidden,' so as to invent lies against Allâh. Verily, those who invent lies against Allâh will never prosper." [An-Nahl: 116]

Likewise it is mentioned in <u>Sahîh Al-Bukhârî</u>, <u>Sahîh Muslim</u> and in other collections, from the narrations of Abû Hurayrah and others, that the Prophet (ﷺ) said:

مَنْ كَذَبَ عَلَيَّ متعمِّداً فليتبوَّأ مقْعَدَه من النار

"Whoever intentionally fabricates a lie against me, let him take his sitting place in the Hell-Fire." [Al-Bukhârî and Muslim]

Likewise the Prophet (ﷺ) has warned against lying when he said:

إِيَّاكُم والكذبَ فإنَّ الكَذِبَ يَهْدِيْ إلى الفُجُورِ وإنَّ الفجورَ يهدِي إلى النار ولا يزالُ الرجلُ يكذِب ويتحرَّى الكذبَ حتى يُكتَبَ عند الله كَذَاباً

"Stay away from lying, for verily lying leads to criminality and criminality leads to the Hell-Fire; and a man will continue to lie and persist in lying until he will be written with Allâh as a liar." [Collected Al-Bukhârî and Muslim]

Also (the fasting person) must abstain from **backbiting**, which is to mention your brother in his absence in a manner that he dislikes. (The ruling is the same) whether what you said about him is something that relates to his physical features such as calling him 'that lamed man, or that one-eyed man, or that blind man in a blemish manner.' (Likewise if you are backbiting him about) something that relates to his character, by saying he is 'stupid, a retard, a sinner etc.' It is the same whether what you are saying about him is true or false. Because the Prophet (ﷺ) said: **"If what you have said about him is true then you have backbitten him. And if what you have said about him is false then you have slandered him."** [Collected by Muslim]

Allâh (ﷻ) has forbidden backbiting in the Qur'ân, resembling it to the ugliest picture. He compared it with a man eating the flesh of his dead brother. As He the Most High said:

﴿ وَلَا يَغْتَب بَّعْضُكُم بَعْضًا أَيُحِبُّ أَحَدُكُمْ أَن يَأْكُلَ لَحْمَ أَخِيهِ مَيْتًا فَكَرِهْتُمُوهُ وَاتَّقُوا اللَّهَ إِنَّ اللَّهَ تَوَّابٌ رَّحِيمٌ ﴿١٢﴾ ﴾

"And do not backbite one another. Would one of you like to eat the flesh of his dead brother? You would hate it (so hate backbiting). And fear Allâh. Verily, Allâh is the One Who accepts repentance, the Most Merciful." [Al-Hujurât: 12]

Also the Prophet (ﷺ) informed us of what he saw the night in which he ascended to the Heaven. He said, **"'He passed by some folk who have nails of brass and they scratched their faces and chests with them.' So he asked: 'Who are these people O Jibrîl!' He said: 'These are those who eat the flesh of the people and transgress against their honor'"** [Collected by Abû Dâwûd]

Likewise (the fasting person) should stay away from **tale-carrying**. It is to narrate one person's statement about another individual to that person in order to bring corruption between them. It is from the major sins. The Prophet (ﷺ) said regarding the tale carrier: **"The tale carrier will not enter paradise."** [Collected by Al-Bukhârî and Muslim]

Likewise it is also mentioned in the authentic books of Al-Bukhârî and Muslim from the narration of 'Abdullâh bin 'Abbâs (ﷺ) that the Prophet (ﷺ) passed by two graves and said: (ﷺ)

إنَّهما لَيُعَذَّبانِ وما يُعَذَّبانِ في كبيرٍ (أي في أمرٍ شاقٌ عليهما)، أمَّا أحَدُهما فكانَ لا يَسْتَنْزِهُ من البولِ، وأمَّا الآخرُ فكانَ يَمْشِي بالنَّميمةِ

"Verily the dwellers of these two graves are being tortured and the reason for their torturing is for something that you consider trifle. As for one of them he used to not avoid soiling himself with his urine. And the other one used to walk around gossiping." [Collected by Al-Bukhârî and Muslim]

Gossiping corrupts the individual as well as society at-large; it divides between the Muslims and creates enmity amongst the believers. Allâh, the Most High, said:

﴿ وَلَا تُطِعْ كُلَّ حَلَّافٍ مَهِينٍ ۝ هَمَّازٍ مَشَّاءٍ بِنَمِيمٍ ۝ ﴾

"And obey not everyone who swears much, and is considered worthless, a slanderer going about with calumnies" [Al-Qalam: 10,11]

Therefore be aware of those who bring tales to you about others because they will tale-carry to others about you.

Likewise the fasting person should stay away from **cheating** in all his dealings and transactions including trading, renting, manufacturing, mortgaging. Likewise (he should stay away from deceit) when advising and counseling. Certainly, cheating is one of the major sins. The Prophet (ﷺ) has freed himself from the cheaters in his statement:

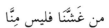

"Whoever cheats us is not from us" and in another wording he said: **"Whoever cheats is not from us"** [Both narrations collected by Muslim]

Cheating is deception and a violation of trust. It causes the people to not have reliance in one another. And any earnings which stem from deceit, is an evil and disgusting earning; it only causes its people to become more remote (and distant) from Allâh.

Also the fasting person must stay away from **stringed instruments**, which include all musical instruments such as the flute, rebec (i.e. a bowed string musical instrument), violin, piano, fiddle, etc. All these instruments are unlawful in their essence. Their impermissibility becomes even worse if they are merged with singing with beautiful and arousing voices. Allâh said regarding the impressibility of music:

$$﴿ وَمِنَ ٱلنَّاسِ مَن يَشْتَرِي لَهْوَ ٱلْحَدِيثِ لِيُضِلَّ عَن سَبِيلِ ٱللَّهِ بِغَيْرِ عِلْمٍ وَيَتَّخِذَهَا هُزُوًا أُوْلَٰٓئِكَ لَهُمْ عَذَابٌ مُّهِينٌ ﴿٦﴾ ﴾$$

"And of mankind is he who purchases idle talks (i.e. Music, singing, etc.) to mislead (men) from the Path of Allâh without knowledge, and takes it (the Path of Allâh, the Verses of the Qur'an) by way of mockery. For such there will be a humiliating torment (in the Hell-fire)." [Luqmân: 6]

It is authentically reported that when Ibn Mas'ûd was asked regarding the meaning of this verse. He (responded) saying, **"I swear by Allâh, the One whom none has the right to be worshipped but He alone, it is (referring to) music."** A similar meaning is narrated from Ibn 'Abbâs and Ibn 'Umar. Ibn Kathîr also mentioned the same meaning from Jâbir bin 'Abdullâh, Ikrimah, Saî'd bin Jubayr, and Mujâhid. Hasan said **"This verse is revealed on the subject matter of music and stringed instruments."** The Prophet (ﷺ) warned us (to stay away from) stringed instruments and connected it with fornication. He (ﷺ) said:

ليكونَنَّ من أُمَّتي أقْوَامٌ يستحلُّونَ الحِرَ والحريرَ والخمرَ والمعازفَ

"There shall be from my nation, some folk who will legalize fornication, the wearing of silk (for men), the usage of intoxicants, and musical instruments" [Collected by Al-Bukhârî]

This has indeed occurred in this era of ours. There are some Muslims who utilize these musical instruments and listen to them as if they are permissible. This is (an example in which) the enemies of Al-Islâm have succeeded in their plots against the Muslims. This, consequently, turns them away from the remembrance of Allâh and causes them to lose focus on their religious and worldly affairs. Many of the Muslims today prefer to listen to music over the Qur'an, the prophetic narrations, and the speech of the scholars which contains the explanation of the Islamic legislations and their wisdoms. Therefore be cautious, O Muslims, of those things which nullify that fast or decrease its reward. Safeguard your fast from false statements and actions. The Prophet (ﷺ) said: **"Whoever did not shun false statements and acting with it, then Allâh is not in need of him leaving his food and his drink"**. [Collected by Al-Bukhârî]

Jâbir (ؓ) said: **"If you fast, then let your hearing, your sight and your tongue fast from lying and unlawful things; and stay away from harming your neighbors. Let tranquility and dignity overshadow you; and the days in which you fast should not be like the days in which you do not fast."** [Ibn Rajab mentioned it in Latâif Al-Mâ'rif page 292]

رَمَضَان Sittings During the Blessed Month of Ramaḍān

O Allāh! Preserve our religion for us and restrain our limbs from falling in to what angers You. Forgive us, our parents, and all the Muslims with your mercy. For verily You are the Most Merciful.

May peace and blessings be upon our Prophet Muhammad (ﷺ), his family members, his Companions, and whoever follows their footsteps until the Day of Judgment.

المَجْلِسُ الحَادِي عَشَر
The Eleventh Sitting
The Recommended Etiquettes of Fasting

All praise is due to Allâh, the One who allows the hopeful person to reach beyond his goal, and gives, the one who asks, more than what he asks. I praise Him for granting me success to (obtain) His guidance, and I testify to His Oneness with a testimony that is based on proofs. I send peace and salutation upon our Prophet Muhammad, His slave and His Messenger, upon his companion Abû Bakr, his consistent companion in all his journeys and while in as a resident, upon 'Umar the defender of Al-Islâm with an unvanquished determination, upon 'Uthmân the forbearer of calamity as it befalls, upon 'Alî the son of Abû Tâlib, the one who terrifies the enemies with his courage before defeating them, and upon all (The Prophet's ﷺ) family members, his companions, those who scored a great success of knowledge in the branches and principles of this religion, and their precedence in this subject matter will continue as long as the breeze continues to blow from all angles.

O My Brothers! This sitting clarifies the second type of etiquettes which the fasting person must observe: the **recommended etiquettes.**

From among the recommended etiquettes of fasting is: "**As-Suhûr:**" eating at the last hours of the night before the rising of dawn. It is called "suhûr" because the time in which this meal is eaten is called "sahar." The Prophet (ﷺ) has commanded us with it in his statement:

تَسَحَّرُوا فَإِنَّ فِي السُّحُورِ بَرَكَةً

"Eat sahûr, for verily in it there blessings." [Collected Al-Bukhârî and Muslim]

In <u>Sahîh Muslim</u> it is narrated by 'Amr bin Al-Aus (ﷺ) that the Prophet (ﷺ) said: **"The difference between our fasting and the fasting of the People of the Book is eating of the sahûr."** [Collected by Muslim]

Likewise the Prophet (ﷺ) has praised the eating of dates for sahûr in his statement:

نِعْمَ سَحُورُ المؤمنِ التمرُ

"The best Sahûr of the believer are dates." [Al-Albânî declared it to be authentic in <u>Sahîh Abû Dâwûd</u>]

Also the Prophet (ﷺ) said:

السُّحُور كله بركةٌ فلا تَدَعوه ولو أن يجرع أحدكم جرعةً من ماءٍ فإن الله وملائكته يُصَلُّون على المتسحرين

"Observing the Suhûr, there lies a blessing in all of it. Therefore do not leave it even if one of you is to take a gulp of water. For verily Allâh and His Angels send salutation to those who eat Sahûr" [Collected by Ahmad. Al-Mundhirî said its chains of narration are strong. Graded Hasan by Al-Albânî in <u>Sahîh Al-Jâmi'</u>]

Likewise the one who eats the Sahûr must intend to implement the Prophet's (ﷺ) command and imitate his action, in order that his Sahûr will be an act of worship. Also he should intend, with his Sahûr, to strengthen himself so that he will be able to observe the fast. By doing this, he will be rewarded upon (his intention).

According to the Sunnah the Saḥûr should be delayed until the last portion of the night except if one fears the rising of the dawn. This is the action of the Prophet (ﷺ). It is narrated from Qatâdah from Anas bin Mâlik who said: **"The Prophet (ﷺ) and Zayd bin Thâbit ate Saḥûr together, and then the Prophet (ﷺ) stood and walked to the Masjid and prayed. We said to him: 'What is the time period between him eating Saḥûr and his prayer?' He said: 'The period of reciting fifty verses of the Qur'ân.'"** [Collected by Al-Bukhârî]

Also it is narrated by 'Âishah (رضي الله عنها) that:

أنَّ بلالاً كان يؤذِّنُ بليْلٍ فقال النبيُّ صلَّى اللهُ عليْهِ وسلَّمَ: «كُلُوا واشرَبُوا حتى يُؤذِّنَ ابن أمِّ مكتومٍ، فإنَّه لا يؤذنُ حتى يطلُعَ الفجر»

"Bilâl used to call the adhân in the night and the Prophet (ﷺ) would say to the people: 'Eat and drink until you hear the adhân of Ibn Ummi Maktûm for verily he would not call the adhân until the rising of the dawn.'" [Collected by Al-Bukhârî]

Delaying the Saḥûr meal is much easier upon the fasting person and safer for him to wake up on time for the dawn prayer. The fasting person can continue to eat and drink even after he has already eaten and intended to fast, until he is certain that dawn has appeared. This is due to Allâh's statement:

﴿ وَكُلُوا۟ وَٱشْرَبُوا۟ حَتَّىٰ يَتَبَيَّنَ لَكُمُ ٱلْخَيْطُ ٱلْأَبْيَضُ مِنَ ٱلْخَيْطِ ٱلْأَسْوَدِ مِنَ ٱلْفَجْرِ ﴾

"Eat and drink until the white thread becomes distinct to you from the black tread of the dawn." [Al-Baqarah: 187]

His certainty must be based on seeing the rising of the sun in the horizon or by being informed by a trustworthy person, whether it is by the adhân or other than that. If the dawn rises he should begin his fast with the intention in his heart without proclaiming it (with his tongue), because proclaiming it (verbally) is an innovation.

Likewise from the recommended etiquettes of fasting is hastening to break the fast when it is confirmed that the sun has set, by way of visual confirmation or by being informed by a trustworthy individual, through the adhân, or other than it. It is narrated by Sahl bin Sa'd (ﷺ) that the Prophet (ﷺ) said:

لا يَزالُ الناسُ بخيرٍ ما عَجَّلُوا الفِطْرَ

"**The people will continue to be upon good as long as they hasten to break their fast**" [Collected by Al-Bukhârî and Muslim]

Likewise the Prophet (ﷺ) said, from what he has narrated from his Lord, the Most High, that He said:

إن أحبَ عبادي إلي أعجلهم فطرا

"**The most beloved of My slaves to Me is the one who is the quickest to break his fast.**" [Collected by Ahmad and At-Tirmidhî. Its chain was graded authentic by Ahmad Shâkir]

According to the Sunnah one should break his fast with wet dates. If there are none then with dry dates, and if not then with water due to Anas' (ﷺ) statement:

كان النبيُّ صَلَّى اللَّهُ عَلَيْهِ وَسَلَّمَ يُفطِرُ قبلَ أن يُصَلِّيَ على رُطباتٍ، فإنْ لَمْ تكنْ رطبات فَتَمَرَات، فإن لم تكن تمرات حَسَا حَسَواتٍ من ماء

"The Prophet used to break his fast with wet dates before he prayed. If there were (no wet dates), (he broke his fast) with the dry dates. If there (were no dry dates) he would break his fast with sips of water" [Collected by Ahmad, Abû Dâwûd, and Tirmidhî. Al-Albânî graded it to be Hasan Sahîh in Sahîh Abû Dâwûd]

If (the fasting person) does not find wet dates, dry dates, or water then he should break his fast with whatever he has of food and drink, as long as it is lawful. If there is nothing with which to break ones fast, the (fasting person) should intend to break his fast within his heart without sucking his finger or swallowing his saliva as some common folk do.

He should invoke Allâh before breaking his fast, asking Allâh of what he wants. It is mentioned in the Sunan of Ibn Mâjah that the Prophet (ﷺ) said: **"The fasting person has an answerable invocation at the time he breaks his fast."** [Graded weak by Al-Albânî in Irwâ Al-Ghalîl]

Abû Dâwûd also narrated from Mu'âdh bin Zahrah: that the Prophet (ﷺ) used to say when he broke his fast:

اللَّهُمَّ لَكَ صُمْتُ وَعَلَى رِزْقِكَ أَفْطَرْتُ

"O Allâh! My fasting is for your sake and with your sustenance I break my fast" [Graded weak by Al-Albânî in Daî'f Abî Dâwûd]

He also mentioned the narration of Ibn 'Umar (ﷺ) that the Prophet (ﷺ) used to say upon breaking his fast:

ذَهَبَ الظَّمَأُ وَابْتَلَّتِ الْعُرُوقُ وَثَبَتَ الْأَجْرُ إِنْ شَاءَ اللهُ

"The thirst has vanished, the veins are moistened, and the reward is affirmed inshâ Allâh" [Graded Hasan by Al-Albânî in Sahîh Abî Dâwûd]

From among the recommended etiquettes of fasting is: increasing in the recitation of the Qur'ân, glorification of Allâh, supplication and praying to Him, as well as giving charity. It is mentioned in Sahîh Ibn Khuzaymah and (Sahîh) Ibn Hibbân that the Prophet (ﷺ) said:

ثلاثةٌ لا ترد دعوتُهم: الصائمُ حتى يُفْطِرَ، والإمامُ العادلُ، ودعوةُ المظلومِ يرْفَعُها اللهُ فوقَ الغمامِ وتُفتَحُ لها أبوابُ السماءِ ويقولُ الرَّبُّ: وعِزَّتي وجَلالِي لأنصُرَنَّكِ ولو بَعدَ حينٍ

"There are three individuals whose invocation will not be rejected: the fasting person until he breaks his fast, a just ruler, and the invocation of the oppressed one. Allâh will raise it above the cloud, and the doors of heaven will be opened for it, and the Lord will say: 'By My Might, and My Greatness I will assist you even if it is after some period of time.'" [Collected by Ahmad and At-Tirmidhî. Graded weak by Al-Albânî in As-Silsilah Ad-Da'îfah]

And in Sahîh Al-Bukhârî and Sahîh Muslim, Ibn 'Abbâs (ﷺ) said: "The Prophet (ﷺ) was the most generous one of us but he was more generous in the month of Ramadân when Jibrîl would meet with him and would study the Qur'ân with him. Verily the Prophet (ﷺ) gave more than the gentle breeze at the time when Jibrîl would come and study the Qur'ân with him." [Collected by Al-Bukhârî and Muslim]

This is because the Prophet's (ﷺ) generosity was all-inclusive, combining all kinds of good including sacrificing his knowledge, soul, and wealth for the sake of Allâh in supporting His religion, guiding His slaves, and benefitting them by all means necessary, including teaching the ignorant ones, fulfilling their needs, and feeding the hungry ones. His philanthropy increased in the month of Ramadân because of the nobility of its time and the multiplicity of its reward. Likewise he helped the worshippers in their acts of worship. Combining between fasting and feeding is one of the means of entering paradise. It is mentioned in <u>Sahîh Muslim</u> from the narrations of Abû Hurayrah (ﷺ) that the Prophet (ﷺ) said:

مَنْ أَصْبَحَ مِنْكُمُ اليومَ صائماً؟ فقال أبو بكر: أنا. قال: فَمَنْ تَبِعَ مِنكم اليومَ جنازةً؟ قال أبو بكر: أنا. قال: فَمَنْ أطعم منكم اليومَ مسكيناً؟ قال أبو بكر: أنا. قال: فَمَنْ عادَ منكم اليومَ مريضاً؟ قال أبو بكر: أنا. قال النبي صلى الله عليه وسلّم: مَا اجتمعْنَ في امرأ إلاَّ دَخَلَ الجنَّةَ

"'Who amongst you is fasting today?' Abû Bakr said: 'I.' And then he said: 'Who amongst you followed a funeral today?' Abû Bakr said: 'I.' Then he said: 'Who amongst you fed the poor today?' Abû Bakr said: 'I.' He said: 'Who amongst you visited the sick today?' Abû Bakr said: 'I.' The Prophet (ﷺ) said: 'No man will have all these qualities in him except that he will enter paradise.'" [Collected by Muslim]

From among the recommended etiquettes of fasting is that the fasting person should recognize the bounty of fasting which Allâh legislated for him. That is because Allâh is the One who granted him the success to fast and made it easy for him to complete his day and month of fasting. There are many people who were deprived the opportunity to fast, either because they died before the month arrived, or because of their inability, misguidance, and negligence of carrying out its responsibility. Therefore the fasting person should be grateful for Allâh's blessing upon him, (by allowing him to) fast, which is a cause for one's sins to be forgiven, shortcomings expiated, and one's rank elevated in the abode of bounty, next to the Lord of Bount(ies).

O my brothers adhere to the etiquettes of fasting, stay away from the causes of anger and revenge. Adorn your selves with the qualities of the pious predecessors. For verily the later generation of this nation will not be successful except with what the former generation was successful, from obedience and staying away from sins.

Ibn Rajab, may Allâh have mercy on him, said: "**Those who fast are of two levels:**

The First Level: Those who refrain from eating, drinking, and following ones desires for the sake of Allâh, hoping for a return of that with paradise. These individuals have indeed bartered with Allâh, and Allâh will not let the deeds of the sincere people go to waste. Rather He will allow them to benefit with a great benefit. The Prophet (ﷺ) said to a man:

إنك لن تدع شيئاً اتقاء الله إلا آتاك الله خيراً منه

"**You will not leave anything out of fear of Allâh, except that Allâh will replace it with what is better.**' [Collected by Ahmad. Muqbil graded it to be authentic in <u>As-Sahîh Al-Musnad</u>]

The fasting person will receive, in paradise, what he desires of food, drink, and women. Allâh said:

﴿ كُلُوا۟ وَٱشْرَبُوا۟ هَنِيٓـَٔۢا بِمَآ أَسْلَفْتُمْ فِى ٱلْأَيَّامِ ٱلْخَالِيَةِ ﴾

"It will be said to him, 'Eat and drink joyfully because of the good deeds you did in the days gone by.'" [Al-Hâqqah: 24]

Mujâhid and others (from the scholars of Tafsîr) said: this verse is referring to those who fast.

Likewise the one who the Prophet (ﷺ) saw in his dream in the hadîth of Abdul-Rahmân bin Samura he said: *"And I saw a man from my ummah panting like a dog out of thirst whenever he approaches The Hawd (i.e. the Prophet's Fountain in the hereafter) to drink from it he will be denied and pushed away, and his fasting in the month of Ramadan came and gave him a drink. So he drank until he quenched his thirst.'* [Collected by At-Tabarânî. Al-Uthaymîn graded its chain to be weak in his collection of Fatâwa]

O my people! Is there anyone who wants to address the Most Merciful in this blessed month? Is there anyone who desires what Allâh prepared for the obedient slaves in the paradise?

> Whoever wants the kingdom of the Paradise
> Then he should abstain from laziness
> And let him rise up in the darkness of the night
> To the illumination of the Qur'ân
> And let him continue to follow fasting with another
> Verily this life is a perishing life
> The real life is the one next to Allâh
> in the abode of Peace

The Second Level: The one who, in the worldly life, abstains from everything other than Allâh. He safeguards his head and what it contains, the belly and what it consumes; and he remembers death and the decaying of his body, and he chooses the hereafter over the luxury of this world. For this individual, his Feast of Fitr is the day he meets his Lord and when he is happy with seeing his Lord.

The Special Group from the Fasting Ones Are those who safeguard their Tongue from Slander and Lying

And the People of Knowledge and Happiness are those Who's Fast is Guarding the Heart from Falsehood and Being Blinded

There is no castle that can cause the people of knowledge to forget about seeing their Creator. And there is no river that (can stand in their way) causing them to deliberate at the expense of seeing Him. Rather their concern is far greater than that.

Whoever abstains, based on Allâh's command, from his desires in this world, will surely obtain it in the hereafter in Paradise. And whoever abstains from everything other than Allâh, his Feast will be the day he meets his Lord.

Allâh said:

﴿ مَن كَانَ يَرْجُواْ لِقَآءَ ٱللَّهِ فَإِنَّ أَجَلَ ٱللَّهِ لَآتٍ وَهُوَ ٱلسَّمِيعُ ٱلْعَلِيمُ ۝ ﴾

"Whoever desires the meeting of Allâh, then verily the appointed term of Allâh will come, and He is the All-Hearer, the All-Knower." [Al-Ankabût: 5]

"O those who turn to their Lord in repentance, fast today from the desires of your soul in order that you will celebrate your feast of Fitr on the Day of Judgment." [A Summary of Ibn Rajab's words from Latâif Al-Mâ'rif pages 295-300]

O Allâh beautify our secrete affairs with sincerity and embellish our deeds by helping us to follow the guidance of Your Messenger. (O Allâh) allow us to adorn ourselves with the etiquettes of Your Messenger. O Allâh, let us awake from our heedlessness, save us from deterioration, expiate our sins, and our shortcomings. Forgive us, our parents, and all the Muslim ummah both the living and the dead with Your mercy. For verily You are the Most Merciful. May the Peace and blessings be upon our Prophet Muhammad (ﷺ), his family members, and all his Companions.

المَجْلِسُ الثَاني عشر
The Twelfth Sitting
The Second Category of Recitation of the Qur'an

All praises are due to Allâh, the One who gives abundantly to those who obey Him, hoping (for His reward). (He) is severe in His punishment of those who turn away from His reminder, disobeying Him. He chooses whom He wills out of His bounty, thus bringing (certain ones) near to Him, while others, out of His justice, He distances them, leaving them to that which they have chosen. He sent down the Qur'ân as a mercy to all the worlds, and as a light for those who tread this path. Whoever holds on to it will achieve their goal. Whoever oversteps its boundaries and neglects its rights has indeed lost his religion and his worldly (life). I praise Him for the bounties He has given. I thank Him for His religious and worldly bounties which He has bestowed upon us. The grateful person is indeed worthy of receiving more. I further bear witness that none has the right to be worshiped but Allâh alone, (He is) without a partner, He has perfect attributes and He is high above all rivals.

I bear witness that Muhammad is His slave and His Messenger. He chose him and gave him preference over all of mankind. May Allâh send His salutation upon him, his family members, his companions, and those who properly follow their footsteps as long as the daylight continues to brighten the universe.

O My Brothers! We have mentioned before in the fifth sitting that the recitation of the Qur'ân is of two types. The first is the verbal recitation which is the oral one and we have explained this in the Fifth Sitting.

The Second Type: Recitation of its rulings by affirming its chronicles, following its legislations, adhering to its commands, and abstaining from its prohibitions. This kind is the utmost goal behind the revelation of the Qur'ân, as Allâh said:

$$\left\{ كِتَابٌ أَنزَلْنَاهُ إِلَيْكَ مُبَارَكٌ لِّيَدَّبَّرُوا آيَاتِهِ وَلِيَتَذَكَّرَ أُولُو الْأَلْبَابِ ﴿٢٩﴾ \right\}$$

"This is a Book which We have revealed to thee, full of excellences, that they may reflect over its verses, and that those gifted with understanding may take heed." [Sâd: 29]

This was the practice of the pious predecessors. They learned the Qur'ân stage by stage, while affirming it and implementing it in their lives with a positive implementation based on firm belief and true certainty. **Abû Abdur Rahmân As-Sulamî**, may Allâh have mercy on him, said: "**Those who used to teach us the Qur'an have informed us (i.e. 'Uthmân bin Affân, 'Abdullâh bin Mas'ûd and other than them) 'When they learned ten verses from the Prophet (ﷺ) they would not exceed them until they studied them and what they contain of knowledge and action.' They said: 'So as a result, we learned the Qur'ân, knowledge, and actions altogether.'"** [Narrated by Ibn Jarîr in his Tafsîr. Ahmad Shâkir graded this narration to be authentic]

This kind of recitation is the one around which our happiness and wretchedness revolve. Allâh said:

$$\left\{ فَإِمَّا يَأْتِيَنَّكُم مِّنِّي هُدًى فَمَنِ اتَّبَعَ هُدَايَ فَلَا يَضِلُّ وَلَا يَشْقَىٰ ﴿١٢٣﴾ وَمَنْ أَعْرَضَ عَن ذِكْرِي فَإِنَّ لَهُ مَعِيشَةً ضَنكًا وَنَحْشُرُهُ يَوْمَ الْقِيَامَةِ أَعْمَىٰ ﴿١٢٤﴾ قَالَ رَبِّ لِمَ حَشَرْتَنِي أَعْمَىٰ وَقَدْ كُنتُ بَصِيرًا ﴿١٢٥﴾ قَالَ كَذَٰلِكَ أَتَتْكَ آيَاتُنَا فَنَسِيتَهَا وَكَذَٰلِكَ الْيَوْمَ تُنسَىٰ ﴿١٢٦﴾ وَكَذَٰلِكَ نَجْزِي مَنْ أَسْرَفَ وَلَمْ يُؤْمِن بِآيَاتِ رَبِّهِ وَلَعَذَابُ الْآخِرَةِ أَشَدُّ وَأَبْقَىٰ ﴿١٢٧﴾ \right\}$$

"And if there comes to you guidance from Me, then whoso will follow My guidance, will not go astray, nor will he come to grief; But whosoever will turn away from My remembrance, his will be a straitened life, and on the Day of Resurrection We shall raise him up blind. He will say, 'My Lord, why hast Thou raised me up blind, while I possessed sight before?' (Allâh) will say, 'Thus did Our Signs come to thee and thou didst ignore them and in like manner wilt thou be ignored this day.' And thus do We recompense him who transgresses the limits of Divine Law and believes not in the Signs of his Lord; and the punishment of the Hereafter is even severer and more lasting."
[Tâhâ: 123-127]

Allâh has clarified in this great verse the reward of those who follow His guidance which He revealed to His Messengers. The greatest of this guidance is the Qur'ân. Likewise He clarified the punishment of those who turned away from His guidance. As for those who follow the guidance, their reward is as Allâh mentioned: they will neither go astray nor will they be wretched. The negation of misguidance and wretchedness from them indicates (that they are upon) perfect guidance and (experience) happiness in this world as well as in the hereafter. As for the punishment of those who turn their backs away from the guidance, their recompense is wretchedness and misguidance in this world and in the hereafter. (This person) will have a narrow life. He will be in constant anxiety and grief. In this world he has neither correct creed nor good deed. He is like the cattle or even worse (and more astray) than them. They are the neglectful ones. (The one who turns away from Allâh's revelation) will live a narrow life in his grave as well. His grave will be narrowed to the point that his ribs will merge in to one another. And on the Day of Resurrection he will be raised up blind, unable to see. As Allâh mentioned in another chapter of the Qur'ân:

$$\text{﴿ وَنَحْشُرُهُمْ يَوْمَ الْقِيَامَةِ عَلَىٰ وُجُوهِهِمْ عُمْيًا وَبُكْمًا وَصُمًّا ۖ مَأْوَاهُمْ جَهَنَّمُ ۖ كُلَّمَا خَبَتْ زِدْنَاهُمْ سَعِيرًا ﴿٩٧﴾ ﴾}$$

"And on the Day of Resurrection We shall gather them together on their faces blind, dumb and deaf. Their abode shall be Hell. Every time it abates, We shall increase for them the flame" [Al-Isrâ: 97]

This is because in this world, (these types of people) were blind from seeing the truth, deaf from hearing it, and they withheld from saying the truth. Allâh mentioned about them in His Book:

$$\text{﴿ وَقَالُوا قُلُوبُنَا فِي أَكِنَّةٍ مِمَّا تَدْعُونَا إِلَيْهِ وَفِي آذَانِنَا وَقْرٌ وَمِنْ بَيْنِنَا وَبَيْنِكَ حِجَابٌ فَاعْمَلْ إِنَّنَا عَامِلُونَ ﴿٥﴾ ﴾}$$

"And they say, 'Our hearts are secure under coverings against that which you call us, and in our ears there is heaviness, and between us and thee is a veil. So carry on your work; we, too, are working.'" [Fussilat: 5]

Thereupon, Allâh (ﷻ) recompensed them according to their deeds in this world, and neglected them as they have neglected His legislations:

$$\text{﴿ قَالَ رَبِّ لِمَ حَشَرْتَنِي أَعْمَىٰ وَقَدْ كُنتُ بَصِيرًا ﴿١٢٥﴾ قَالَ كَذَٰلِكَ أَتَتْكَ آيَاتُنَا فَنَسِيتَهَا ۖ وَكَذَٰلِكَ الْيَوْمَ تُنسَىٰ ﴿١٢٦﴾ ﴾}$$

"He will say: 'O my Lord! Why did you raise me up blind when I used to have sight?' And Allâh will say to him: 'like that, Our revelations have come to you but you have neglected them and for that reason you will be neglected this day.'" [Tâhâ: 125-126]

This is an exact recompense according to their evil crime. Whoever does an evil deed will be recompensed according to what he used to do.

It is mentioned in Sahîh Al-Bukhârî from the narration of Samura bin Jundub (ﷺ): "The Prophet (ﷺ) used to ask his companions after the fajr prayer if any of them saw a dream. Those who saw the dream would narrate to him what they saw. The Prophet (ﷺ) said to us one morning: '**Two visitors came to me last night and told me to proceed with them.** So we proceeded until we came across a man who was lying down on his side and another man standing over him with a big rock in his hand, and behold, he threw the rock to the man's head and smashed his head. Then the rock bounced here and there. He followed the rock and picked it up and by the time he would return back to him, his head would heal and return back to its normal state, and he would smash his head again, and this repeated over and over. I (i.e. Prophet Muhammad ﷺ) said to my Companions (i.e. the Angels) 'Glory be to Allâh! What is the matter with these two people?' They said to me 'proceed.' And then they informed the Prophet (ﷺ) at the end. They said: 'But as for that man whom you came across with his head being smashed, that is the individual who receives the knowledge of the Qur'ân and then rejects it, and he sleeps without praying the obligatory prayers.'" [Collected by Al-Bukhârî]

It is also narrated by 'Abdullâh bin 'Abbâs (ﷺ) that the Prophet (ﷺ) gave a speech to the people in the farewell pilgrimage and said to them: "**The devil has given up the hope of him being worshipped in your land, but he is pleased to be obeyed in other than that from among your deeds that you belittle. Therefore be aware of his plot! I have indeed left with you two things which if you hold on to them, you will never go astray: the Book of Allâh and the Sunnah of His Prophet**". [Graded authentic by Al-Albânî in Sahîh At-Targhîb]

It is also narrated by 'Amr bin Shu'ayb from his father, from his grandfather who said that the Prophet (ﷺ) said: **"The Qur'ân will come in the appearance of a man on the Day of Judgment along with a man who bore it but did not implement it and they will come for litigation before Allâh. Then the Qur'ân will say: 'O Allâh you made this man carry me, but what an evil carrier he is! He transgressed my set limits, neglected my obligations, committed my prohibitions and disobeyed my commands.' It will continue to throw evidences against him until it will be said to him: 'Deal with him according to what he deserved.' Then he will be dragged on his nose and be flung in to the Hell-Fire"**. [Al-Uthaymîn graded it weak in his Collection of Fatâwa]

It is also narrated in <u>Sahîh Muslim</u> from the narration of Abû Mâlik Al-Ash'arî (﴾) that the Prophet (ﷺ) said:

القرآن حُجَّةٌ لك أو عليك

"The Qur'ân is either a proof for or against you." [Collected by Muslim]

Also Ibn Mas'ûd (﴾) said: **"The Qur'an intercedes, likewise intercession is granted for its sake. Whoever places the Qur'ân before him, it will guide him to Paradise. And whoever places the Qur'ân behind him it will lead him to the hell-fire."**

O he who the Qur'an is his litigant! How could you hope to obtain intercession from something that you have made to be your litigant? Woe to he whose interceders will become his litigants on the day of benefiting from the item.

O Slaves of Allâh! This is the Book of Allâh that is being recited to you which you can hear. It is the Qur'ân which if it was to be revealed to the mountains, you would have seen the mountains humbling themselves, crumbling to dust. Even though this is the fact about the Qur'ân, the ears do not listen, the eyes do not shed tears, the heart is not affected by it, and the people do not adhere to its teaching in order that it will be the means of intercession. The hearts are void of the fear of Allâh and are ruined and overshadowed with the darkness of sins. As a result they neither see nor hear. How many times do we hear the Qur'ân being recited, but yet our hearts are as hard as rocks or even harder. And how many times does Ramadân reach us, yet our conditions are like the conditions of the wretched ones. The youth do not desist from their youthful passions and desires, nor do the elders desist from their evil actions and (strive to) catch up with the pious ones. Where are we from those people whom when they heard the call of Allâh they answered it, and when His revelations were recited to them they had tranquility in their hearts. They are the ones whom Allâh (ﷻ) has bestowed His bounties upon. Consequently, they knew Allâh's right and they chose the best deeds.

Ibn Mas'ûd said: "**The Qur'ân bearer must be known by his night while the people are sleeping, by his day while the people are eating, by his crying while the people are laughing, by his cautiousness while the people are careless, by his silence while the people are chatting, by his humbleness while the people are being proud, and by his sadness while the people are happy.**" [Ibn Rajab Reported in <u>Latâif Al-Mâ'rif</u>]

O my soul, the righteous are successful with piety
And they saw the truth while my heart is blinded from it
How beautiful they are when they are covered by the darkness of the night
And you see their glow brighter than the radiance of the stars
They hymn the praise of their Lord in their evenings
Their life is indeed pleasant with the glorification of their Lord
Their hearts are occupied with the remembrance of Allâh
Their tears are like arranged pearls
Their dawn is illuminated with their light

> Being forgiving is the best apportionment
> They have preserved their fasting from absurdity
> They humble themselves in the night in their remembrance
> Woe to you O soul! Will you not awake?
> Towards what will benefit you before the instability of your feet
> Many years have passed by in our negligence and desire,
> Therefore catch up with what is left from your age and take advantage

[See Ibn Rajab's <u>Latâif Al-Mâ'rif</u> pages 232, 324]

O My Brothers, memorize the Qur'ân before you lose the ability. Preserve its set limits, not transgressing against them and disobeying them. Know that this Qur'ân will bear witness for you or against you in front of the King, the Judge. Being grateful to Allâh for revealing this Book means that we should not throw it behind our backs. And honoring Allâh's commandments comprises not taking (the religious) rulings as an object of mockery.

﴿ وَيَوْمَ يَعَضُّ ٱلظَّالِمُ عَلَىٰ يَدَيْهِ يَقُولُ يَٰلَيْتَنِى ٱتَّخَذْتُ مَعَ ٱلرَّسُولِ سَبِيلًا ۝ يَٰوَيْلَتَىٰ لَيْتَنِى لَمْ أَتَّخِذْ فُلَانًا خَلِيلًا ۝ لَّقَدْ أَضَلَّنِى عَنِ ٱلذِّكْرِ بَعْدَ إِذْ جَآءَنِى ۗ وَكَانَ ٱلشَّيْطَٰنُ لِلْإِنسَٰنِ خَذُولًا ۝ وَقَالَ ٱلرَّسُولُ يَٰرَبِّ إِنَّ قَوْمِى ٱتَّخَذُوا۟ هَٰذَا ٱلْقُرْءَانَ مَهْجُورًا ۝ وَكَذَٰلِكَ جَعَلْنَا لِكُلِّ نَبِىٍّ عَدُوًّا مِّنَ ٱلْمُجْرِمِينَ ۗ وَكَفَىٰ بِرَبِّكَ هَادِيًا وَنَصِيرًا ۝ ﴾

"On that day the wrongdoer will bite his hands and will say, 'O, would that I had taken a way along with the Messenger! O, woe is me! Would that I had never taken so and so as a friend! He led me astray from the Reminder after it had come to me.' And Satan always deserts man in the hour of need. And the Messenger will say, 'O my Lord, my people indeed treated this Qur'ân as a thing to be discarded.' Thus did We make for every Prophet an enemy from among the sinners; and sufficient is thy Lord as a Guide and a Helper." [Al-Furqân: 27-31]

O Allāh, allow us to recite Your book as it should be recited. Make us among those who obtained success and happiness with it. O Allāh allow us to establish its words and meanings, (and allow us) to preserve its limits. O Allāh make us from among those who are firmly grounded in knowledge, those who believe in both the clear and the unclear verses. (O Allāh, make us from those who) affirm its chronicles and implement its commands.

Forgive us, our parents, and the rest of the Muslim Ummah with Your Mercy, for verily You are the Most Merciful. O Allāh! Send Your salutations upon our Prophet Muhammad (ﷺ), his family, and all his companions.

المَجْلِسُ الثَّالِثَ عَشَرَ
The Thirteenth Sitting
The Etiquettes of Reciting the Qur'ân

All praise is due to Allâh, the One whom every true worshiper humbles to His legislation and everyone who bows and prostrates yields to His sovereignty. And due to the sweetness of holding a conversation with Him, (every true worshipper) stays up in the night, forsaking his bed. And due to the quest to obtain His reward, the striver sacrifices his soul and toils. He, Glory be to Him, speaks in a manner that is far from resembling the Speech of the creatures. From among His Speech is His Book that was revealed to His Prophet Muhammad (ﷺ). We repeatedly recite it throughout the day and the night. It does not get faded due to continuous repetition and neither does it get boring. I praise Him with the praises of the one who hopes to stand at His door without being forsaken. And I bear witness that none has the right to be worshipped but Allâh alone without a partner. I bear witness that Muhammad is His slave and His Messenger, the one who carried out the responsibility of worshiping the Creator and prepared for the hereafter. May Allâh bless him, his companion Abû Bakr, the one who filled the hearts of his haters with an exhausting ulcer, 'Umar, the one who continued to support and strengthen Al-Islâm, 'Uthmân, the one who was not hesitant at his martyrdom, 'Alî the one who winnowed the plants of disbelief with his sword and harvested them, and the rest of his family and his companions, we ask for them a continuing blessing and mercy forever.

O My Brothers! This Qur'ân which is before you, which you recite, listen to it being recited, and which you memorize and write, it is the Speech of your Lord, the Lord of the worlds, the Lord of the first and last generations. It is His firm rope and the straight path. It is the blessed reminder and the book giving light. Allâh has spoken with it in truth in a manner that befits his

Majesty and His Sovereignty. He sent it with Jibrîl the Trustworthy and Honorable Angel, who is close to Allâh. He sent it down to the heart of Muhammad (ﷺ) in order that he be from those who warn, in an eloquent Arabic Language. Allâh has described this Book with great attributes in order for you to honor and respect it. He, the Most High, said:

$$﴿ شَهْرُ رَمَضَانَ ٱلَّذِىٓ أُنزِلَ فِيهِ ٱلْقُرْءَانُ هُدًى لِّلنَّاسِ وَبَيِّنَٰتٍ مِّنَ ٱلْهُدَىٰ وَٱلْفُرْقَانِ ۚ ﴾$$

"The month of Ramadân in which was revealed the Qur'ân, a guidance for mankind and clear proofs for the guidance and the criterion (between right and wrong)" [Al-Baqarah: 185]

Allâh said:

$$﴿ ذَٰلِكَ نَتْلُوهُ عَلَيْكَ مِنَ ٱلْءَايَٰتِ وَٱلذِّكْرِ ٱلْحَكِيمِ ﴾$$

"This is what We recite to you (O Muhammad) of the Verses and the Wise Reminder (i.e. the Qur'ân)." [Āli Imrân: 58]

Allâh said:

$$﴿ يَٰٓأَيُّهَا ٱلنَّاسُ قَدْ جَآءَكُم بُرْهَٰنٌ مِّن رَّبِّكُمْ وَأَنزَلْنَآ إِلَيْكُمْ نُورًا مُّبِينًا ﴾$$

"O mankind! Verily, there has come to you a convincing proof (Prophet Muhammad) from your Lord, and We sent down to you a manifest light (this Qur'ân)." [An-Nisâ: 174] Allâh said:

$$﴿ يَٰٓأَهْلَ ٱلْكِتَٰبِ قَدْ جَآءَكُمْ رَسُولُنَا يُبَيِّنُ لَكُمْ كَثِيرًا مِّمَّا كُنتُمْ تُخْفُونَ مِنَ ٱلْكِتَٰبِ وَيَعْفُواْ عَنْ$$

$$\text{كَثِيرٍ ۚ قَدْ جَاءَكُم مِّنَ ٱللَّهِ نُورٌ وَكِتَابٌ مُّبِينٌ ﴿١٥﴾ يَهْدِي بِهِ ٱللَّهُ مَنِ ٱتَّبَعَ رِضْوَانَهُ سُبُلَ ٱلسَّلَامِ وَيُخْرِجُهُم مِّنَ ٱلظُّلُمَاتِ إِلَى ٱلنُّورِ بِإِذْنِهِ وَيَهْدِيهِمْ إِلَىٰ صِرَاطٍ مُّسْتَقِيمٍ ﴿١٦﴾}$$

"O people of the Scripture (Jews and Christians)! Now has come to you Our Messenger (Muhammad) explaining to you much of that which you used to hide from the Scripture and passing over (i.e. leaving out without explaining) much. Indeed, there has come to you from Allâh a light (Prophet Muhammad) and a plain Book (this Qur'ân)". Wherewith Allâh guides all those who seek His Good Pleasure to ways of peace and He brings them out of darkness by His Will unto light and guides them to a Straight Way (Islamic Monotheism). [Al-Mâidah: 15-16] Allâh said:

$$\text{وَمَا كَانَ هَٰذَا ٱلْقُرْآنُ أَن يُفْتَرَىٰ مِن دُونِ ٱللَّهِ وَلَٰكِن تَصْدِيقَ ٱلَّذِي بَيْنَ يَدَيْهِ وَتَفْصِيلَ ٱلْكِتَابِ لَا رَيْبَ فِيهِ مِن رَّبِّ ٱلْعَالَمِينَ ﴿٣٧﴾}$$

"And this Qur'ân is not such as could ever be produced by other than Allâh, but it is a confirmation of (the revelation) which was before it [i.e. the Taurat (Torah), and the Injîl (Gospel), etc.], and a full explanation of the Book (i.e. laws and orders, etc, decreed for mankind) wherein there is no doubt from the Lord of all that exists." [Yûnûs: 37] Allâh said:

$$\text{يَا أَيُّهَا ٱلنَّاسُ قَدْ جَاءَتْكُم مَّوْعِظَةٌ مِّن رَّبِّكُمْ وَشِفَاءٌ لِّمَا فِي ٱلصُّدُورِ وَهُدًى وَرَحْمَةٌ لِّلْمُؤْمِنِينَ ﴿٥٧﴾}$$

"O mankind! There has come to you good advice from your Lord (i.e. the Qur'ân, ordering all that is good and forbidding all that is evil), and a healing for that (disease of ignorance, doubt, hypocrisy and differences, etc.) in your breasts, a guidance and a mercy (explaining lawful and unlawful things, etc.) for the believers." [Yûnûs: 57] Allâh said:

$$\bigl\{ \text{الٓرٰ ۚ كِتَٰبٌ أُحْكِمَتْ ءَايَٰتُهُۥ ثُمَّ فُصِّلَتْ مِن لَّدُنْ حَكِيمٍ خَبِيرٍ ۝} \bigr\}$$

"Alif Lâm Râ (This is) a Book, the Verses whereof are perfected (in every sphere of knowledge, etc.), and then explained in detail from One (Allâh), Who is All-Wise and Well-Acquainted (with all things)." [Hûd: 1] Allâh said:

$$\bigl\{ \text{إِنَّا نَحْنُ نَزَّلْنَا ٱلذِّكْرَ وَإِنَّا لَهُۥ لَحَٰفِظُونَ ۝} \bigr\}$$

"Verily We: It is We Who have sent down the Dhikr (i.e. the Qur'ân) and surely, We will guard it (from corruption)" [Al-Hijr:9] Allâh said:

$$\bigl\{ \text{وَلَقَدْ ءَاتَيْنَٰكَ سَبْعًا مِّنَ ٱلْمَثَانِى وَٱلْقُرْءَانَ ٱلْعَظِيمَ ۝ لَا تَمُدَّنَّ عَيْنَيْكَ إِلَىٰ مَا مَتَّعْنَا بِهِۦٓ أَزْوَٰجًا مِّنْهُمْ وَلَا تَحْزَنْ عَلَيْهِمْ وَٱخْفِضْ جَنَاحَكَ لِلْمُؤْمِنِينَ ۝} \bigr\}$$

"And indeed, We have bestowed upon you seven of Al-Mathânî (the seven repeatedly recited Verses), (i.e. Surat Al-Fâtihah) and the Grand Qur'ân. Look not with your eyes ambitiously at what We have bestowed on certain classes of them (the disbelievers), nor grieve over them. And lower your wings for the believers (be courteous to the fellow-believers)." [Al-Hijr: 87-88] Allâh said:

$$\text{﴿ وَيَوْمَ نَبْعَثُ فِى كُلِّ أُمَّةٍ شَهِيدًا عَلَيْهِم مِّنْ أَنفُسِهِمْ وَجِئْنَا بِكَ شَهِيدًا عَلَىٰ هَـٰٓؤُلَآءِ ۚ وَنَزَّلْنَا عَلَيْكَ ٱلْكِتَـٰبَ تِبْيَـٰنًا لِّكُلِّ شَىْءٍ وَهُدًى وَرَحْمَةً وَبُشْرَىٰ لِلْمُسْلِمِينَ ۝ ﴾}$$

"And We have sent down to you the Book (the Qur'ân) as an exposition of everything, a guidance, a mercy, and glad tidings for those who have submitted themselves (to Allâh as Muslims)". [An-Nahl: 89] Allâh said:

$$\text{﴿ إِنَّ هَـٰذَا ٱلْقُرْءَانَ يَهْدِى لِلَّتِى هِىَ أَقْوَمُ وَيُبَشِّرُ ٱلْمُؤْمِنِينَ ٱلَّذِينَ يَعْمَلُونَ ٱلصَّـٰلِحَـٰتِ أَنَّ لَهُمْ أَجْرًا كَبِيرًا ۝ وَأَنَّ ٱلَّذِينَ لَا يُؤْمِنُونَ بِٱلْـَٔاخِرَةِ أَعْتَدْنَا لَهُمْ عَذَابًا أَلِيمًا ۝ ﴾}$$

"Verily, this Qur'ân guides to that which is most just and right and gives glad tidings to the believers (in the Oneness of Allâh and His Messenger, Muhammad, etc.). Who work deeds of righteousness, that they shall have a great reward (Paradise). And that those who believe not in the Hereafter (i.e. they disbelieve that they will be recompensed for what they did in this world, good or bad, etc.), for them We have prepared a painful torment (Hell). [Al-Isrâ: 9-10] Allâh said:

$$\text{﴿ وَنُنَزِّلُ مِنَ ٱلْقُرْءَانِ مَا هُوَ شِفَآءٌ وَرَحْمَةٌ لِّلْمُؤْمِنِينَ ۙ وَلَا يَزِيدُ ٱلظَّـٰلِمِينَ إِلَّا خَسَارًا ۝ ﴾}$$

"And We send down from the Qur'an that which is a healing and a mercy to those who believe (in Islâmic Monotheism and act on it), and it increases the Thâlimûn (polytheists and wrong-doers) nothing but loss" [Al-Isrâ: 82] Allâh said:

$$\text{﴿ وَلَقَدْ صَرَّفْنَا لِلنَّاسِ فِى هَٰذَا ٱلْقُرْءَانِ مِن كُلِّ مَثَلٍ فَأَبَىٰٓ أَكْثَرُ ٱلنَّاسِ إِلَّا كُفُورًا ۝ ﴾}$$

"And indeed We have fully explained to mankind, in this Qur'ân, every kind of similitude, but most mankind refuse (the truth and accept nothing) but disbelief" [Al-Isrâ: 89] Allâh said:

$$\text{﴿ مَآ أَنزَلْنَا عَلَيْكَ ٱلْقُرْءَانَ لِتَشْقَىٰٓ ۝ إِلَّا تَذْكِرَةً لِّمَن يَخْشَىٰ ۝ تَنزِيلًا مِّمَّنْ خَلَقَ ٱلْأَرْضَ وَٱلسَّمَٰوَٰتِ ٱلْعُلَى ۝ ﴾}$$

"We have not sent down the Qur'ân unto you (O Muhammad) to cause you distress, But only as a Reminder to those who fear Allâh. A revelation from Him (Allâh) Who has created the earth and high heavens." [Tâhâ: 2-4] Allâh said:

$$\text{﴿ تَبَارَكَ ٱلَّذِى نَزَّلَ ٱلْفُرْقَانَ عَلَىٰ عَبْدِهِۦ لِيَكُونَ لِلْعَٰلَمِينَ نَذِيرًا ۝ ﴾}$$

"Blessed be He Who sent down the criterion (of right and wrong, i.e. this Qur'ân) to His slave (Muhammad) that he may be a warner to the 'Alamîn (mankind and jinns)." [Al-Furqân: 1] Allâh said:

﴿ وَإِنَّهُ لَتَنزِيلُ رَبِّ ٱلْعَٰلَمِينَ ۝ نَزَلَ بِهِ ٱلرُّوحُ ٱلْأَمِينُ ۝ عَلَىٰ قَلْبِكَ لِتَكُونَ مِنَ ٱلْمُنذِرِينَ ۝ بِلِسَانٍ عَرَبِيٍّ مُّبِينٍ ۝ وَإِنَّهُ لَفِى زُبُرِ ٱلْأَوَّلِينَ ۝ أَوَلَمْ يَكُن لَّهُمْ ءَايَةً أَن يَعْلَمَهُۥ عُلَمَٰٓؤُاْ بَنِىٓ إِسْرَٰٓءِيلَ ۝ ﴾

"And truly, this (the Qur'ân) is a revelation from the Lord of all that exists. Which the trustworthy Rûh [Jibraîl (Gabriel)] has brought down, upon your heart (O Muhammad) that you may be (one) of the warners. In the plain Arabic language. And verily, it (the Qur'ân, and its revelation to Prophet Muhammad) is (announced) in the Scriptures [i.e. the Taurat (Torah) and the Injîl (Gospel)] of former people. Is it not a sign to them that the learned scholars (like "Abdullâh bin Salam who embraced Islâm) of the Children of Isrâîl knew it (as true)? [Ash-Shu'arâ: 192-197] Allâh said:

﴿ وَمَا تَنَزَّلَتْ بِهِ ٱلشَّيَٰطِينُ ۝ وَمَا يَنۢبَغِى لَهُمْ وَمَا يَسْتَطِيعُونَ ۝ ﴾

"And it is not the Devils who have brought it (this Qur'ân) down. Neither would it suit them, nor can they (produce it)." [Ash-Shu'arâ 210-211] Allâh said:

﴿ بَلْ هُوَ ءَايَٰتٌۢ بَيِّنَٰتٌ فِى صُدُورِ ٱلَّذِينَ أُوتُواْ ٱلْعِلْمَ ۚ وَمَا يَجْحَدُ بِـَٔايَٰتِنَآ إِلَّا ٱلظَّٰلِمُونَ ۝ ﴾

"Nay, it is a collection of clear Signs in the hearts of those who are given knowledge. And none but the wrongdoers deny Our Signs" [Al-Ankabût: 49] Allâh said:

Sittings During the Blessed Month of Ramaḍān رَمَضَان

﴿ وَمَا عَلَّمْنَٰهُ ٱلشِّعْرَ وَمَا يَنۢبَغِى لَهُۥٓ إِنْ هُوَ إِلَّا ذِكْرٌ وَقُرْءَانٌ مُّبِينٌ ۝ لِّيُنذِرَ مَن كَانَ حَيًّا وَيَحِقَّ ٱلْقَوْلُ عَلَى ٱلْكَٰفِرِينَ ۝ ﴾

"And We have not taught him (Muhammad) poetry, nor is it suitable for him. This is only a Reminder and a plain Qur'ân. That he or it (Muhammad or the Qur'ân) may give warning to him who is living (a healthy minded the believer), and that Word (charge) may be justified against the disbelievers (dead, as they reject the warnings)." [Yâsîn: 69-70] Allâh said:

﴿ كِتَٰبٌ أَنزَلْنَٰهُ إِلَيْكَ مُبَٰرَكٌ لِّيَدَّبَّرُوٓا۟ ءَايَٰتِهِۦ وَلِيَتَذَكَّرَ أُو۟لُوا۟ ٱلْأَلْبَٰبِ ۝ ﴾

"(This is) a Book (the Qur'ân) which We have sent down to you, full of blessings that they may ponder over its Verses, and that men of understanding may remember." [Sâd: 29] Allâh said:

﴿ قُلْ هُوَ نَبَؤٌا۟ عَظِيمٌ ۝ ﴾

"Say: 'It (i.e. this Qur'ân) is a great news'" [Sad: 67] Allâh said:

﴿ ٱللَّهُ نَزَّلَ أَحْسَنَ ٱلْحَدِيثِ كِتَٰبًا مُّتَشَٰبِهًا مَّثَانِىَ تَقْشَعِرُّ مِنْهُ جُلُودُ ٱلَّذِينَ يَخْشَوْنَ رَبَّهُمْ ثُمَّ تَلِينُ جُلُودُهُمْ وَقُلُوبُهُمْ إِلَىٰ ذِكْرِ ٱللَّهِ ذَٰلِكَ هُدَى ٱللَّهِ يَهْدِى بِهِۦ مَن يَشَآءُ وَمَن يُضْلِلِ ٱللَّهُ فَمَا لَهُۥ مِنْ هَادٍ ۝ ﴾

"Allâh has sent down the best statement, a Book (this Qur'ân), its parts resembling each other in goodness and truth, oft-repeated. The skins of those who fear their Lord shiver from it (when they recite it or hear it). Then their skin and their heart soften to the remembrance of Allâh. That is the guidance of

Allâh. He Guides therewith whom He pleases and whomever Allâh sends astray, for him there is no guide" [Az-Zumar: 23] Allâh said:

$$﴿ إِنَّ ٱلَّذِينَ كَفَرُوا۟ بِٱلذِّكْرِ لَمَّا جَآءَهُمْ ۖ وَإِنَّهُۥ لَكِتَٰبٌ عَزِيزٌ ۝ لَّا يَأْتِيهِ ٱلْبَٰطِلُ مِنۢ بَيْنِ يَدَيْهِ وَلَا مِنْ خَلْفِهِۦ ۖ تَنزِيلٌ مِّنْ حَكِيمٍ حَمِيدٍ ۝ ﴾$$

"Verily, those who disbelieved in the Reminder (i.e. the Qur'ân) when it came to them (shall receive the punishment) And verily, it is an honorable respected Book (because it is Allâh's Speech, and He has protected it from corruption, etc.). Falsehood cannot come to it from before it or behind it (it is) sent down by the All-Wise, Worthy of all praise" [Fussilat: 41-42] Allâh said:

$$﴿ وَكَذَٰلِكَ أَوْحَيْنَآ إِلَيْكَ رُوحًا مِّنْ أَمْرِنَا ۚ مَا كُنتَ تَدْرِى مَا ٱلْكِتَٰبُ وَلَا ٱلْإِيمَٰنُ وَلَٰكِن جَعَلْنَٰهُ نُورًا نَّهْدِى بِهِۦ مَن نَّشَآءُ مِنْ عِبَادِنَا ۚ ﴾$$

"And thus We have sent to you, a Rûh of Our Command. You knew not what is the Book, nor what is Faith? But We have made it (this Qur'ân) a light wherewith We guide whosoever of Our slaves We will" [Al-Shûrâ: 52] Allâh said:

$$﴿ وَإِنَّهُۥ فِىٓ أُمِّ ٱلْكِتَٰبِ لَدَيْنَا لَعَلِىٌّ حَكِيمٌ ۝ ﴾$$

"And Verily, it (this Qur'ân) is in the Mother of the Book (i.e. The Preserved Tablet), before Us, indeed Exalted, full of Wisdom" [Az-Zukhruf: 4] Allâh said:

$$﴿ هَٰذَا بَصَٰٓئِرُ لِلنَّاسِ وَهُدًى وَرَحْمَةٌ لِّقَوْمٍ يُوقِنُونَ ۝ ﴾$$

"This (Qur'ân) is a clear insight and evidence for mankind, and a guidance and a mercy for people who have Faith with certainty". [Al-Jâthiyah: 20] Allâh said:

$$\bigl\{ ق ۚ وَالْقُرْآنِ الْمَجِيدِ ۝ \bigr\}$$

"Qâf, By the Glorious Qur'ân" [Qâf:1] Allâh said:

$$\bigl\{ ۞ فَلَا أُقْسِمُ بِمَوَاقِعِ النُّجُومِ ۝ وَإِنَّهُ لَقَسَمٌ لَّوْ تَعْلَمُونَ عَظِيمٌ ۝ إِنَّهُ لَقُرْآنٌ كَرِيمٌ ۝ فِي كِتَابٍ مَّكْنُونٍ ۝ لَا يَمَسُّهُ إِلَّا الْمُطَهَّرُونَ ۝ تَنزِيلٌ مِّن رَّبِّ الْعَالَمِينَ ۝ \bigr\}$$

"So I swear by the setting of the stars. And verily, that is indeed a great oath, if you but know. That (this) is indeed an honorable recital. In a Book well-guarded (with Allâh in the heaven i.e. The Preserved Tablet). Which none can touch but the purified. A Revelation from the Lord of the all that exists." [Al-Wâqi'ah 75-80] Allâh said:

$$\bigl\{ لَوْ أَنزَلْنَا هَٰذَا الْقُرْآنَ عَلَىٰ جَبَلٍ لَّرَأَيْتَهُ خَاشِعًا مُّتَصَدِّعًا مِّنْ خَشْيَةِ اللَّهِ ۚ وَتِلْكَ الْأَمْثَالُ نَضْرِبُهَا لِلنَّاسِ لَعَلَّهُمْ يَتَفَكَّرُونَ ۝ \bigr\}$$

"Had We sent down this Qur'ân on a mountain, you would surely have seen it humbling itself and rending asunder by the fear of Allâh. Such are the parables which We put forward to mankind that they may reflect" [Al-Hashr: 21] Allâh said:

$$\{ قُلْ أُوحِيَ إِلَيَّ أَنَّهُ اسْتَمَعَ نَفَرٌ مِنَ الْجِنِّ فَقَالُوا إِنَّا سَمِعْنَا قُرْآنًا عَجَبًا ۝ يَهْدِي إِلَى الرُّشْدِ فَآمَنَّا بِهِ وَلَنْ نُشْرِكَ بِرَبِّنَا أَحَدًا ۝ \}$$

"Say (O Muhammad): "It has been revealed to me that a group of Jinns listened (to this Qur'ân). They said: 'Verily! We have heard a wonderful Recital! 'It guides to the Right Path. So we believed in it. And we will not associate partners with our Lord in worship." [Al-Jinn:1-2] Allâh said:

$$\{ بَلْ هُوَ قُرْآنٌ مَجِيدٌ ۝ فِي لَوْحٍ مَحْفُوظٍ ۝ \}$$

"Nay! This is a Glorious Qur'ân, (Inscribed) in The Preserved Tablet!" [Al-Burûj: 22-21] Allâh said:

These great attributes which we have mentioned to you along with the ones which we have not mentioned, all of them indicate the greatness of this Qur'ân, the obligation of honoring it, and the proper behavior (one must have) while reciting it (including) staying away from jest and play.

From among the etiquettes of reciting the Qur'ân is making the intention to recite sincerely for Allâh. For indeed, recitation is from the great acts of worship, as we have previously mentioned when talking about its virtuous. Allâh states in His Book:

$$\{ فَادْعُوا اللَّهَ مُخْلِصِينَ لَهُ الدِّينَ \}$$

"Invoke Allâh making religion pure and sincerely for Him" [Ghâfir: 14]

And a similar command is directed to the Prophet (ﷺ) in (the chapter entitled) Az-Zumar verse two in His statement, the Most High:

$$\text{﴿ فَٱعْبُدِ ٱللَّهَ مُخْلِصًا لَّهُ ٱلدِّينَ ﴾}$$

"Worship Allâh making religion pure for Him alone" [Az-Zumar: 2]

Likewise Allâh the Most High said:

$$\text{﴿ وَمَآ أُمِرُوٓاْ إِلَّا لِيَعْبُدُواْ ٱللَّهَ مُخْلِصِينَ لَهُ ٱلدِّينَ حُنَفَآءَ ﴾}$$

"They are not commanded with anything but to worship Allâh Alone making religion purely and sincerely for Him and being upright and firm upon worshipping (Allâh) alone" [Al-Bayyinah: 5]

The Prophet (ﷺ) said: **"Read the Qur'ân seeking with it the Face of Allâh before there come some folk, who will establish it like the establishment of an arrow, they hasten its reward in this world and not the hereafter"** [Collected by Ahmad. Al-Albânî graded it to be sound]

From among the etiquettes of reciting the Qur'ân is to recite it with a conscious heart, contemplating its meaning, seeking to comprehend them.

(Likewise from the etiquettes of reciting the Qur'ân is) having tranquility in the heart and bearing in mind that Allâh, the Most High, is addressing (the reader). For indeed the Qur'ân is the Speech of Allâh (ﷻ).

From among the etiquettes of reciting the Qur'an is that you should recite it while in a state of ritual purity. By doing this you are honoring Allâh's speech (ﷻ). Likewise, one should not recite the Qur'ân while in a state of major ritual impurity until after performing the full body wash, if water is available. Otherwise perform tayammum with clean dirt, if you are unable to use water due to sickness or due to it not being available.

However (even in a state of major ritual impurity) one may glorify Allâh and invoke Him with the invocations mentioned in the Qur'ân, as long as one's intentions are not to actually *recite* the Qur'ân. An example of this is when one says:

﴿ لَّآ إِلَٰهَ إِلَّآ أَنتَ سُبْحَٰنَكَ إِنِّى كُنتُ مِنَ ٱلظَّٰلِمِينَ ۝ ﴾

"None has the right to be worshipped but You alone. Verily I am among those who wrong themselves." [Al-Anbiyâ: 87] The invocation of Yûnus (ﷺ)

Or to say (for example):

﴿ رَبَّنَا لَا تُزِغْ قُلُوبَنَا بَعْدَ إِذْ هَدَيْتَنَا وَهَبْ لَنَا مِن لَّدُنكَ رَحْمَةً إِنَّكَ أَنتَ ٱلْوَهَّابُ ﴾

"O our Lord! Do not cause our heart to divert from the straight path after you have guided us, and give us mercy from you verily you are the Giver" [Âli 'Imrân:8]

From among the etiquettes of reciting the Qur'ân is that one should not recite the Qur'ân in filthy areas or in a sitting where the people will not keep quiet and listen to the recitation. By (reciting the Qur'ân in such a gathering) you are humiliating the Book of Allâh. Likewise one should not recite the Qur'ân in the bathroom or places that are made for the sole purpose of defecation and urinating; this is not befitting for the Glorious Qur'ân.

From among the etiquettes of reciting the Book of Allâh is that one must seek refuge with Allâh from the devil when intending to recite. This is based on Allâh's statement:

$$\text{﴿ فَإِذَا قَرَأْتَ ٱلْقُرْءَانَ فَٱسْتَعِذْ بِٱللَّهِ مِنَ ٱلشَّيْطَانِ ٱلرَّجِيمِ ۝ ﴾}$$

"When you recite the Qur'ân seek refuge with Allâh from the Satan, the outcast" [Al-Nahl: 98]

By doing this (the reciter) will be safe from the devil's plot which turns him away from reciting the Book of his Lord or from completing it. But as for the "basmalah" and that is saying "bismillahi Rahmân Rahîm" if he starts his recitation from other than the beginning of the chapter, then he should not say the basmalah. But if he starts his recitation in the beginning of the chapter then he should begin it with the basmalah except when reciting the beginning of Surah Al-Tawbah, because it does not have a basmalah in its beginning. This is because it was difficult upon the companions to determine whether it is a chapter by itself or whether it was a continuation of Surah Al-Anfâl. So they have separated between them without basmalah.

And what they have agreed upon is the right decision without doubt. Because if there was basmalah in its beginning it will have been preserved, because Allâh (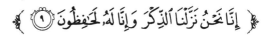) has guaranteed to preserve this Book. As He, the Most High, said:

$$\text{﴿ إِنَّا نَحْنُ نَزَّلْنَا ٱلذِّكْرَ وَإِنَّا لَهُۥ لَحَافِظُونَ ۝ ﴾}$$

"Verily it is We who revealed the Book and it is We who will preserve it" [Al-Hijr:9]

Also from among the etiquettes (of reciting the Qur'ân) is to beautify ones voice, reciting it in a beautiful melody. This is based on what is mentioned in Sahîh Al-Bukhârî and Sahîh Muslim from the hadîth of Abû Hurayrah (ﷺ) who said that the Prophet (ﷺ) said: "**Allâh did not listen to anything more than His listening to the Prophet who has a beautiful voice, reciting the Book of Allâh in a beautiful melody and proclaiming it.**" [Collected by Al-Bukhârî and Muslim]

It is also mentioned in Sahîh Al-Bukhârî and Sahîh Muslim from the narration of Jubayr bin Mut'im (ﷺ) who said: "**I heard the Prophet of Allâh (ﷺ) reciting Surah At-Tûr in the Maghrib prayer. I have never heard anyone who has better recitation than him (ﷺ).**" [Collected by Al-Bukhârî and Muslim]

However, if there are people around him who may be disturbed with his loud voice such as the one who is praying, the one who is sleeping and those similar to them, in this case he should not raise his voice in a manner that disturbs or harms them. This is because the Prophet (ﷺ) once came out to the people and found them praying, raising their voices while reciting. So the Prophet (ﷺ) said: "**The one who prays is holding a conversation with his Lord, therefore let him see with what does he converse his Lord, and let not some of you raise their voices over the other when reciting the Qur'ân.**" [Narrated by Mâlik in Al-Muwattah and Ibn 'Abdul Barr said it is authentic]

From the etiquettes of reciting the Book of Allâh is to recite it slowly in a manner that is clear and touching. This is because of Allâh's statement:

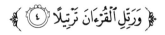

"Recite the Qur'ân (aloud) in a slow, (pleasant tone and) style" [Al-Muzammil: 4]

This is because by reciting it in that manner it will help you to ponder and contemplate more on its meaning and give its letters and words their right(s) of articulation.

It is mentioned in <u>Sahîh Al-Bukhârî</u> from the narration of Anas bin Mâlik (ﷺ) when he was asked about the recitation of the Prophet (ﷺ) he replied: **"He used to recite deliberately."** And then he recited Sûratu Al-Fâtihah to demonstrate to (the people) how the Prophet (ﷺ) used to recite. [Narrated by Ahmad, Abû Dâwûd, and At-Tirmidhî]

Ibn Mas'ûd (ﷺ) said: **"Do not spread it like the spreading of the dust, and do not recite it very fast like the way they say a poem. Stand by its wonders and shake the hearts with it. Let not your concern base on completing the entire Qur'ân."**

There is nothing wrong with reciting it fast as long as it does not affect the wording, lead to dropping out of some letters, or merging together letters that are not supposed to be merged. If it leads to violation of its wording then it is impermissible because this changes the meaning of the Qur'ân.

From among the etiquettes of reciting the Qur'ân is to prostrate upon reciting verses of prostration as long as a person is upon ritual purity, regardless of whether the verse is recited during the day or night. One should say the takbîr (before) prostrating and then say: "Glorified is my Lord the Most High." Then one should invoke Allâh and then raise his head up, without saying the takbîr and without (concluding with the) salâms. That is because the Prophet (ﷺ) only declared the taslîm and the takbîr (upon raising up from prostration) when he was in the prayer. As it is narrated in the hadîth of Abû Hurayrah (ﷺ) that he used to say the takbîr whenever he rose up and went down in his prayer. [Collected by Muslim]

Also Ibn Mas'ûd said: **"I saw the Prophet (ﷺ) saying the takbîr in every rising and falling, and every standing and sitting."** [Narrated by Ahmad, An-Nasâî', and At-Tirmidhî graded it to be authentic]. This includes the prostration while praying along with the prostration of recitation (outside of the prayer).

These are some of the etiquettes of recitation. Therefore discipline yourselves with them, preserve them, and seek with it Allâh's Bounties.

O Allâh make us among those who honor Your sanctity, those who are successful with Your gifts, the inheritors of Your gardens. And forgive us, our parents, and all the Muslims with Your mercy. For verily You are the Most Merciful. May Allâh shower His blessings on His Prophet Muhammad, his family, and all his Companions.

المَجْلِسُ الرَّابِعَ عَشَرَ
The Fourteenth Sitting

Praise be to Allâh, the One who sees that which is apparent and that which is hidden, the One who knows the secret and the open affairs of His slaves as well as their inner thoughts, the Only Originator of the Universe and its Decorator, the One who decrees the movements of the creatures and their stillness. He has perfected everything that He created; He carved the ears and eyes. He encompasses the number of leaves of the trees. He stretched out the earth and stabilized it. He expanded the sky and raised it up. He makes the stars move and exposes them in the darkness of the night; He sent down the rain from the sky pouring and drizzling. And He protects, with it, the seeds from dehydration.

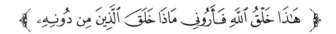

"This is the creation of Allâh, so show me the creation of those (whom they worship) besides him" [Luqmân: 11]

I thank Him for His generosity and kindness. I also bear witness that none has the right to be worshiped but He Alone, without a partner in His (unique right) to be worshipped and nor in His sovereignty. And I also bear witness that Muhammad (ﷺ) is His slave and His Messenger, the one who is supported with proofs from Allâh, peace be upon him, his companion Abû Bakr, in all his affair, 'Umar, the one who terrified the Persian king in his palace, 'Uthmân, the one who revived his night in recitation of the Qur'ân, 'Alî, the one who exterminated the door of khaybar and shook its fortress, upon his family, and his companions, those who strived hard to be obedient to their Lord in their movements and in their stillness.

رَمَضَان Sittings During the Blessed Month of Ramaḍān

O My Brothers! Allâh (ﷻ) said:

﴿ فَٱلْـَٔنَ بَـٰشِرُوهُنَّ وَٱبْتَغُوا۟ مَا كَتَبَ ٱللَّهُ لَكُمْ وَكُلُوا۟ وَٱشْرَبُوا۟ حَتَّىٰ يَتَبَيَّنَ لَكُمُ ٱلْخَيْطُ ٱلْأَبْيَضُ مِنَ ٱلْخَيْطِ ٱلْأَسْوَدِ مِنَ ٱلْفَجْرِ ۖ ثُمَّ أَتِمُّوا۟ ٱلصِّيَامَ إِلَى ٱلَّيْلِ ﴾

"So now have sexual relations with them and seek that which Allâh has ordained for you (offspring), and eat and drink until the white thread (light) of dawn appears to you distinct from the black thread (darkness of night), then complete your Fast till the nightfall." [Al-Baqarah: 187]

In this verse Allâh (ﷻ) mentioned the fundamental nullifiers of the fast. And the Prophet (ﷺ) mentioned in the Sunnah the remaining nullifiers.

There are seven things which nullify the fast:

The First: Sexual intercourse, which is the penetration of the penis into the vagina. This is the major nullifier, as well as a major sin for the one who perpetrates such an act. Whenever the fasting person has intercourse, his fast becomes nullified, whether it is an obligatory or voluntary fast. If this happened in the day time of Ramaḍân, one must make up that day along with a severe penalty, which is to free a slave. If he does not have any slaves, then he must fast two months consecutively without breaking his fast within this period except if he has a valid excuse: such as the days of the 'Eîd, the three days after the sacrificial feast, the days of tashrîq, or if he is sick or traveling on a journey in which he travels merely to break the fast.

If he breaks his fast without a valid excuse, even if it is a single day, he must start all over again from scratch. If he is unable to fast two months continuously then he should feed sixty poor people, for every poor person 510 grams of good barley (or 750 ml of any appropriate food item, regardless of the difference in weight). It is reported in Sahîh Al-Bukhârî that a man had intercourse with his wife in the daytime of Ramadân. So he came and asked the Prophet (ﷺ) the ruling on that. The Prophet (ﷺ) asked him '**Can you find a slave to free?**' He said "**no.**" He said to him: '**Can you fast two months continuously?**' He said: 'no.' He said to him: '**Then feed sixty poor people.**' And the details of this hadîth can be found in the Sahîh Al-Bukhârî and Sahîh Muslim.

The Second: Intentional ejaculation from kissing, masturbating, or that which is similar to this. This is one of the desires that must be abstained from while fasting, as it is mentioned in the hadîth qudsî: "**He leaves his food, drink, and his desire(s) for My sake.**" [Collected by Al-Bukhârî]

As for kissing and touching *without* ejaculation, this does not nullify the fast, based on what is mentioned in Sahîh Al-Bukhârî and Sahîh Muslim from the narration of 'Âîshah (رضي الله عنها):

أَنَّ النبيَّ صلى الله عليه وسلّم كان يُقَبِّلُ وهو صائمٌ ويباشر وهو صائمٌ، ولكِنَّه كان أَمْلَكَكُمْ لإِرِبه

"The Prophet (ﷺ) used to kiss and fondle while fasting, but he can control himself more than you can."[Collected by Al-Bukhârî and Muslim]

In Sahîh Muslim it is narrated from 'Umar bin Abî Salamah that he asked the Prophet (ﷺ): "Is it permissible for the fasting person to kiss (his spouse)? The Prophet (ﷺ) said to him: '**Ask this lady.**' He meant (his wife) Umm Salamah. She informed him that the Prophet (ﷺ) used to do that. So ('**Umar bin Abî Salamah**) said, 'O Messenger of Allâh, you have been forgiven for your past and future sins.' Then the Prophet (ﷺ) said: "**Indeed I am the most pious and the most righteous of you all.**" [Collected by Muslim]

However, if the fasting person fears for himself ejaculation by kissing and fondling, or fears that it may lead to actual intercourse due to his weakness of controlling his desires, then it will be impermissible for him to fondle as a precautionary measure, in order to preserve his fast from being corrupted. This is the reason why the Prophet (ﷺ) commanded the fasting person not to aggressively inhale water in to one's nostrils when performing the ablution for fear that the water may travel to his stomach.

As for ejaculation caused by a wet dream or mere thinking (without any actions), this will not nullify your fast, because the fasting person has no control over his dream. As for thinking (about intimacy with one's wife) it is also forgiven, based on the Prophet's statement:

إنَّ الله تَجَاوزَ عن أمَّتي ما حدَّثَتْ به أنْفُسَهَا ما لم تَعْمَلْ أوْ تتكلمْ

"Allâh has forgiven my Ummah their evil thoughts as long as they did not say it or act upon it." [Collected by Al-Bukhârî and Muslim]

The Third: Eating or drinking: by passing the food through your mouth or nose (and eventually) arriving into your stomach. This includes all kinds of foods and drinks, based on Allâh's statement:

﴿ وَكُلُواْ وَٱشْرَبُواْ حَتَّىٰ يَتَبَيَّنَ لَكُمُ ٱلْخَيْطُ ٱلْأَبْيَضُ مِنَ ٱلْخَيْطِ ٱلْأَسْوَدِ مِنَ ٱلْفَجْرِ ﴾

"And eat and drink until the white thread (light) of dawn appears to you distinct from the black thread (darkness of night)" [Al-Baqarah: 187]

This includes inhaling through the nose based on the Prophet's (ﷺ) statement in the hadith of Laqît bin Sabrah:

وَبَالِغْ فِي الاسْتِنْشَاقَ، إِلاَّ أَنْ تَكُونَ صَائِماً

"Sniff water up high to the nostril except if you are fasting."
[Authenticated by Al-Albânî in Irwâ Al-Ghalîl]

As for smelling fragrances (and scents), this will not nullify the fast because (scents) are not a (physical substance).

The Forth: Anything that replaces eating or drinking also nullifies the fast. **They are of Two Types:**

1st: Injecting blood. For example if the fasting person is suffering from hemorrhage and is injected with blood, this will nullify his fast. That is because blood is the goal of eating and drinking. Therefore by injecting the blood you have nourished the fasting person.

2nd: The nourishing injection that suffices you from eating and drinking, if a person uses them, his fast is nullified. Although it is not actual food, it replaces eating and drinking and serves the same function.

As for injections which are not for the purpose of nourishment, it will not nullify the fast whether one took it through his muscles or his veins. Even if he felt the taste in his throat it will still not nullify his fast because it is neither food nor drink, and does not serve the same purpose as food or drink. Thus it cannot take the same ruling (i.e. meaning it does not invalidate the fast).

And no attention is given to the presence of the taste of a substance inside one's throat, if it is not food or drink. For this reason, our scholars have mentioned: **"If a person were to stomp their foot on colocynth, and found the taste of it inside his throat, it would not break his fast."**

Sheikh Al-Islâm Ibn Taymiyyah said in his letter entitled The Reality of Fasting: "There is no proof which indicates that Allâh and His Messenger have made the nullifiers of the fast anything which reaches the brain, the body, goes through the body, or reaches the stomach as those people presume. (Due to them thinking that a nullifier of the fast is everything that shares these aforementioned descriptions)." He said: "And if Allâh and His Messenger did not make the (legislative ruling of breaking the fast) connected with these meanings, then the statement of those who say: 'Allâh and His Messenger made this thing as a nullifier of fasting due to such and such of a reason, is merely speaking without any knowledge."

The Fifth Nullifier: Cupping. Based on the Prophet's statement (ﷺ): "**The fast of both the one who received the cupping and the one who gave it is broken.**" [This hadîth is narrated by Ahmad and Abû Dâwûd from the hadîth of Shaddâd bin Auws. Al-Bukhârî said: "**This is the most authentic narration concerning this issue.**"]

This is the school of thought of Al-Imâm Ahmad and the majority of the scholars of hadîth. Included in the meaning of removing blood by way of cupping, is to remove blood by way of phlebotomy and that which is similar to that, from those things which weaken the body as cupping does.

So based on this, it is also not permissible for the one who is observing the obligatory fast to donate blood except in case of necessity. There is no sin upon the fasting person who has blood taken from him (in such a case), it is permissible in time of need. He should break his fast for that day and make it up later. But the blood that comes out due to nasal hemorrhage, coughing, hemorrhoid, tooth pulling, a cut in one's wound, blood test, injections, and things similar to this, these things do not nullify the fast because they are not like cupping and neither are they similar to cupping; they do not affect the body in the same way as cupping.

The Sixth Nullifier is: Disgorging intentionally, which is to release the food and drink which is inside the statement via the mouth. This is based on the Prophet's (ﷺ) statement:

مَنْ ذَرَعه الْقَيْءُ فليس عليه قضاءٌ ومَن استقاءَ عمداً فلْيَقِض

"Whoever is unintentionally overcome by vomiting does not have to make up his fast, but whoever regurgitated intentionally (i.e. he made himself vomit) must make up (his fast)." [Narrated by the five scholars of hadîth except Al-Imâm Nasâ'î. Al-Hâkim declared it authentic. Al-Albânî graded it to be authentic in Sahîh At-Tirmidhî]

As for the one who intentionally vomits, either by an action such as squeezing his belly, dipping his finger in his throat, by smelling, such as smelling something that will make him vomit, or by looking, such as intentionally looking at a thing that will cause him to vomit, this person has broken his fast.

But if one vomits without any specific reason, this does not harm his fast. If your stomach surges by itself then you should not try to stop yourself from vomiting because it may be harmful to your health, rather leave it alone. (So in summary): do not make yourself vomit and do not stop yourself from vomiting (if your stomach is beginning to surge).

The Seventh Nullifier: Menstrual or Postpartum bleeding based on the Prophet's (ﷺ) statement regarding the woman: **"Does not she avoid praying and fasting when she sees her menses?"** [Collected by Al-Bukhârî and Muslim]

Her fast is corrupt at the moment she sees her menses or the postpartum bleeding, whether it is at the beginning of the day, the end of the day, or even if it is just a moment before sunset. However, if she felt the coming of the blood, but it did not become distinctively clear until after sunset, her fast (for that day) is still valid.

It is forbidden for the fasting person, observing an obligatory fast, to fall into any of these aforementioned nullifiers. (Examples of obligatory fasting) includes: fasting the month of Ramadân, fasting to fulfill a penalty, fasting to fulfill a vow with Allâh etc. (One may not break his fast) except if he has a legislative excuse allowing him to do so, such as traveling, sickness, etc. That is because whoever initiates an obligation must complete it, except if he has a valid excuse.

Also, whoever breaks his fast in the day time of Ramadân without a valid excuse must refrain from eating the rest of the day and he must make that day up later. But if it is (an obligatory fast) outside of Ramadân, (and he breaks his fast) he just has to make it up (and does not have to refrain from food and drink after breaking the fast that day).

If his fasting is supererogatory, it is permissible for him to break his fast even without a valid excuse, but it is better to complete it.

O My Brothers! Safeguard the righteous acts of obedience, stay far away from sins and abominations. Supplicate to the Originator of the heavens and earth, and hasten towards His Bounties; for verily He gives abundantly. And know that all you have in this world is whatever you have spent in the obedience of your Lord. Therefore rush to the treasure! Rush to the treasure before it is too late. Rush to the great gain, rush to the great gain, before the arrival of loss.

O Allāh grant us success to benefit from our time, keeping it busy with good deeds. O Allāh give us from Your Bounty and generosity, and deal with us with pardoning and forgiveness. O Allāh grant us ease in all our affairs, keep us far away from hardship, and forgive us the previous and latter sins that we have committed. O Allāh we ask You to provide us with the intercession of our Prophet (on the Day of Judgment), allow us to come and drink from his fountain. Give us a drink from it that will keep us hydrated forever, (we ask You) O Lord of the worlds!

O Allāh, bless us and send the peace and blessings upon Your slave, your Prophet Muhammad (ﷺ), his family members, and all his Companions.

المَجْلِسُ الخَامِسُ عشر
The Fifteenth Sitting
The Conditions that must be Fulfilled in order for something to actually break the fast & The things that are permissible for the fasting person to do

All praise is due to Allâh, the Wise, the Creator, the Almighty, the Patient, the Truthful, the Most Merciful, the Most Bounteous, the Provider, He raised the seven ascending stairs without any pillar or hook holding them, and He stabilized the earth with the mountains. He made Himself known to the creatures by proofs and evidences, and He guaranteed to provide for all His creatures. He created man from a gushing fluid, and obligated the legislation on him, and He forgave him what he did wrong out of error or forgetfulness. I will continue to praise Him as long as one remains silent and as long as one continues to talk.

I also bear witness that none has the right to be worshipped but Allâh alone without a partner, a sincere testimony that is free from hypocrisy, and I also bear witness that Muhammad is His slave and His Messenger, the one whose call includes every descending and ascending (creature). Peace be upon him, upon Abû Bakr, his companion the one who stood firm on the Day of the battle of apostasy, upon 'Umar, the exterminator of the disbelievers and the opener of the locks, upon 'Uthmân, the one who none violates his right but the rebellion, upon 'Alî the One who took risks due to his courage, upon (the Prophet's ﷺ) family members, and his companions who preceded those who came after them in virtue.

O My Brothers! The aforementioned nullifiers of fasting, with the exclusion of menses and postpartum bleeding, only nullify the fast if one commits them with knowledge, while remembering he is fasting, and willingly.

These are three conditions:

The First Condition: To commit these nullifiers knowingly. If you committed them unknowingly you will not be held accountable for it, because of Allâh's statement (informing about the supplication of the believers):

$$\{ \text{رَبَّنَا لَا تُؤَاخِذْنَا إِن نَّسِينَا أَوْ أَخْطَأْنَا} \}$$

"O our Lord! Do not hold us accountable if we forget or made a mistake" [Al-Baqarah: 286]

Allâh said: "I have indeed done that." [Collected by Muslim] Likewise Allâh's statement:

$$\{ \text{وَلَيْسَ عَلَيْكُمْ جُنَاحٌ فِيمَا أَخْطَأْتُم بِهِ وَلَٰكِن مَّا تَعَمَّدَتْ قُلُوبُكُمْ ۚ وَكَانَ ٱللَّهُ غَفُورًا رَّحِيمًا} \}$$

"There is nothing wrong on you regarding the things that you do by mistake except the things that you do intentionally, and He Allâh is Oft-Forgiving Most Merciful" [Al-Ahzâb:5]

(This applies) whether the person is ignorant of the religious ruling connected to the issue, like a person who actually does not know that a certain things nullifies the fast or whether the person is ignorant of the time, like an individual who does not know that dawn has appeared, thus he eats while dawn has appeared. Also an individual who thinks that the sun has set, so he eats although the sun has not yet set. None of these things will nullify your fast. The proof being what is mentioned in Sahîh Al-Bukhârî and Sahîh Muslim from the narration of 'Adî bin Hâtim (ﷺ) who said: "When (the verse) was revealed:

$$\{ \text{وَكُلُوا۟ وَٱشْرَبُوا۟ حَتَّىٰ يَتَبَيَّنَ لَكُمُ ٱلْخَيْطُ ٱلْأَبْيَضُ مِنَ ٱلْخَيْطِ ٱلْأَسْوَدِ مِنَ ٱلْفَجْرِ ثُمَّ أَتِمُّوا۟ ٱلصِّيَامَ إِلَى ٱلَّيْلِ} \}$$

'Eat and drink until the white thread (light) of dawn appears to you distinct from the black thread (darkness of night), then complete your fast till the nightfall.' [Al-Baqarah:187]

('Adî said): 'I went and got me a white and a black thread and placed them under my pillow and continued to look at them until when I was able to differentiate between them. (Once I was able to differentiate) I would commence my fast. When I reached the morning I went to the Messenger of Allâh and informed him about what I did.

The Prophet (ﷺ) said: 'Your pillow must be very wide if the white and black thread could be placed under it! The black and white threads are none other than the light of dawn and the darkness of the night.'" [Collected by Al-Bukhârî and Muslim]

Surely 'Adî ate after the appearance dawn and did not seize from eating until when he was able to differentiate between the two threads, but the Prophet (ﷺ) did not command him to make up his fast. This is because he was ignorant of the religious ruling.

Also it is reported in <u>Sahîh Al-Bukhârî</u> from the narration of Asmâ the daughter of Abû Bakr (ﷺ), who said: **"We broke our fast during the time of the Prophet (ﷺ) on a cloudy day (thinking that the sun had set) then after a while the sun appeared."** [Collected by Al-Bukhârî]

She did not mention that the Prophet (ﷺ) commanded them to make up that day (even though they ate before sunset). This is because they were ignorant of the time. Had they been commanded to make it up, it would have certainly been narrated for verily this is an important issue that cannot be neglected. Rather, Ibn Taymiyyah mentioned in his book entitled <u>The Reality of Fasting</u>, that Hishâm bin 'Urwah, one of the narrators of this hadîth, narrated from his father that **"They were not commanded to make up the fasting of that day."**

However, if an individual is aware that the sun has not yet set, he must wait until it sets.

For example: If a person unknowingly ate after the rising of the dawn and then discovers afterwards that the dawn has risen, his fast is still valid and he does not have to make up that day, because he was ignorant of the time. And Allâh has made it permissible for him to eat and drink until it becomes clear that dawn has appeared. So a person is not commanded to make up for something which he was legislatively allowed to do.

The Second Condition: That a person must remember (he is fasting). If a person eats due to forgetfulness his fast is still valid, and he does not have to make it up. The proof for this is what is previously mentioned in Al-Baqarah as well as the hadîth which is narrated by Abû Hurayrah (﴾﴿) that the Messenger of Allâh (﴾﴿) said:

من نَسِيَ وهُوَ صَائِمٌ فأكَلَ أو شرِبَ فليُتِمَّ صَوْمَهُ فإنَّما أطْعَمَهُ اللهُ وسقاه

"Whoever ate while fasting out of forgetfulness or drank then he should complete his fast for verily it is Allâh who fed him and gave him drink" [Collected by Al-Bukhârî and Muslim]

The Prophet's (﴾﴿) command to complete the fast (although a person ate or drank) is proof that the fast is still valid. And attributing the eating and drinking to Allâh is proof that the fasting person will not be held accountable for it. However, whenever an individual remembers or is reminded (that he is fasting) he should stop eating and spit out whatever is in his mouth, because the excuse (of forgetfulness) is no longer present. Likewise, it is a must upon whoever sees the fasting person eating or drinking to remind him, based on Allâh's statement:

$$﴿ وَتَعَاوَنُوا۟ عَلَى ٱلْبِرِّ وَٱلتَّقْوَىٰ ۝ ﴾$$

"Help one another upon good and piety" [Al-Mâi'dah: 5]

The Third Condition: Breaking one's fast willingly, meaning he chooses out of his own free-will to break his fast. However, if a fasting person is (forcefully) compelled to break the fast, his fast is still valid. Surely Allâh has pardoned the individual who is compelled to disbelieve as long as his heart is at rest with true faith. (This is found) in Allâh's statement:

$$﴿ مَن كَفَرَ بِٱللَّهِ مِنۢ بَعْدِ إِيمَٰنِهِۦٓ إِلَّا مَنْ أُكْرِهَ وَقَلْبُهُۥ مُطْمَئِنٌّۢ بِٱلْإِيمَٰنِ ﴾$$

"Whoever disbelieved in Allâh after his belief, except him who is forced thereto and whose heart is at rest with Faith" [An-Nahl: 106]

So if Allâh (pardons) the one who is compelled to disbelieve, then whatever is less than that is, with greater reason, to be overlooked. Also based on the Prophet's (ﷺ) statement:

$$إنَّ الله تجاوز عن أمَّتي الْخَطأَ والنسيانَ وما استُكرهوا عليه$$

"Indeed Allâh has forgiven my ummah the wrong things which they do out of error, forgetfulness, or compulsion." [Narrated by

Ibn Mâjah, Al-Bayhaqî, and An-Nawawî graded it sound. Al-Albânî graded it to be authentic in Sahîh Ibn Mâjah].

If a man forced his wife to have intercourse with him while she was fasting, her fast is still valid; she does not have to make it up. Although it is not permissible for him to compel her while she is fasting, unless she is observing a supererogatory fast, without his permission, while he is present.

If dust or anything flew into a person's mouth reaching his stomach unwillingly, or passes through his throat while sniffing the water and rinsing out his mouth, his fast is still valid. He does not have to make it up.

Also applying eye-liner or eye drops in will not nullify your fast even if you found the taste in your throat, because they are neither food nor drink, nor do they function as food or drink.

Likewise using ear drops or putting medicine in your injury for treatment will not break your fast even if you found the taste in your throat because they are neither food nor drink, and they do not function as food or drink.

Sheikh Al-Islâm Ibn Taymiyyah said in his book entitled The Reality of Fasting: "We know that there is no proof from the Book or the Sunnah that indicates that the above-mentioned (things) break the fast. Therefore we know that they do not break the fast."

Then he said: "Indeed fasting is from the religious acts of worship which every Muslim is obligated to have knowledge of. If these things were from that which Allâh and His Messenger have made impermissible upon the fasting person, because they corrupt the fast, then it would have been obligatory for the Messenger (ﷺ) to clarify it. And if it were mentioned, the Companions would have known of it, and they would have conveyed it to the

Ummah, as they have conveyed the other acts of worship. But since it was the case that no one conveyed it from the people of knowledge, reporting it from the Prophet (ﷺ), not an authentic or weak narration, and neither a connected nor disconnected narration, with this it becomes known that nothing of the sort was mentioned. As for the narration reported about (the permissibility of wearing) eye-liner in the night when sleeping and forbade it for the fasting person, this narration is weak. Abû Dâwûd said: Yaḥyâ bin Ma'în informed me that: **"This hadîth is munkar (i.e. a narration in which a weak narrator opposes the reliable narrators)."**

Sheikh Al-Islâm said: "**The rulings that the Muslims need to know regarding their religion, it is a must that they be clarified by the Prophet (ﷺ) and conveyed by his companions. Therefore if there is not any clarification from the Prophet (ﷺ) and (the Companions did not) convey (these matters), then it must be known that these things are not from the religion.**" This statement of Ibn Taymiyyah is very strong and it is based on clear evidence and firm principles.

Likewise tasting food without swallowing it or smelling oils or fragrances (this does not nullify the fast). But he should not sniff incense's smoke because it may go through the throat and into the stomach. Likewise rinsing the mouth out, and sniffing water in order to clean the nostrils, do not nullify the fast. However (the fasting person) should not sniff the water up high in his nostril in order to avoid water from passing through his throat to his stomach. The proof for this is the narration of Laqît bin Sabra (ﷺ) who reported that the Prophet (ﷺ) said:

أَسْبِغِ الوضوء وخَلِّلْ بينَ الأصابع وبالِغْ في الاستنشاق إلاَّ أنْ تكون صائماً

Sittings During the Blessed Month of Ramaḍān رَمَضَانَ

"Perform ablution perfectly and use your finger to clean between your fingers and sniff the water up high in your nostril unless you are fasting" [Narrated by Abû Dâwûd and An-Nasâî'. Ibn Khuzaymah graded it to be authentic. Authenticated by Al-Albânî in Sahîh Al-Jâmi']

Likewise using the miswâk will not break your fast. As a matter of fact it is recommended in the beginning of the day *and* the end of the day, whether one is fasting or not. This is based on the Prophet's (ﷺ) statement:

لولا أنْ أشقَّ على أمَّتِي لأمرْتُهم بالسواكِ عندَ كلِّ صلاةٍ

"Had it not been because I do not want to make it hard upon my ummah, I would have commanded them to use the miswâk before each prayer" [Graded authentic by Al-Albânî in Sahîh At-Tirmidhî]

This hadîth is general. Therefore it is applied to both the fasting person and the one who is not fasting at any time. Also Āmir bin Rabî'ah (ؓ) said: "I saw the Prophet (ﷺ) a number of times using the miswâk while fasting." [Narrated by Ahmad and Abû Dâwûd and At-Tirmidhî. Al-Albânî graded it to be weak in Irwâ Al-Ghalîl]

The fasting person should not use toothpaste to clean his mouth because it has a very strong sway and may possibly sway with your saliva to your stomach. Therefore stick to the miswâk and that is sufficient for you.

Also it is permissible for the fasting person to do that which will ease the severity of heat and thirst, for example, taking a cold shower and that which is similar to that. The proof for it is what is narrated by Mâlik and Abû Dâwûd from some of the Companions of the Prophet (ﷺ) who said: "I saw the Messenger of Allâh (ﷺ) at Urj 'a name of a place' pouring water on his head while fasting due to thirst and heat." [Al-Albânî graded this narration to be authentic in Sahîh Abî Dâwûd]

Likewise Ibn 'Umar (ﷺ) soaked his garment with water and put it on while fasting. Also Anas bin Mâlik (ﷺ) used to have a carved-out rock, which resembled a pool. When he felt very hot while fasting, he would enter in it.

Hasan Al-Basrî also said: **"There is nothing wrong with rinsing the mouth and cooling down the body while fasting."**

Al-Imâm Al-Bukhârî reported these (aforementioned) narrations in his Authentic Collection, with disconnected chains. [See the Book of Fasting, Section: "The Ritual Body Wash of the One Observing the Fast"]

O My Brothers! seek the understanding of Allâh's Book in order that you may worship Him upon knowledge. For verily those who know are not equal to those who do not know; and if Allâh loves goodness for his slave He gives him understanding of the religion.

O Allâh, give us understanding of this religion and help us to implement it in our lives. Keep us firm upon it, take our souls while we are believers, and join us with the pious. Forgive us, our parents, and all the Muslims, with Your Mercy. For verily You are the Most Merciful.

May the peace and blessings of Allâh be upon our Prophet Muhammad, upon his family members, and his Companions.

Sittings During the Blessed Month of Ramaḍān رَمَضَان

المَجْلِسُ السَّادِسُ عَشَرَ
The Sixteenth Sitting
Regarding Alms giving

All praises and thanks are due to Allâh, the One who wipes away the slave's shortcomings and overlooks them. (He) forgives their sins and pardons them. Whoever depends upon Him becomes successful, and whoever trades with Him becomes profitable. He raised up the sky without any pillars holding it, therefore ponder over it. He sent down the rain and then behold, the plants shoot out from the ground, and the animals are delighted, after suffering a period of drought. He enriches and impoverishes. And perhaps poverty is better than wealth. How many wealthy people have we seen who were destroyed by their riches, due to their arrogance and stinginess. (Take for example) Qârûn, who possessed tons of wealth, but he was too stingy to give a little. He was reminded but he did not take heed. Thus he was censured, but censuring did not benefit him when his people advised him saying **"do not be boastful."** I praise Allâh as long as the day and night continues to alternate; and I further bear witness that none has the right to be worshipped but Allâh Alone, the Independent the Generous, He gives abundantly.

I also bear witness that Muhammad is His slave and His Messenger, the one who strived in the path of Allâh with his soul, his wealth, and clarified the truth. May the peace and blessings of Allâh be upon him, his companion Abû Bakr, the one who accompanied him while as a resident and while traveling, 'Umar, the one who constantly toiled in order to elevate the religion, 'Uthmân the one who spent a lot for the sake of Allâh, and rectified; 'Alî the son of (the Prophet's ﷺ) uncle the one who freed himself from the extremism of those who have exaggerated about him, and on the rest of the companions, and those who followed them correctly until the Day of Judgment.

O My Brothers! Allâh (ﷻ) said:

﴿ وَمَا أُمِرُوٓا۟ إِلَّا لِيَعْبُدُوا۟ ٱللَّهَ مُخْلِصِينَ لَهُ ٱلدِّينَ حُنَفَآءَ وَيُقِيمُوا۟ ٱلصَّلَوٰةَ وَيُؤْتُوا۟ ٱلزَّكَوٰةَ ۚ وَذَٰلِكَ دِينُ ٱلْقَيِّمَةِ ۞ ﴾

"And they were commanded not, but that they should worship Allâh, and worship none but Him Alone (abstaining from ascribing partners to Him), establish the Salât and give the Zakât: and that is the upright religion." [Al-Bayyinah: 5] Allâh said:

﴿ وَأَقِيمُوا۟ ٱلصَّلَوٰةَ وَءَاتُوا۟ ٱلزَّكَوٰةَ وَأَقْرِضُوا۟ ٱللَّهَ قَرْضًا حَسَنًا ۚ وَمَا تُقَدِّمُوا۟ لِأَنفُسِكُم مِّنْ خَيْرٍ تَجِدُوهُ عِندَ ٱللَّهِ هُوَ خَيْرًا وَأَعْظَمَ أَجْرًا ۚ وَٱسْتَغْفِرُوا۟ ٱللَّهَ ۖ إِنَّ ٱللَّهَ غَفُورٌ رَّحِيمٌ ۞ ﴾

"Establish the prayer, give the charity, and lend to Allâh a goodly loan. And whatever good you send before you for yourselves, you will certainly find it with Allâh, better and greater in reward. And seek Allâh's Forgiveness. Verily, Allâh is Oft-Forgiving, Most-Merciful." [Al-Muzammil: 20] Allâh said:

﴿ وَمَآ ءَاتَيْتُم مِّن رِّبًا لِّيَرْبُوَا۟ فِىٓ أَمْوَٰلِ ٱلنَّاسِ فَلَا يَرْبُوا۟ عِندَ ٱللَّهِ ۖ وَمَآ ءَاتَيْتُم مِّن زَكَوٰةٍ تُرِيدُونَ وَجْهَ ٱللَّهِ فَأُو۟لَٰٓئِكَ هُمُ ٱلْمُضْعِفُونَ ۞ ﴾

"And that which you give in gift (to others), in order that it may increase (your wealth by expecting to get a better one in return) from other people's property, has no increase with Allâh, but that which you give in Zakât seeking the Face of Allâh, then those, they shall have manifold increase" [Ar-Rûm: 39]

The verses which indicate the obligation of giving charity are many. Likewise there are many prophetic narrations that indicate the obligation of zakât. Some of these prophetic traditions are reported in Sahîh Muslim from the narrations of 'Abdullâh bin 'Umar (ﷺ) who said that the Messenger of Allâh (ﷺ) said:

بُنِيَ الإِسلامُ على خمسةٍ: على أَنْ يُوحَّدَ اللهُ، وإقامِ الصلاةِ، وإيتاءِ الزكاةِ، وصيامِ رمضانَ، والحجِّ

"Al-Islâm is built upon five pillars: 'Singling out Allâh alone with worship, establishing the prayer, paying the zakât, fasting in the month of Ramadân, and performing pilgrimage to the sacred house of Allâh.' Then a man asked: Performing the pilgrimage and *then* fasting? He said no fasting and performing the pilgrimage, this is how I heard from the Messenger of Allâh (ﷺ)."

In another narration it says: "**Testifying that none has the right to be worshipped but Allâh and that Muhammad is his Messenger.**"

Therefore zakât is one of the pillars of Al-Islâm and (one of) its great foundations. It is connected to the prayer in many places in the Book of Allâh (ﷺ). There is a decisive consensus amongst the Muslims about the obligation of given the Zakât. Therefore, whoever knowingly denies the obligation of zakât has disbelieved and is out of the realm of Al-Islâm. But the one who was stingy in giving zakât or did not give its due right, will be considered among the wrong doers, worthy of being punished and made an example of.

<u>Zakât is obligatory in Four Things</u>

The First: The **plants and seeds** that shoot out of the ground, based on Allâh's statement:

$$\{ \text{يَا أَيُّهَا الَّذِينَ آمَنُوا أَنفِقُوا مِن طَيِّبَاتِ مَا كَسَبْتُمْ وَمِمَّا أَخْرَجْنَا لَكُم مِّنَ الْأَرْضِ} \}$$

"O you who believe! Spend of the good things which you have (legally) earned, and of that which We have produced from the earth for you" [Al-Baqarah: 267] Allâh said:

$$\{ \text{كُلُوا مِن ثَمَرِهِ إِذَا أَثْمَرَ وَآتُوا حَقَّهُ يَوْمَ حَصَادِهِ وَلَا تُسْرِفُوا إِنَّهُ لَا يُحِبُّ الْمُسْرِفِينَ} \}$$

"Eat of their fruit when they ripen, but pay the due thereof (its Zakât, according to Allâh's Orders 1/10th or 1/20th) on the day of its harvest, and waste not by extravagance. Verily, He likes not Al-Musrifûn (those who waste by extravagance)" [Al-An'âm:141]

The Greatest Right Due from the Wealth is the Obligatory Charity (i.e. zakât): The proof for this from the Sunnah is the statement of the Prophet (ﷺ):

$$\text{فِيمَا سَقَتِ السَّمَاءُ أَوْ كَانَ عَثَرِيًّا الْعُشْرُ وَفِيمَا سُقِيَ بِالنَّضْحِ نِصْفُ الْعُشْرِ}$$

"Give one tenth of your plants that are watered by the rain, and one fifth from the ones that you watered" [Collected by Al-Bukhârî]

Zakât is only obligatory in this wealth when it reaches the nisâb (i.e. the minimal amount that one must have in order for zakât to become obligatory for him). The **nisâb is five wasaq** and **a wasaq equals sixty sâ'**. Therefore a nisâb is equal to three hundred sâ'. (A single sâ' if weighed in barley equals) 2040 grams of pure barely, which is equivalent to 2.04 kilos. So a nisâb weighed with pure barley is equal to six hundred and twelve kilos and (in volume it is 900 liters). There is no zakât below this amount. The percentage of zakât in this amount is one tenth as long as it is watered by rain without (the person) having to put any effort towards watering it. But if he watered it by his effort then he will give half of one tenth. There is no zakât on fruits and vegetables because of the statement of 'Umar (☙) *"There is no zakât in vegetables."* Likewise due to 'Alî's statement *"There is no zakât in apples and that which is similar to that."* This is because they are neither seeds nor grains. However if they were sold and cash was made, and the cash reached the nisâb then one must give the zakât of that money after a year has passed, without the wealth decreasing.

The Second: Cattle which include the camel, cow, sheep, and goat. If these cattle are livestock meaning they are raised for the purpose of milking and reproduction and they only graze from the grass that grows from the ground, and they reached the nisâb then the zakât due for them must be paid. The minimum number of the nisâb is five for camels, thirty for cows, and forty for sheep or goat.

If they are not livestock, then there is no zakât in them. However, if these cattle are prepared for trade, there is zakât due in them whether they graze freely from the pasture or are fed by their owner. If it reaches the nisâb of business items or if they were added to ones business items then the zakât of that wealth should be paid.

The Third: Gold & silver regardless of what state it is in. The proof for it is Allâh's statement:

$$\{ \text{وَالَّذِينَ يَكْنِزُونَ الذَّهَبَ وَالْفِضَّةَ وَلَا يُنفِقُونَهَا فِي سَبِيلِ اللَّهِ فَبَشِّرْهُم بِعَذَابٍ أَلِيمٍ ۝ يَوْمَ يُحْمَىٰ عَلَيْهَا فِي نَارِ جَهَنَّمَ فَتُكْوَىٰ بِهَا جِبَاهُهُمْ وَجُنُوبُهُمْ وَظُهُورُهُمْ ۖ هَٰذَا مَا كَنَزْتُمْ لِأَنفُسِكُمْ فَذُوقُوا مَا كُنتُمْ تَكْنِزُونَ ۝ \}$$

"And those who hoard up gold and silver [Al-Kanz: the money, the Zakât of which has not been paid], and spend it not in the Way of Allâh, announce unto them a painful torment. On the Day when that (Al-Kanz: money, gold and silver, etc., the Zakât of which has not been paid) will be heated in the Fire of Hell and with it will be branded their foreheads, their flanks, and their backs, (and it will be said unto them): "This is the treasure which you hoarded for yourselves. Now taste of what you used to hoard." [At-Tawbah: 34-35]

This means: saving it without spending it in the cause of Allâh. The greatest way of spending in the cause of Allâh is by paying the obligatory charity.

It is reported in Sahîh Muslim from the narration of Abû Hurayrah (ﷻ) who said the Prophet (ﷺ) said:

$$\text{مَا مِنْ صَاحِبِ ذَهَبٍ ولا فضةٍ لا يُؤَدِّي منها حقَّها إلَّا إذا كان يومُ القيامةِ صُفِّحَتْ له صفائحُ من نارٍ فأُحمي عليها في نار جهنم فيكوى بها جَنْبُه وجبينُه وظهرُه كلَّما بَرَدَتْ أُعيدت له في يوم كان مِقْدارُه خمسينَ ألفَ سَنَةٍ حتَّى يُقْضى بَيْنَ العبادِ}$$

"No one will possess gold or silver and then keep it with him without giving its right of zakât except that they would be turned to trays of fire and will be used as an iron to iron his side, his forehead, and his back, whenever it cools down it will be turned on again on the day whose period equals fifty thousand years (of the counting of this world) and this will continue until Allâh judges between the people." [Collected by Muslim]

It is obligatory to give the zakât due on gold and silver whether it is a coin, raw-gold, ornaments that are worn, lent out, or other than the abovementioned. This is due to the generality of the proofs about the obligation of giving the charity due for gold and silver, without any specification.

It is narrated by 'Abdullâh bin 'Amr bin Aws (ﷺ) who said: "A lady came to the Prophet (ﷺ) along with her daughter who was carrying two chunks of thick gold (bracelets) in her hand. So the Prophet (ﷺ) asked her: 'Do you give the zakât due for this?' She said: 'No.' He said: 'Would you be glad to be adorned with two bracelets of fire in the hereafter?' Upon hearing this, she took them off and threw them to the Prophet (ﷺ). She then said: 'They now belong to Allâh and His Messenger.'" [Collected by Ahmad, Abû Dâwûd, An-Nasâ'î and At-Tirmidhî. Ibn Hajar said in his book Bulugh Al-Marâm it has strong chains of narrations. Graded authentic by Al-Albânî in Sahîh Abû Dâwûd]

It is also narrated by 'Âishah (رضي الله عنها) that: "The Prophet (ﷺ) entered upon me and saw some silver in my hand. So he said: 'what is this?' I said: 'With it, I beautify myself for you.' He said: 'Do you give the zakât due for this silver?' I said: 'No.' He said: 'Then it will suffice you in the hell.'" [Collected by Abû Dâwûd, Al-Bayhaqî, and Al-Hâkim. Al-Hâkim graded it authentic and said: it is according to the conditions of Al-Bukhârî and Muslim. Ibn Hajar also said in his book At-Talkhîs: "It is (authentic) according to the conditions of the Sahîh." Ibn Daqîq also said "it is (authentic) based on the conditions of Muslim."]

It is obligatory to give the zakât due for gold when it reaches the nisâb which is twenty dinar (one dinar equals approximately 4.235 grams of gold). The Prophet (ﷺ) said regarding the nisâb of Gold:

$$\text{وَلَيْسَ عَلَيْكَ شَيْءٌ يَعْنِي فِي الذَّهَبِ حَتَّى يَكُونَ لَكَ عِشْرُونَ دِينَارًا}$$

"There is nothing on you until the amount reaches twenty dinar." [Collected by Abû Dâwûd. Graded authentic by Al-Albânî]

That which is intended by Ad-Dinâr, is the Islâmic Dinâr which equals a Mithqâl (i.e. 1440 grains of barley) which is equal to 4.2535 grams of pure gold. So a nisâb of gold equals approximately 85 grams of pure gold. In Saudi Pounds this equates to 11 3/7 pounds. Likewise the zakât due for silver is also obligatory when it reaches the nisâb. And that is five awâq. Based on the Prophet's (ﷺ) statement: **"There is no zakât due for that which is less than five (awâq)."** [Collected by Al-Bukhârî and Muslim]

Al-Awqiyah is equivalent to 40 Islâmic Dirhâms (one dirham equals 2.9645 grams). A Nisâb is equal to 200 Islâmic Dirham (i.e. 40 dirham multiplied by 5 awâq). A Dirham is equal to 7/10 of a mithqâl, so it equates to 140 mithqâl which is 595 grams or 56 Arab Riyals of Silver. The percentage due in charity of gold and silver is only one-fourth of a tenth or 2.5 %.

Also zakât is obligatory in paper currency, because it replaces silver. Therefore if it reaches the nisâb of silver then it becomes obligatory to pay its due charity. Also it is obligatory to pay the charity due for gold, silver, and paper currency, regardless of whether it is in the hands of the owner or in the possession of others (due to loan, debt, rent etc).

So Based on this: (The Muslim paying zakât) has the option of giving the zakât in advance before he gets hold of it and he has the option of waiting till he grasps it. He must give the zakât of the years that he missed in which he did not give the due zakât as well.

But if his wealth is in the hand of an oppressor who does not want to give him his right or in the hands of the poor who does not have the money to pay him, there is no zakât in that money until he gets hold of it and if he did (give the charity in the presence of such circumstances) he only has to give the zakât due for that year not the previous.

Zakât is only obligatory in gold and silver, but as for the other metals, there is no zakât on them even if they are more expensive than gold and silver.

The Fourth Thing in Which Zakât is due: Business Commodities. This includes anything that is prepared for business transactions including real estate, animals, food, drinks, cars, and more. Each year you determine the value of the items at the beginning of the new year, then give the due charity at a rate of 2.5% of its value regardless of whether it is more than, equal to, or less than the amount the items were purchased for.

It is incumbent upon business owners who deal with groceries, spare parts, appliances, electronics, and other items, to make sure they calculate their wealth carefully including every minor and major item in order to ensure that they accurately pay the zakât for it. But if they are not able to calculate everything, they should avoid risk (and estimate what they think is the right amount) and then give out the amount which will definitely free them from this legislative debt (with Allâh).

There is no zakât on the things which a person possesses for his own personal need such as one's food, drinks, furniture, house,

رَمَضَان Sittings During the Blessed Month of Ramaḍān

cars, animals, and clothes, except the ornaments of gold and silver. This is based on the Prophet's statement (ﷺ):

$$\text{ليس على المُسْلِمِ في عبدِهِ ولا فَرَسِهِ صدقةٌ}$$

"The Muslim does not have to give zakât on his slave or his ride"
[Collected Al-Bukhârî and Muslim]

Likewise, there is no zakât on the things that are prepared for rent, like real estate, automobiles, etc.

The zakât is only due out of the *money* that is earned from these rental items if it is monetary currency which reaches the nisâb and an entire lunar year goes by without (it decreasing in value). In such a case one would pay the zakât due. Likewise in the case where by combining the money earned from rental properties and taxis, with money from other sources and it reached a nisâb, and a lunar year goes by without the money decreasing, in such a case one would also pay the zakât due.

O My brother! Pay the zakât due from your wealth and be happy with that. For verily it is an achievement and not failure; it is a gain and not a loss. Count all the wealth which you possess that you have to pay zakât for. Ask Allâh (ﷻ) to accept what you have given out and to bless what has remained.

All praise is due to Allâh, Lord of all the worlds. And may peace and blessings be upon our Prophet, his family members, and all his companions.

المَجْلِسُ السَّابِعَ عَشَر
The Seventeenth Sitting
Those Entitled to Receive the Zakât

All praise is due to Allâh, the One whom none can bring down what He has elevated, and none can elevate what He has brought down. None can give what He has withheld or withhold what He has given. No one can connect what He has cut, or disconnect what he has connected. Glorified is He for these wonderful arrangements, the Wise and Merciful Deity. It is with His wisdom that calamity befalls, and it is with His mercy that benefit (reaches the slaves). I praise Him for His actions and thank Him for His bounties. And I bear witness that none has the right to be worshiped but Allâh Alone without a partner. He has perfected His legislation and beautified his creation.

I also bear witness that Muhammad (ﷺ) is His slave and His Messenger. He sent him at the time when the banner of disbelief was raised up high and the people were united upon it. But he exterminated it from above it, uprooted it from beneath it, and dispersed their unity. Peace and blessings of Allâh be upon him, his companion Abû Bakr, the one whose star of bravery shined up on the day of the battle of apostasy, upon 'Umar through whom Al-Islâm became elevated and protected, upon 'Uthmân the one who was oppressively killed, upon 'Alî the one who abolished disbelief and combated it with his Jihâd, upon the rest of his family members, and companions as long as the people continue to bow and prostrate to their Lord.

O My brothers! Allâh mentioned in His Book:

$$\left\{ \begin{array}{c} \text{إِنَّمَا الصَّدَقَاتُ لِلْفُقَرَاءِ وَالْمَسَاكِينِ وَالْعَامِلِينَ عَلَيْهَا وَالْمُؤَلَّفَةِ قُلُوبُهُمْ وَفِي الرِّقَابِ وَالْغَارِمِينَ وَفِي سَبِيلِ اللَّهِ وَابْنِ السَّبِيلِ فَرِيضَةً مِنَ اللَّهِ وَاللَّهُ عَلِيمٌ حَكِيمٌ ۝} \end{array} \right\}$$

"The Charity (i.e. the Obligatory Zakât) is only for the Fuqara' (poor), Al-Masâkîn (indigent), those employed to collect (the funds); and in order to attract the hearts of those who have been inclined (towards Al-Islâm), in order to free the captives; (it is) for those in debt; for Allâh's Cause, and for the wayfarer (cut off from everything); a duty imposed by Allâh. Allâh is All-Knower, All-Wise" [At-Tawbah: 60]

In this verse Allâh has mentioned where to spend your charity and (has outlined) those who deserve to receive the obligatory charity, (which is all) based on His knowledge, wisdom, justice and mercy. He also restricted it to these eight categories of people and clarified that giving zakât to these categories is obligatory. Therefore it is not permissible to ignore this obligation, spending your charity on other than the abovementioned. That is because Allâh is aware of the best interests of His slaves and He is the Most Wise, the One who places things in their appropriate locations. As Allâh said:

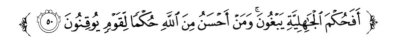

"And who is better in judgment than Allâh for a people who have firm Faith" [Al-Mâi'dah: 50]

The Eight Categories of People Entitled to Receive the Zakât

The First and Second categories: "The Poor and Destitute"

They are those who do not have what is sufficient for them and their dependents. They do not have any savings, a permanent sufficient salary, a running business, and they do not have a compulsory support from any one. So these people are in need of support and help. The scholars said they should be given from the Zakât money enough to suffice them and their dependents for the period of a year. If a poor person needs help from the zakât money to get married, it must be granted to him. Likewise a student of knowledge who needs some of the zakât money to get some books must be helped. And the one who works but does not make enough to cover his needs must also receive some help from the zakât money enough to cover their needs, because he (and all the aforementioned) are needy people.

As for the one who has enough to cover his needs, it is not permissible to give such an individual from the zakât money even if he asks for it. Rather he should be admonished and warned against asking for something which he does not deserve to receive. It is narrated from 'Abdullâh bin 'Umar (ﷺ) that the Messenger of Allâh (ﷺ) said:

لَا تَزَالُ المَسْأَلَةُ بِأَحَدِكُم حتّى يَلْقَى اللهَ عزَّ وجلَّ وليس في وجهِهِ مُزعةُ لحمٍ، رواه البخاري

"One of you will continue to ask until he meets Allâh with a boney face without any flesh covering it" [Collected by Al-Bukhârî].

Likewise, on the authority of Abû Hurayrah (ﷺ) he reported that the Prophet (ﷺ) said:

Sittings During the Blessed Month of Ramaḍān

مَنْ سَأَلَ النَّاسَ أَمْوَالَهُم تَكَثُّراً فَإِنَّمَا يَسْأَلُ جَمْراً فَلْيَسْتَقِلَّ أَوْ لِيَسْتَكْثِرْ رواه مسلم.

"The one who asks the people for help while having what is enough, he is only asking for a coal of fire. Therefore let him ask for more or desist from doing so." [Collected by Muslim]

Likewise it is also narrated by Hakîm bin Hizâm (ﷺ) who reported that the Prophet (ﷺ) said:

إِنَّ هَذَا المَالَ خَضِرَةٌ حُلْوَةٌ فَمَنْ أَخَذَهُ بِسَخَاوَةِ نَفْسٍ بُورِكَ فِيهِ، وَمَنْ أَخَذَهُ بِإِشْرَافِ نَفْسٍ لَمْ يُبَارَكْ لَهُ فِيهِ وَكَانَ كَالَّذِي يَأْكُلُ وَلَا يَشْبَعُ، وَالْيَدُ الْعُلْيَا خَيْرٌ مِنَ الْيَدِ السُّفْلَى

"Surely this wealth is sweet green foliage (i.e. very delightful). Whoever controls it with a generous heart then it will be blessed for him, but whoever holds it with selfishness then it will be deprived of blessing. Thus he will eat but will not be satisfied. And the upper-hand is better than the lower hand" [Collected by Al-Bukhârî and Muslim]

It is also narrated by Abdur Rahmân bin 'Awf (ﷺ) that the Prophet (ﷺ) said:

لَا يَفْتَحُ عَبْدٌ بَابَ مَسْأَلَةٍ إِلَّا فَتَحَ اللهُ عَلَيْهِ بَابَ فَقْرٍ

"A slave will not open a door to begging except that Allâh will open for him a door of poverty" [Narrated by Al-Imâm Ahmad. Al-Albânî graded it to be authentic due to other texts, as found in Sahîh At-Targhîb]

If an unknown person comes with an appearance of a rich man asking for zakât, it is permissible to give him after informing him that the rich does not have a portion from it, likewise the strong man who is able to cover his needs. This is because two men came to the Prophet (ﷺ) asking him for the zakât money, and he looked at them and saw the signs of richness on them. So he said:

إِنْ شِئْتُما أَعْطَيْتُكُما وَلا حَظَّ فيها لِغَنِيٍّ وَلا لِقَوِيٍّ مُكْتَسِبٍ

"If you will I will give it to you but know that: the rich and the strong who is able to work and cover his needs do not have a portion from the zakât money" [Narrated by Ahmad, Abû Dâwûd, and An-Nasâî. Al-Albânî graded it to be authentic in Sahîh Abû Dâwûd and Sahîh An-Nasâî].

The Third Category: "The Caretakers of the Zakât Money"

They are those who are given the authority by the ruler to collect the zakât money, preserve it, and give it away to the poor. These people should be given their portion from the zakât money according to their efforts even if they are rich. As for the individuals who give zakât on behalf of some individuals, they will not be considered under this category. If a person volunteered to distribute the zakât money with honesty and sincerity he will share the reward with the giver. As it is narrated by Al-Bukhârî from the narration of Abû Mûsâ Al-Ash'arî (رضي الله عنه) that the Prophet (ﷺ) said:

الْخازِنُ الْمُسْلِمُ الأَمينُ الَّذي يُنَفِّذُ أَو قَالَ: يُعْطي ما أُمِرَ بِهِ كامِلاً مُوفَّراً طَيِّباً بِهِ نَفْسُهُ فَيَدْفَعُهُ إِلى الَّذي أَمَرَ بِهِ أَحَدُ الْمُتَصَدِّقينَ، وَإِنْ لَمْ يَتَبَرَّعوا بِتَفريقِها أَعْطاهُمْ صاحِبُ الْمالِ مِنْ مالِهِ لا مِنَ الزَّكاةِ

"The trustworthy Muslim treasurer who executed sincerely what he is commanded with in full, by giving it to the needy even though they are not the donors, should be given some help from the money of the donors and not from the zakât money" [Collected by Al-Bukhârî]

The Fourth Category: Attracting the Hearts of those Inclined toward Al-Islâm (i.e those who are weak in faith or even the disbelievers who it is desired that they will embrace Al-Islâm)

The zakât money should be given to them in order to bring their hearts closer to Al-Islâm, increase their faith, or to be safeguarded from their criminality if they are criminals, as long as it is known that giving them the money will stop them from their criminality.

The Fifth Category: To Free the Slaves

Those who have a deal with their masters to free themselves from slavery. It is permissible to give them from the zakât money in order for them to free themselves from slavery. This also includes freeing the Muslim captives, in the hands of the enemy.

The Sixth Category: Those who are overburdened with debt

They are of two kinds: **The I**st: The one who carries the burden of reconciling between the people. This individual deserves to be given from the zakât according to his effort in order to encourage him to continue this wonderful job that is needed in the society to preserve the unity of the people, reconciling between them, eradicating the enmity and rancor from the society.

It is narrated by Qabîsah Al-Hilâlî who said: "I have carried the burden of reconciling between the between the people. So I came to the Prophet (ﷺ) asking him about the ruling regarding that, and he said to me: '**Stay with us, if somebody brings his zakât we** will give you a share from it.' Then he said: "O Qabîsah! Verily begging is impermissible except in one of these three occasions: A man who has carried the burden of reconciling between the people until he becomes poor, it is permissible for him to take from the zakât money until he is no longer in need of it and then he mentioned the rest of the narration. [Collected by Muslim]

The 2nd: The one who carries a burden of debt upon himself and is unable to pay it. This individual deserves to receive money from the zakât enough to pay off his debt. (Instead of giving the money to him) one may pay his debt directly to the one he owes using the zakât money without giving the money to him, because the goal is to pay his debt.

The Seventh Category: In the Path of Allâh

Those who work on the path of Allâh and strive hard so that the word of Allâh will be victorious, not those who strive for their pride, their race, or tribe to become victorious. The one who fights in the path of Allâh must be given from the zakât money what is sufficient for him to buy the materials that he needs for his work, including weapons and ammunition. This is in order that they can defend and protect the religion of Allâh from the enemies and to help the religion of Allâh to be victorious.

The Eighth Category: The Wayfarer

This is the traveler who got stuck in the middle of his journey, due to lack of provisions. This individual must be given from the zakât money what will cover his trip, even if he is rich (back home in) his country. However (it is important to note that) it is not permissible for (a person) to carry few provisions while on a journey if one's intentions are merely to receive zakât money when his provision are exhausted. Because this is a form of deception and we are forbidden from that.

Also it is not permissible to give zakât money to the disbeliever except if there is hope that he will accept Al-Islâm.

Likewise it is not permissible to give the zakât money to the individual who has a business, industry, or skill, except if he is among those who work on the zakât committee, is amongst those who go out for jihâd, or is from those who have dedicated their time to reconcile between the people.

Also, the zakât money must not be given to replace another obligation with it. Therefore you should not take from the zakât money to feed your guest because this is a separate obligation that must be carried out with (other) money.

Likewise you cannot give your wife, your children, or relatives whom you are responsible for (from the zakât money) because it is a must on you to spend on them (regardless).

However it *is* in fact permissible to spend the zakât on your wives, your parents, or your relatives if it is being used for things outside of your obligatory responsibility, such as to pay one of their debts that they are not able to fulfill.

Likewise it is permissible for one to give the zakât to his poor relatives who (he is not responsible for) if they do not have enough to spend on their dependents.

Also, it is permissible for the wife to give her zakât money to her poor husband in order for him to pay his debt and cover some of his needs. This is because Allâh (ﷻ) has given a general description of those who deserve the zakât. Therefore whoever falls under this description is entitled to receive the zakât. Therefore no one should be excluded except with a clear text or the consensus of the scholars.

Sittings During the Blessed Month of Ramaḍān رَمَضَان

It is also reported in Sahîh Al-Bukhârî and Sahîh Muslim from the hadîth of Zaynab Al-Thaqafiyyah, the wife of 'Abdullâh bin Mas'ûd (ﷺ) that the Prophet (ﷺ) commanded the women to give charity. So she came to the Prophet (ﷺ) and asked him saying: "O messenger of Allâh! You have indeed commanded us to give charity and I have some ornaments that I want to give away in charity, but Ibn Mas'ûd claimed that he and his children deserve this charity more than anyone else.' Then the Prophet (ﷺ) said: 'Ibn Mas'ûd has said the truth. Your husband and your child deserve your charity more than anyone else.'" [Collected by Al-Bukhârî and Muslim]

It is also narrated by Salmân bin 'Āmir (ﷺ) that the Prophet (ﷺ) said: **"Giving charity to the poor is a charity and giving it to your poor close and distant relatives is a charity along with keeping the ties of kinship."** [Collected by An-Nasâ'î, At-Tirmidhî, Ibn Khuzaymah, and Al-Hâkim. Al-Hâkim said its chain is authentic.]

(Note): It is not permissible to pardon a poor person who is indebted to you, with the intention that (you are fulfilling your obligatory Zakât duty), because zakât is take and give. As Allâh (ﷻ) said:

﴿ خُذْ مِنْ أَمْوَالِهِمْ صَدَقَةً تُطَهِّرُهُمْ وَتُزَكِّيهِم بِهَا وَصَلِّ عَلَيْهِمْ إِنَّ صَلَوٰتَكَ سَكَنٌ لَّهُمْ وَٱللَّهُ سَمِيعٌ عَلِيمٌ ﴿١٠٣﴾ ﴾

"Take Sadaqah (alms) from their wealth in order to purify them and sanctify them with it, and invoke Allâh for them. Verily! Your invocations are a source of security for them, and Allâh is All-Hearer, All-Knower" [At-Tawbah: 103]

Also the Prophet (ﷺ) said:

أن الله افتَرَضَ عليهم صدقةٌ في أموالِهم ، تُؤْخَذُ مِن أغنيائِهم وتُرَدُّ على فقرائِهم

"Verily Allâh has obligated on them the giving of charity, which must be taken from the rich from amongst them and given to the poor." [Collected by Al-Bukhârî and Muslim]

Discharging of a debt owed to you by a poor person is not considered taking and giving, because a debt is absent money that cannot be spent. Therefore it cannot replace money that is present and consumable. Therefore zakât cannot be replaced with debt. This is because debt is of less value than the money that is available in your possession. For that reason replacing the zakât with debt is like replacing that which is superior with that which is inferior or replacing good with bad.

If an individual tries his best to give the zakât to those he thinks are worthy of it, but it ends up (with those who do not deserve it), his zakât is still valid because he feared Allâh to the best of his ability. And Allâh does not place a burden on a soul which it cannot bear.

It is reported in Sahîh Al-Bukhârî and Sahîh Muslim from the narration of Abû Hurayrah (﷜) who said that the Prophet (ﷺ) said: "That a man swore by Allâh that he will give charity to the right person. So he ended up giving his charity to the rich. (At that point) the people complained saying: 'his charity was given to the rich.' So he said: 'All praise is due to Allâh.' Somebody came to him and said: 'Perhaps that rich man will learn from your generosity and be generous like you.' And in the narration of Muslim, it says, it was said to him: 'But as for your charity, it is accepted.'" [Collected by Al-Bukhârî and Muslim]

Also it is narrated by Ma'nu bin Yazîd (﷜) who said:

Sittings During the Blessed Month of Ramaḍān رَمَضَانْ

كَانَ أَبِي يُخْرِجُ دَنانِيرَ يتصدقُ بِهَا فوضعها عندَ رجُلٍ في المسجد، فجئتُ فأخَذْتُها فأتيتُه بِهَا فقال: واللهِ ما إيَّاكَ أَرَدْتُ فخاصَمتُه إلى النبيِّ صلى الله عليه وسلّم، فقال النبيُّ صلى الله عليه وسلّم: «لك ما نَوَيْتَ يا يزيدُ ولك ما أَخَذْتَ يا مَعْنُ»، رواه البخاريُّ.

"My dad used to give out dinars as charity. So (one day) he gave them to a poor man in the Masjid. So I arrived at the Masjid and the dinars were given to me by the (poor) man as a charity. So I came home (to my dad) with the dinars. My dad said: 'By Allâh I did not intend to give this charity to you.' So I raised this complaint to the Prophet (ﷺ). So the Prophet (ﷺ) sad: 'O Yazîd yours is what you have intended. And O Ma'nu yours is what you have taken.'" [Collected by Al-Bukhârî]

O My Brothers! Know that zakât will not be accepted except if it is placed where Allâh (ﷻ) commanded for it to be placed. Therefore try your best, may Allâh have mercy on you all, and be eager to place the zakât in its right places in order that you will not be held accountable before Allâh, and in order that your wealth will be purified. By doing that you have executed your Lord's command and your charity will be accepted.

May Allâh grant us success. And all praise is due to Allâh, Lord of the worlds. And may peace be upon our Prophet Muhammad, his family members, and all his Companions.

الـمَجْلِسُ الثَامِنَ عشر

The Eighteenth Sitting
The Battle of Badr

All praise and thanks are due to Allâh, the Strong, the Omnipotent, the Most High, the True King. The whimpering of the whimper is not hidden from His hearing, and the movement of the fetus in the belly of its mother is not hidden from His sight. The tyrannical leaders humble themselves to His glory. He is the One who decreed the destiny based on His wisdom and He is the Most Wise. I praise Him with the praise of the thankful ones, and I ask Him the support of the forbearing ones. I bear witness that none has the right to be worshipped but Allâh alone and I bear witness that Muhammad is His slave and His Messenger, the one who is given preference over all the Messengers, the one who was aided on the Day of Badr with descending angels, may Allâh (ﷻ) shower His blessings and favor on him, his family members, his companions, and those who follow their footsteps till the Day of Judgment. To proceed:

O My Brothers! In this Blessed Month, Allâh (ﷻ) aided the Muslims in the great battle of Badr against their enemies, the polytheist, and He named that day "The Day of Al-Furqân" (i.e. the day in which truth was distinguished from falsehood). That is because Allâh (ﷻ) separated between the truth and the falsehood by making His Messenger and the believers victorious over the disbelievers.

This happened in the month of Ramadân in **the Second Year following the Prophet's migration to Al-Madinah.**

The Reason For This Battle: A message reached the Prophet (ﷺ) that Abû Sufyân was coming from Syria towards Mecca with the business caravan of the Quraysh. So he told his companions to go and take the items from them, because Quraysh were at war against the Messenger of Allâh (ﷺ) and his companions and there was not any covenant between them. For verily, Quraysh had dispelled (the Muslims) from their home, seized their wealth, and stood against their call of truth.

The Prophet (ﷺ) went out with almost three hundred and twenty of his companions, on two horses and seventy camels, being followed by seventy men from the Ansâr and the rest from the Muhâjirûn, to capture the items from the caravan, not intending war. But Allâh (ﷻ), from His wisdom, caused them to meet their enemies with war which was not prearranged in order to decree something that was already predestined.

When the news of the Muslims reached Abû Sufyân, he sent messengers to Quraysh informing them to arm themselves and come and defend their properties from the Muslims. But Abû Sufyân had managed to escape by changing the regular route of the people and traveled by the sea shore.

As for the tribes of Quraysh, when the news had reached them that the Muslims were taking their property, all of them came out with their honorable ones without exception. Almost a thousand (people), they had with them one hundred horses, seven hundred camels, and they came out in a state of arrogance, showing off in order to be seen of men. This is as Allâh (ﷻ) states:

﴿ وَلَا تَكُونُوا۟ كَٱلَّذِينَ خَرَجُوا۟ مِن دِيَٰرِهِم بَطَرًا وَرِئَآءَ ٱلنَّاسِ وَيَصُدُّونَ عَن سَبِيلِ ٱللَّهِ وَٱللَّهُ بِمَا يَعْمَلُونَ مُحِيطٌ ۝٤٧ ﴾

"And be not like those who come out of their homes boastfully and to be seen of men, and hindering (men) from the Path of Allâh" [Al-Anfâl: 47]

Along with them were songstresses, who sang songs insulting the Muslims. When Abû Sufyân heard of their raid he sent a messenger to Quraysh informing them of his escape and told them to return back to their homes without involving in a war. But they refused that and Abû Jahl, their leader, said: **"By Allâh we will not return until we arrive at Badr, and we will remain there for three days, slaughter our cattle, eat, and drink wine in order to demonstrate to the Arabs our power; and they will continue to be afraid of us."**

When the Messenger of Allâh (ﷺ) knew that Quraysh were on their way to fight the Muslims, he gathered his companions, discussed the issue with them saying: **"Allâh (ﷻ) has promised me one of the two, either the business caravan or victory against them in war."** Upon saying that, Miqdâd bin Al-Aswad, one of the immigrants, stood up and said: **"O Messenger of Allâh! execute what you are commanded with by your Lord, by Allâh we will not say to you as the children of Isrâîl said to Mûsâ, 'Go and fight with your Lord we will be right here sitting and watching.' Rather we will fight with you on your left and your right, in front of you and behind you."** So Sa'd bin Mu'âdh, the leader of Aws from among the Ansâr, stood up and said: **"O Messenger of Allâh! Perhaps you think that the Ansâr will not fight with you because they promised to defend you in their homes based on the bonds of the pledge. I am speaking on behalf of the Ansâr: 'Take us to where you will, connect whom you will amongst us and disconnect whom you will, take what you will from our money and spare what you will, and what you will take from our money is more beloved to us than what you will leave for us, and your command is our will. By Allâh if you were to travel with us until you reach the pool of Ghamdân we will travel with you, and if you take us to this sea and plunge into it, we will plunge with you, and we will not have a problem with the enemies tomorrow. For verily we are firm and patient at war, and may be Allâh (ﷻ) show you in this war what will please your eyes about us."** Upon hearing this, the Prophet (ﷺ) was very happy with both the Ansâr and the Muhâhjirîn (﷠). He then he said: **"Get ready for the fight and rejoice. By Allâh it is as if I can see the dying spots of the enemies."** So the Prophet (ﷺ) proceeded with the companions until they arrived at one of the rivers of Badr. Then the Prophet settled before the river. So Hubbâb bin Al-Mundhir bin 'Amr bin Al-Jamûh said: **'O Messenger of Allâh! Are we settling here because you are inspired to do so or it is just based on your opinion and your strategy of war?"** The Prophet (ﷺ) said: **"Rather it is my opinion and my war strategy."** Then he said: **"O Messenger of Allâh! I do not think this is the best place to settle, let us cross to the other side of the river so that the water will be behind us, and then build a pond from it, so that we will be able to drink if we are thirsty but they will not be able to drink."** The Prophet (ﷺ) chose (Hubbâb's) opinion and proceeded with them till they crossed the river and kept it behind them to the direction of Al-Madinah. Quraysh settled at the furthermost of the riverbank to the direction of Mecca. Then Allâh (ﷻ) sent down heavy rain, making the disbelievers' journey very complicated and the ground very muddy and slippery. As a result they were very exhausted. As for the believers the rain had cleansed them, made the ground firm and stable for them, and stabilized their feet. Then the Muslims built a tent for the Prophet on the battlefield. The Prophet (ﷺ) arranged his Companions' rows, prepared them for the battle, and then proceeded to the battlefield pointing with his fingers at the spots where the disbelievers would die, saying: **"this is the spot in which so and so will die"** and it happened as the Prophet (ﷺ) said. Then the Prophet (ﷺ) looked at his Companions, then he looked at Quraysh, and then he said: **"O Allâh here is Quraysh: she came out with her pride and arrogance, and their archers are here opposing You and rejecting Your Messenger. O Allâh we are asking You for victory which You have promised me. O Allâh execute what You have promised me with, O Allâh if You will, You will not be worshipped, O Allâh if this group of Muslims are destroyed today, You will not be worshipped!'** So the Muslims sought the help and support of

رَمَضَان Sittings During the Blessed Month of Ramaḍān

their Lord. And He (indeed) answered (their invocation). As Allâh (ﷻ) states:

﴿ إِذْ يُوحِى رَبُّكَ إِلَى ٱلْمَلَٰٓئِكَةِ أَنِّى مَعَكُمْ فَثَبِّتُوا۟ ٱلَّذِينَ ءَامَنُوا۟ۚ سَأُلْقِى فِى قُلُوبِ ٱلَّذِينَ كَفَرُوا۟ ٱلرُّعْبَ فَٱضْرِبُوا۟ فَوْقَ ٱلْأَعْنَاقِ وَٱضْرِبُوا۟ مِنْهُمْ كُلَّ بَنَانٍ ۝ ذَٰلِكَ بِأَنَّهُمْ شَآقُّوا۟ ٱللَّهَ وَرَسُولَهُۥۚ وَمَن يُشَاقِقِ ٱللَّهَ وَرَسُولَهُۥ فَإِنَّ ٱللَّهَ شَدِيدُ ٱلْعِقَابِ ۝ ذَٰلِكُمْ فَذُوقُوهُ وَأَنَّ لِلْكَٰفِرِينَ عَذَابَ ٱلنَّارِ ۝ ﴾

"(Remember) when your Lord inspired the angels, 'Verily, I am with you, so keep firm those who have believed. I will cast terror into the hearts of those who have disbelieved, so strike them over the necks, and smite over all their fingers and toes.' This is because they defied and disobeyed Allâh and His Messenger. And whoever defies and disobeys Allâh and His Messenger, then verily, Allâh is Severe in punishment. This is the torment, so taste it, and surely for the disbelievers is the torment of the Fire. [Al-Anfâl: 12-14]

The two parties clashed and the battle became severe. The Prophet (ﷺ) was in the tent with Abû Bakr and Sa'd bin Mu'âdh who were guarding him. While the battle began to intensify the Prophet (ﷺ) continued to invoke his Lord for the help and victory which Allâh promised him. And then he dozed off and then woke up and walked out saying:

﴿ سَيُهْزَمُ ٱلْجَمْعُ وَيُوَلُّونَ ٱلدُّبُرَ ۝ ﴾

"The enemies will be defeated and they will turn their backs and run away." [Qamar: 45] He then encouraged his Companions to fight saying: "I swear by Him in Whose Hand is the soul of

Muhammad, whoever got killed by the disbelievers today while sincerely fighting them attacking and defending without running away from the battlefield, Allâh (ﷻ) will grant him Paradise." Then 'Umayr bin Al-Himâm Al-Ansârî said: "O Messenger of Allâh! You mean the Paradise that is more spacious than the Heavens and the Earth?' He said: 'Yes.' Then 'Umayr said: 'bakhin, bakhin' (i.e. a phrase they used to express their strong desire of something.) Then he said: "O Messenger of Allâh! Between me and paradise is only if I am killed by these people?!" Then he threw away the dates that he had in his hand and then said: **"It will be a waste of time for me to finish eating these dates."** Then he went and fought until he was martyred (ﷺ).

Then the Prophet (ﷺ) took a grasp of dirt in his hand and threw it at the enemies, it filled up all of their eyes. So they could not see and were defeated as a result of that. This is a miracle from his Lord. The disbelievers were defeated and turned their backs and ran away. The Muslims followed them, killing some of them and capturing others. They killed seventy people from the polytheist and captured seventy. There were twenty seven leaders of Quraysh who were killed from the seventy and were thrown in to a ditch. Some of those leaders who were killed included Abû Jahl, Shaybah bin Rabî'ah, his brother 'Utbah, and his son Walîd bin 'Utbah.

It is reported in <u>Sahîh Al-Bukhârî</u>, from the narration of 'Abdullâh bin Mas'ûd (ﷺ) who said: **"The Prophet (ﷺ) turned to the direction of the Ka'bah and invoked his Lord against these four people whose names were mentioned above."** He (Abdullah bin Mas'ûd) said: **"I swear by Allâh that I saw all of them dead, their nature was altered by the Sun's heat and that was a very hot day."** [Collected by Al-Bukhârî]

It is also reported in <u>Sahîh Al-Bukhârî</u> from the narration of Abû Talhah (ﷺ): "On the day of Badr, the Prophet (ﷺ) ordered that the corpses of twenty four leaders of Quraysh should be thrown into one of the dirty dry wells of Badr. It was a habit of the Prophet (ﷺ) that whenever he conquered some people, he used to stay at the battle-field for three nights. So, on the third day of the Battle of Badr, he ordered that his she-camel be saddled, then he set out, and his companions followed him saying among themselves: **'Definitely he (i.e. the Prophet) is proceeding for some great purpose.'** When he halted at the edge of the well, he addressed the corpses of the Quraysh infidels by their names and their fathers' names, **'O so-and-so, son of so-and-so and O so-and-so, son of so-and so! Would it have pleased you if you had obeyed Allâh and His Messenger? We have found true what our Lord promised us. Have you too found true what your Lord promised you?'** Umar said, **'O Allâh's Messenger (ﷺ)! You are speaking to bodies that have no souls!"** Allah's Messenger (ﷺ) said, **'By Him in Whose Hand is Muhammad's soul, you do not hear what I say better than they do.'** (Qatada said, **'Allâh brought them to life (again) to let them hear him, in order to be reprimanded, slight them, take revenge over them, and cause them to feel remorse and regret.'"** [Collected by Al-Bukhârî, Muhsin Khan's Translation. Hadîth Number 3976, page 188]

The Prophet (ﷺ) asked the companions regarding what they should do with the war captives. So **Sa'd bin Muâdh**, who disliked what the Quraysh did, said: **"This is the first battle that our enemies were defeated, and I'd rather have them killed than to keep them alive."**

'Umar bin Al-Khattâb (ﷺ) said: "I think you should allow us to strike their necks, let 'Alî strike the neck of 'Aqîl, and let me strike the neck of so and so (i.e. a relative of his). For verily these people are the leaders of disbelief."

Abû Bakr said, "These men are our cousins and our countrymen. I see it most appropriate that the Muslims should take ransom from them and thus this will be strength for the Muslims over the disbelievers. And perhaps Allâh will guide them to Al-Islâm."

The Prophet (ﷺ) inclined to the opinion of Abû Bakr and accepted the ransom money from them. Most of them were ransomed with four thousand dirham and some of them with one thousand dirham. And some of them were ransomed for teaching the children of Al-Madînah how to read and write. Some of them were also exchanged with the Muslim captives that were in the hands of Quraysh. Some of them were killed by the Prophet (ﷺ) due to the severity of their harm against the Muslims. And some of them were released without any ransom money, but for the interest of the Muslims.

This is the Battle of Badr, the battle in which a small group gained victory over a big group.

"A group fighting for the sake of Allâh, whereas the others were disbelievers." [Āli Imrân: 13]

However the small group was victorious only because they were supporting the religion of Allâh. They were fighting to make the word of Allâh victorious, and to defend His religion. Therefore establish your religion O Muslims, so that you will be helped against your enemies. Be patient and stand firm upon your religion and fear Allâh so that you will be successful.

O Allâh help us with Al-Islâm. Make us amongst those who support Al-Islâm, and keep us firm upon it till we meet You. May the Almighty shower His mercy and peace on our Prophet Muhammad, his family members, and all his Companions.

المَجْلِسُ التَّاسِعَ عَشَرَ
The Nineteenth Sitting
The Battle of the Meccan Conquest

All praise is due to Allâh, the One who created everything and ordained. He knows the source of every creation. He affirmed what He wanted to affirm in the Mother of the Books (i.e. the Preserved Tablet), no one can set back what He has put forward, and no one can put forward what He has set back. No one can help the one whom He has forsaken, and no one can defeat the one whom He has aided. He has the exclusive possession of kingdom and eternity, the exclusive possession of honor and glory. Therefore whoever tries to claim possession of glory with Him will be humiliated by Him. He is the Only One Deity (who has the right to be worshiped in truth), He is the Lord, the Self-sufficient. There is no partner with Him in what He has created and originated. He is the Ever-Living, the Caretaker of His Creatures and the Ever-Watchful over their affairs. He is the All-Knower, the Well-Acquainted. Whatever the slaves hide in their hearts is not hidden from Him. I praise Him for what He has bestowed on us of His bounties.

Likewise I bear witness that none has the right to be worship but Allâh alone without a partner, the One who accepted the repentance of the sinner and overlooked his sins and forgave him. I also bear witness that Muhammad (ﷺ) is His slave and His Messenger. (He is) the one through whom the path of guidance became clear and illuminated, the one who eradicated the darkness of polytheism, conquered Mecca and purified the Ka'bah from the idols (ﷺ). (May the peace and blessings of Allâh be upon him) his family members, his pious companions, and those who follow their footsteps till the Day of Judgment.

O My Brothers! Just as the Battle of Badr occurred in this blessed month, in which Allâh (ﷺ) made Al-Islâm victorious and raised its minarets, it was in the same month that the Battle of the Meccan conquest occurred. (It was) in the eighth year of the Islâmic calendar. Allâh (ﷻ) saved Mecca from polytheism with this great victory; Mecca became an Islâmic state replacing polytheism with monotheism, disbelief with belief, and objection of Tawhîd to total submission to the will of Allâh (ﷻ). The worship of Allâh, the Only One deity, the Omnipotent was announced on that day, and the idols were broken into pieces.

The Reason for this Battle: When the Prophet (ﷺ) was making a peaceful agreement with the Quraysh at Hudaybiyah, from among the bonds of the treaty is that: whoever wants to ally the Muslims in their agreement is welcome and whoever wants to ally with Quraysh in their agreement is also welcome. So the tribe of Khuzâ'ah allied the Muslims and the tribe of Banû Bakr allied the Quraysh, and there was bloodshed between the two tribes. So the tribe of Banû Bakr had taken the advantage of their alliance with the Quraysh and laid an ambush against the tribe of khuzâ'ah in their peaceful abode, and Quraysh also supported them with men and weapons secretly. When Quraysh did that they broke their peaceful agreement with the Prophet. So some men from the tribe of Khuzâ'ah came to the Prophet (ﷺ) and informed him of what Banû Bakr did and the support that Quraysh gave them.

But as for Quraysh they had the guilty conscious within themselves that they have broken their agreement with the Prophet (ﷺ). So they sent their leader Abû Sufyân to come and reassure the agreement between them and the Muslims and extend the period of the agreement. He came and spoke to the Prophet (ﷺ) but the Prophet (ﷺ) did not respond to him, then he spoke to Abû Bakr and 'Umar in order that they will intercede for him with the Prophet (ﷺ) but he was not successful. Then he spoke to 'Alî but to no avail. Then he said to 'Alî: **"O Abâl- Hasan! What would you suggest for me to do?"** 'Alî said to him, **"I do not think that there is anything that you can do to get out of this, however, since you are the leader of the people I will suggest for** you to seek protection with the people." So he said to 'Alî: "Do you think that will benefit me?" 'Alî said "No. But this is the best thing I can suggest for you." So he did as 'Alî told him and then returned back to Mecca. So Quraysh said to him: "What did you bring back with you?" He said: "I came and spoke to Muhammad; by Allâh he did not respond to me with anything. Then I came to (Abû Bakr) bin Abî Quhâfah and ('Umar) bin Al-Khattâb but did not find any good from them either. Then I came to 'Alî and he suggested for me to seek the protection of the people, and I did it." They said, "Did Muhammad accept that from the people?" He said "No." They said, "Woe to you, this man just played with your mind (they meant 'Alî)." [Review Zâd Al-Ma'âd 3/387,398]

But as for the Prophet (ﷺ), he commanded his Companions to prepare for the Battle and informed them with what he intended. He called out the neighboring tribes of Al-Madinah to fight with him. He supplicated to his Lord saying: "O Allâh! Keep Quraysh unaware and uninformed with our affair until we arrive at their hometown unexpectedly." He then left Al-Madinah with ten thousand fighters and put 'Abdullâh bin Ummi Maktûm in charge of Al-Madinah. While he was on his way to Mecca he met his uncle Al-Abbâs at a place named Juhfah migrating to Al-Madinah with his wife and children as Muslims. Likewise he met his cousin Abû Sufyân bin Al-Hârith bin Abdul-Muttalib and his maternal cousin 'Abdullâh bin Abî Umayyah at "Al-Abwâ." These two cousins of his were his worst enemies, but they also embraced Al-Islâm . The Prophet (ﷺ) accepted it from them and then said regarding Abû Sufyân, "I hope he will replace Hamzah." [Review Zâd Al-Ma'âd 3/401]

When the Prophet (ﷺ) arrived at a place called Marri At-Thahrân, he commanded the fighters to light ten thousand fires and he made 'Umar to be his guard. Al-Abbâs, his uncle, rode on the Prophet's (ﷺ) mule, looking for somebody to inform Quraysh to come out and make a peaceful treaty with the Prophet

(ﷺ) in order to prevent war from occurring in Mecca, the peaceful land. While he was on the mule he heard the voice of Abû Sufyân bin Harb saying to Budayl bin Warqâ: "**I have never seen in my life this many fires.**" So Budayl said to him: "**this is the tribe of Khuzâ'ah.**" Abû Sufyân said to him: "**Khuzâ'ah are fewer than this and are more inferior.**" So Al-Abbâs recognized his voice and he called him. Then Abû Sufyân responded and said: "**What is the matter with you O Abâl Fadl?**" So Abbâs said to him: "**This is the Messenger of Allâh (ﷺ) with the people.**" He said to him: "**What is the way out then?**" Al-Abbâs said to him: "**Get on the ride so that I will take you to the Prophet (ﷺ) to seek protection for you.**" So when they came to the Prophet (ﷺ) he said to Abû Sufyân: "**Woe to you. Is it not yet time for you to (recognize openly) that none has the right to be worshipped but Allâh alone?**" Then Abû Sufyân replied: "**I will ransom you with my father and mother, how patient and how generous and how kind you are! I know for sure that if there had been a god besides Allâh, that god would have benefitted me.**" Then the Prophet (ﷺ) said to him: "**Is it not yet time for you to (acknowledge openly) that I am a Messenger of Allâh?**" So he paused for a minute, then Abbâs said to him: "**Woe to you, embrace Al-Islâm!**" Then Abû Sufyân became Muslim and testified to the true testimony. Then the Prophet (ﷺ) commanded Al-Abbâs to stand with Abû Sufyân at the narrow path of the valley by the peak of the mountain so that the Muslims will come and pass by him. So the Muslims came and passed by him tribe by tribe each tribe carried their banner with them. Whenever a tribe passed by, Abû Sufyân would ask Al-Abbâs about it and then would say: "**I have nothing to do with them.**" Until when a huge battalion came and passed by which he never saw before, he said to Al-Abbâs: "**What tribe is this?**" Al-Abbâs said: "**These are the Ansârs led by Sa'd bin Ubâdah carrying the banner.**" And when Sa'd passed by Abû Sufyân he said to him: "**Today is a day of butchery, today butchery will be permissible in the Ka'bah.**" Then another battalion came and passed by, it was the smallest but the honorable, among them is the Messenger of Allâh (ﷺ) and his companions. Zubayr bin Awâm was the one carrying the banner of the Immigrants. When the Prophet (ﷺ) passed by Abû Sufyân, he informed him with what Sa'd said. So the Prophet (ﷺ) said: **"Sa'd was wrong for (what) he has said, rather today is the day in which Allâh (ﷻ) will venerate the Ka'bah. This day is the day in which the Ka'bah will be draped."** [Collected by Al-Bukhârî]

Then the Prophet (ﷺ) commanded that the Banner should be taken away from Sa'd and transferred to his son Qays, so that Sa'd will not think that the banner is totally taken away from him as long as it ended up in the hands of his son. Then the Prophet (ﷺ) continued his journey and commanded the people to pitch his banner at Al-Hajûn. Then he entered Mecca conquering it with victory. He bent his head down to show humbleness to Allâh (ﷻ) to the point that his forehead almost touched his ride while he was reciting the verse and repeating it:

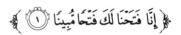

"Verily, We have given you (O Muhammad) a manifest victory" [Al-Fath: 1]

Then the Prophet (ﷺ) sent Khâlid bin Walîd and Zubayr bin 'Awâm against two flanks of armies of the disbelievers who came out to fight the believers, and then said: **"Whoever enters the Masjid is safe, and whoever enters the house of Abû Sufyân is safe, and whoever enters his house and locks the door is safe."** [Collected by Al-Bukhârî]

Then the Prophet (ﷺ) proceeded to the Sacred Masjid and circumambulated the Masjid while riding on his ride. There were three hundred and sixty idols around the sacred house. So the Prophet (ﷺ) shot them with his arrows saying:

$$\left\{ \text{وَقُلْ جَاءَ ٱلْحَقُّ وَزَهَقَ ٱلْبَاطِلُ إِنَّ ٱلْبَاطِلَ كَانَ زَهُوقًا} \; \textcircled{\scriptsize ٨١} \right\}$$

"And say: 'Truth has come and falsehood has vanished. Surely! Falsehood is ever bound to vanish.'" [Al-Isrâ: 81]

$$\left\{ \text{قُلْ جَاءَ ٱلْحَقُّ وَمَا يُبْدِئُ ٱلْبَاطِلُ وَمَا يُعِيدُ} \; \textcircled{\scriptsize ٤٩} \right\}$$

"Say (O Muhammad): 'The truth has come, and falsehood can neither create anything nor resurrect (anything).'" [Saba': 49] Then the idols started to fall on their faces. [Collected by Al-Bukhârî and Muslim]

The Prophet (ﷺ) entered the Ka'bah and found some pictures. So he commanded that those pictures be wiped out and then he prayed in it. When he was done praying he turned around in the Ka'bah, glorified Allâh, and singled him out alone (in worship). While he was in the Ka'bah the Quraysh were waiting out to see the reaction he will take towards them. He then held by the doorjamb and said: **"None has the right to be worshipped but Allâh alone without a partner, His is the sovereignty, and His is the praise and He is able to do all things. He fulfilled His promise, helped His slave, and overcame the confederate by Himself."** Then he said, "O group of Quraysh! Allâh (ﷻ) has taken away from you the haughtiness of the pre-Islamic era, and the ancestral pride. All the people are from Ādam and Ādam is from dust." He then recited:

$$\left\{ \text{يَا أَيُّهَا ٱلنَّاسُ إِنَّا خَلَقْنَاكُم مِّن ذَكَرٍ وَأُنثَىٰ وَجَعَلْنَاكُمْ شُعُوبًا وَقَبَائِلَ لِتَعَارَفُوا إِنَّ أَكْرَمَكُمْ عِندَ ٱللَّهِ أَتْقَاكُمْ إِنَّ ٱللَّهَ عَلِيمٌ خَبِيرٌ} \; \textcircled{\scriptsize ١٣} \right\}$$

"Oh Mankind! Indeed We have created you all from a male and female, and We have made you into Tribes and nations in order that you can get to know one another. Indeed the most honorable of you with Allâh is the (believer) who has the most Taqwâ." [Al-Hujurât: 13]

(He said): "O group of Quraysh! What do you think I will do to you?" They said: "Good, O our generous brother, the son of our kind brother." Then he said, "I will say to you just as Yusuf said to his brothers:

$$\left\{ \text{قَالَ لَا تَثْرِيبَ عَلَيْكُمُ ٱلْيَوْمَ يَغْفِرُ ٱللَّهُ لَكُمْ} \right\}$$

"He said: 'No reproach on you this day, may Allâh forgive you.'" [Yusuf: 92]

'Go, for verily all of you are free.'"

On the Second Day of the Meccan conquest the Prophet (ﷺ) stood up and gave them a speech. He thanked and praised Allâh and then said: "Indeed Allâh (ﷺ) is the One who made Mecca sacred and not the people. Therefore it is not permissible for a man who believes in Allâh and the Last Day to shed blood in Mecca or to cut its trees. And if anyone justifies the permissibility of doing so because of the fighting of the Messenger of Allâh (ﷺ), say to such an individual: 'Allâh has made it permissible for His Messenger but did not make it permissible for you.' He has only made it permissible for me for some hours of the day. And today its sacredness has returned back like it was yesterday. So let the one who is present convey the message to the one who is absent." [Collected by Al-Bukhârî and Muslim]

The period of hours that was made permissible for the Prophet (ﷺ) was from sunrise until 'Asr Prayer on the day of the conquest. Then the Prophet (ﷺ) remained in Mecca for nineteen days shortening his prayers. [Collected by Al-Bukhârî]

(This was the case) because he intended to continue his travel. He remained in Mecca for that period of time for the purpose of stabilizing Islâmic monotheism and the teachings of Al-Islâm. Likewise (he remained there) to strengthen (the people's) faith and to take their pledges.

It is reported in the Sahîh that Majâshi' said: "I came to the Prophet (ﷺ) with my brother in order for him to give the pledge of allegiance to the Prophet (ﷺ) upon migrating. So the Prophet (ﷺ) said: 'The immigrants have already carried out what is needed to be carried out in the Hijrah. However, I will take a pledge with him on Al-Islâm, Al-Imân, and Al-Jihâd.'" [Collected by Al-Bukhârî and Muslim]

It is with this great triumph that Allâh (ﷻ) completed His victory for this religion. And the people entered Allâh's religion in droves. Allâh's Land returned back to what it was before, an Islamic state where Islâmic Monotheism is announced openly. The Prophet (ﷺ) was accepted, the Book of Allâh became their constitution, and Al-Islâm became the religion of the state. Polytheism, on the other hand, deteriorated and its darkness dispersed. So, glory be to Allâh and all praise belongs to Him. That is from Allâh's great bounties upon His slaves until the Day of Judgment.

O Allâh allow us to be grateful for this great bounty. Allow us to actualize victory for the Islâmic Ummah at all times and in all places. O Allâh, with Your Mercy, forgive us, our parents, and all the Muslims. For verily You are the Most Merciful. May peace and blessings be upon our Prophet Muhammad, his family members, and all his Companions.

المَجْلِسُ الْعِشْرُونُ
The Twentieth Sitting
The Means of True Victory

All praise is due to Allâh, the One who's Status is Magnificent, the Mighty in His Omnipotence, the Knower of the slave's secrets and open affairs, the One who is kind towards whoever strives in His cause by assisting him, and He is (generous) towards the one who humbles himself for His sake by elevating him. He hears the creaking of the pen upon writing with it. And He sees the creeping of the ant on a desert land. From among His signs is the standing of the heaven and the earth by His command. I praise Him for His decree, both the good and bad. I further bear witness that none has the right to be worshipped but Allâh Alone without a partner. And I also bear witness that Muhammad is His slave and His Messenger who was sent with goodness to the creatures. May the peace of Allâh be upon him, his companion Abû Bakr, the one who surpassed the ummah after the Prophet with the faith which settled in his heart, upon 'Umar, the one who elevated Al-Islâm with his strong determination and strength, upon 'Uthmân, the owner of two lights, the one who was patient with his affair although it was bitter, upon 'Alî the son of the Prophet's uncle and his son-in-law, upon his family members, his companions, and those who follow their footsteps in a good manner as long as the cloud continues to shower its generosity.

O My Brothers! Allâh (ﷻ) has helped the believers in various occasions. He granted them victory over their enemies in the Battle of Badr, Ahzâb, Al-Fath, Hunayn, and more. Allâh (ﷻ) granted them victory as a fulfillment of His promise to them. As He, the Most High, said:

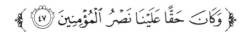

"And it was certainly incumbent upon Us to help the believers" [Ar-Rûm: 47] Allâh said:

$$\text{﴿ إِنَّا لَنَنصُرُ رُسُلَنَا وَٱلَّذِينَ ءَامَنُوا۟ فِى ٱلْحَيَوٰةِ ٱلدُّنْيَا وَيَوْمَ يَقُومُ ٱلْأَشْهَـٰدُ ۝ يَوْمَ لَا يَنفَعُ ٱلظَّـٰلِمِينَ مَعْذِرَتُهُمْ ۖ وَلَهُمُ ٱللَّعْنَةُ وَلَهُمْ سُوٓءُ ٱلدَّارِ ۝ ﴾}$$

"Most, surely, We help Our Messengers and those who believe, both in the present life and on the day when the witnesses will stand forth. The day when their pleading will not profit the wrongdoers, and for them will be the curse and for them will be the evil abode." [Ghâfir: 51-52]

Allâh (ﷻ) aided them because they were firm upon His religion, which is victorious over any other religion. Therefore whoever holds on to this religion will be victorious over all the nations. As Allâh the Most High states:

$$\text{﴿ هُوَ ٱلَّذِىٓ أَرْسَلَ رَسُولَهُۥ بِٱلْهُدَىٰ وَدِينِ ٱلْحَقِّ لِيُظْهِرَهُۥ عَلَى ٱلدِّينِ كُلِّهِۦ وَلَوْ كَرِهَ ٱلْمُشْرِكُونَ ۝ ﴾}$$

"He is the One who sent His Messenger with guidance and the religion of truth, to make it apparent over all religions, even if the polytheists hate it." [As-Saff: 9]

Allâh (ﷻ) helped them only because they have taken the true means of victory: the spiritual and the physical means. They had strong determination with which they overcame their enemies, implementing the instruction(s) of Allâh (ﷻ) and walking with His guidance, and with the stability that is giving to them by Allâh the Most High. As He, the Most High, said:

﴿ وَلَا تَهِنُوا۟ وَلَا تَحْزَنُوا۟ وَأَنتُمُ ٱلْأَعْلَوْنَ إِن كُنتُم مُّؤْمِنِينَ ۞ إِن يَمْسَسْكُمْ قَرْحٌ فَقَدْ مَسَّ ٱلْقَوْمَ قَرْحٌ مِّثْلُهُۥ ۚ وَتِلْكَ ٱلْأَيَّامُ نُدَاوِلُهَا بَيْنَ ٱلنَّاسِ ﴾

"Slacken not nor grieve; and you shall certainly have the upper hand, if you are true believers. If you have received an injury, surely the disbelieving people have already received a similar injury. And such days We cause to alternate among men" [Āli Imrân: 139-140] And Allâh said:

﴿ وَلَا تَهِنُوا۟ فِى ٱبْتِغَآءِ ٱلْقَوْمِ ۖ إِن تَكُونُوا۟ تَأْلَمُونَ فَإِنَّهُمْ يَأْلَمُونَ كَمَا تَأْلَمُونَ ۖ وَتَرْجُونَ مِنَ ٱللَّهِ مَا لَا يَرْجُونَ ۗ وَكَانَ ٱللَّهُ عَلِيمًا حَكِيمًا ۞ ﴾

"And slacken not in seeking these people. If you suffer, they too suffer even as you suffer. But you hope from Allâh what they hope not. And Allâh is All-Knowing, Wise" [An-Nisâ: 104] And Allâh said:

﴿ فَلَا تَهِنُوا۟ وَتَدْعُوٓا۟ إِلَى ٱلسَّلْمِ وَأَنتُمُ ٱلْأَعْلَوْنَ وَٱللَّهُ مَعَكُمْ وَلَن يَتِرَكُمْ أَعْمَـٰلَكُمْ ۞ ﴾

"So be not slack and sue not for peace, for you will, certainly, have the upper hand. And Allâh is with you, and He will not deprive you of the reward of your actions" [Muhammad: 35]

It is with this fortification and stabilization that they moved on with power, strong determination, and seriousness. They held on to all means of power, implementing Allâh's (ﷺ) statement:

Sittings During the Blessed Month of Ramaḍān رَمَضَانْ

﴿ وَأَعِدُّواْ لَهُم مَّا ٱسۡتَطَعۡتُم مِّن قُوَّةٖ وَمِن رِّبَاطِ ٱلۡخَيۡلِ تُرۡهِبُونَ بِهِۦ عَدُوَّ ٱللَّهِ وَعَدُوَّكُمۡ وَءَاخَرِينَ مِن دُونِهِمۡ لَا تَعۡلَمُونَهُمُ ٱللَّهُ يَعۡلَمُهُمۡۚ وَمَا تُنفِقُواْ مِن شَيۡءٖ فِي سَبِيلِ ٱللَّهِ يُوَفَّ إِلَيۡكُمۡ وَأَنتُمۡ لَا تُظۡلَمُونَ ۝ ﴾

"And make ready for them, who fight you, whatever you can of strength and of mounted pickets at the frontier, whereby you may frighten the enemy of Allâh and your enemy and others besides them whom you know not, but Allâh knows them. And whatever you spend in the way of Allâh, it shall be paid back to you in full, and you shall not be wronged." [Al-Anfâl: 60]

The 'strength' intended in the verse includes both the spiritual and physical strength: having strong faith along with having ammunition. Allâh (ﷻ) only helped them because they carried out the responsibility of helping His religion. As He (ﷻ) promised to do so in His statement:

﴿ وَلَيَنصُرَنَّ ٱللَّهُ مَن يَنصُرُهُۥٓۚ إِنَّ ٱللَّهَ لَقَوِيٌّ عَزِيزٌ ۝ ٱلَّذِينَ إِن مَّكَّنَّٰهُمۡ فِي ٱلۡأَرۡضِ أَقَامُواْ ٱلصَّلَوٰةَ وَءَاتَوُاْ ٱلزَّكَوٰةَ وَأَمَرُواْ بِٱلۡمَعۡرُوفِ وَنَهَوۡاْ عَنِ ٱلۡمُنكَرِۗ وَلِلَّهِ عَٰقِبَةُ ٱلۡأُمُورِ ۝ ﴾

"(And certainly) Allâh will, surely, help him who helps Him. Allâh is, indeed, Powerful and Mighty. Those who, if We empower them in the earth, will observe Prayer and pay the Zakât and enjoin good and forbid evil. And with Allâh rests the final issue of all affairs." [Al-Hajj: 40-41]

In these two noble verses, Allâh (ﷻ) has promised to grant victory to whoever helps Him (by supporting His religion) with an assured promise emphasized by words and meanings. He emphasized it by swearing, and by using particles of emphasis like "surely" and by saying He is the Powerful and the Mighty. He, the Glorified, is strong without weakness and Mighty without humiliation. And every power or exultance that confronts with His power and exultance will be weakened and humiliated. And in His statement:

$$﴿ وَلِلَّهِ عَاقِبَةُ ٱلْأُمُورِ ﴾$$

"And unto Allâh is the return of affairs" [Al-Hajj:41]

This statement stabilizes the believer, and keeps him firm at a time when the believer (may have lost) hope in being victorious, because he does not have all the means of victory. The believer, however, understands from this verse that, the finality of affairs is with Allâh, He changes what he wants based on His wisdom.

In these two verses Allâh mentions some of the qualities through which victory can be obtained. These are qualities that the believer has, after being established on the earth. Therefore, this authority which Allâh gives to (a particular person) must not be a cause of him being oppressive, boastful, arrogant, and a mischief-maker. Rather it should increase his strength in Allâh's religion.

The First Characteristic is the statement of Allâh:

$$﴿ ٱلَّذِينَ إِن مَّكَّنَّـٰهُمْ فِى ٱلْأَرْضِ أَقَامُوا۟ ٱلصَّلَوٰةَ ﴾$$

"Those who, if We empower them in the earth, will observe Prayer"

(True) Empowerment cannot be attained on the earth until monotheism is actualized, as Allâh (ﷻ) said:

$$﴿ وَعَدَ ٱللَّهُ ٱلَّذِينَ ءَامَنُوا۟ مِنكُمْ وَعَمِلُوا۟ ٱلصَّـٰلِحَـٰتِ لَيَسْتَخْلِفَنَّهُمْ فِى ٱلْأَرْضِ كَمَا ٱسْتَخْلَفَ ٱلَّذِينَ مِن قَبْلِهِمْ وَلَيُمَكِّنَنَّ لَهُمْ دِينَهُمُ ٱلَّذِى ٱرْتَضَىٰ ﴾$$

$$\text{هُمْ وَلَيُبَدِّلَنَّهُم مِّنۢ بَعْدِ خَوْفِهِمْ أَمْنًا ۚ يَعْبُدُونَنِي لَا يُشْرِكُونَ بِي شَيْئًا ۚ وَمَن كَفَرَ بَعْدَ ذَٰلِكَ فَأُولَٰئِكَ هُمُ ٱلْفَٰسِقُونَ ۞}$$

"Allâh has promised those among you who believe, and do righteous good deeds, that He will certainly grant them succession to (the present rulers) in the earth, as He granted it to those before them, and that He will grant them the empowerment to practice their religion, that which He has chosen for them (i.e. Islam). And He will surely give them in exchange a safe security after their fear (provided) they (believers) worship Me and do not associate anything (in worship) with Me. But whoever disbelieved after this, they are the Fasiqûn (rebellious, disobedient to Allâh)" [An-Nûr: 55]

So, when the slave establishes the worship of Allâh alone, being sincere to Him in his statements and actions, and seeking with that Allâh's pleasure and the abode of the hereafter, he does not seek with it fame, praise from the people, wealth, or any worldly glitter. And he is to be persistent upon that at times of fortune and misfortune, times of ease and hardship. Then Allâh the (ﷻ) will empower him and establish him on the face of the earth.

Therefore being empowered in the earth has some characteristics that precedes it and are prerequisites of it, and they are: **the worship of Allâh** alone without ascribing partners with Him, along with sincerity. This worship must continue after being empowered in the earth as well.

The Second Characteristic: Establishing the prayer by carrying it out in a required manner, fulfilling its conditions, pillars, and obligations. The perfection of that is by fulfilling its recommendations. Therefore one should perform the ablution in a perfect manner, likewise one's bowing, prostration, standing and sitting. And (the Muslim) should preserve the Friday prayer, congregational prayer, and maintain his tranquility in his prayer by focusing with his heart and tranquilizing his limbs. This is because tranquility is the spirit of the prayer and its core. Prayer without tranquility is like a body without a spirit. Ammâr bin Yâsir (ﷺ) said: I heard the Messenger of Allâh (ﷺ) saying: "**Indeed a man will finish his prayer and only one tenth of it will be written for him, or one eighth, one seventh, one sixth, one fifth, one fourth, one third, or half of it.**" [Narrated by Abû Dâwûd and An-Nasâ'î. Al-Irâqî said: its chains of narration is authentic.]

The Third Characteristic: Giving the Zakât. This is by giving it to those who deserve it, being pleased while giving it (not angry), giving it to them in full without deducting from it, seeking with it Allâh's pleasure and bounty.

So (the believers) purify their souls with it, clean their wealth, and benefit their brothers who are poor and needy. We have already mentioned the categories of those who receive zakât in the seventeenth sitting.

The Fourth Characteristic: Commanding with the good, which includes all that Allâh (ﷺ) and His Messenger (ﷺ) commanded us with of obligations and recommendations. (The believers are to) do this in order to revive Allâh's religion (ﷺ), rectify His slaves' affairs, and to seek His mercy and pleasure. This is because the believers to one another are like fortified bricks, each one strengthens the other. Just as the believer loves for himself to be obedient to his Lord, he should love the same for his brothers. His command of the good must be based on faith and truthfulness, by implementing what he commanded the people with and being convinced with its benefits and fruits in this world and the hereafter.

The Fifth Characteristic: Forbidding the evil, which is anything that is Allâh and His Messenger forbade of the major and minor sins regarding any act of worship, characteristic, or transactions. They prevent all these evils in order to preserve Allâh's religion (ﷻ), to preserve His slaves, and in order to avoid the causes of corruption, and punishment.

Commanding the good and forbidding the evil are two strong fundamentals that maintain the Muslim Ummah's honor and unity, (assuring that they will) not be divided by the evil desires and (to guarantee that they will not be) disseminated in different paths. This is the reason why commanding the good and forbidding the evil is one of the religious duties which is a must upon every Muslim man and woman as long as they have the ability to do it. Allâh (ﷻ) said:

﴿ وَلْتَكُن مِّنكُمْ أُمَّةٌ يَدْعُونَ إِلَى ٱلْخَيْرِ وَيَأْمُرُونَ بِٱلْمَعْرُوفِ وَيَنْهَوْنَ عَنِ ٱلْمُنكَرِ وَأُوْلَٰٓئِكَ هُمُ ٱلْمُفْلِحُونَ ۝ ﴾

"Let there arise out of you a group of people inviting to all that is good, enjoining Al-Ma'rûf (i.e. Islamic Monotheism and all that Islam orders one to do) and forbidding Al-Munkar (polytheism and disbelief and all that Islam has forbidden). And it is they who are the successful." [Āli Imrân: 104]

Had it not been for commanding with the good and forbidding the evil, the people would have been divided into groups and sects, each group being proud with what they have. It is with the principle of commanding the good and forbidding the evil that this nation is given preference over other nations. As He, the Most High, mentioned in His Glorious Book:

﴿ كُنتُمْ خَيْرَ أُمَّةٍ أُخْرِجَتْ لِلنَّاسِ تَأْمُرُونَ بِٱلْمَعْرُوفِ وَتَنْهَوْنَ عَنِ ٱلْمُنكَرِ وَتُؤْمِنُونَ بِٱللَّهِ ﴾

"You [true believers in Islamic Monotheism, and real followers of Prophet Muhammad and his Sunnah (legal ways, etc.)] are the best of peoples ever raised up for mankind; you enjoin Al-Ma'rûf (i.e. Islâmic Monotheism and all that Islâm has ordained) and forbid Al-Munkar (polytheism, disbelief and all that Islam has forbidden), and you believe in Allâh" [Āli Imrân: 110]

It is by abandoning (this foundation) that some of the Children of Isrâîl were cursed, as He the Most High said:

$$\lbrace لُعِنَ الَّذِينَ كَفَرُوا مِنْ بَنِي إِسْرَائِيلَ عَلَىٰ لِسَانِ دَاوُودَ وَعِيسَى ابْنِ مَرْيَمَ ۚ ذَٰلِكَ بِمَا عَصَوا وَّكَانُوا يَعْتَدُونَ ۝ كَانُوا لَا يَتَنَاهَوْنَ عَن مُّنكَرٍ فَعَلُوهُ ۚ لَبِئْسَ مَا كَانُوا يَفْعَلُونَ ۝ \rbrace$$

"Those among the Children of Isrâîl who disbelieved were cursed by the tongue of Dâwûd (David) and 'Isa (Jesus), the son of Maryam (Mary). That was because they disobeyed (Allâh and the Messengers) and were ever transgressing beyond bounds. They used not to forbid one another from the Munkar (wrong, evil-doing, sins, polytheism, disbelief, etc.) which they committed. Vile indeed was what they used to do" [Al-Mâi'dah: 78-79]

Whenever these five (aforementioned) characteristics are found, and when strong determination and high ambition are carried out, along with preparation of the physical power, the triumph will materialize by Allâh's permission. This is because Allâh does not break his promise. As He, the Most High, said:

$$\lbrace وَعْدَ اللَّهِ ۖ لَا يُخْلِفُ اللَّهُ وَعْدَهُ وَلَٰكِنَّ أَكْثَرَ النَّاسِ لَا يَعْلَمُونَ ۝ \rbrace$$

"Allâh promised, Allâh does not break His promise, but most of mankind know not" [Ar-Rûm: 6]

Allâh's help for the Ummah occurs in a manner which they may not (even) perceive. The believer who is sure and certain of

Allâh's promise must know that the material means of triumph are nothing (in comparison) to Allâh's Power, regardless of how mighty these material means may be. After all, who created them and brought them in to existence?

The tribe of 'Ād were boastful of their strength. They said: "Who is more powerful than us!!" So Allâh, the Most High, said:

﴿ فَأَمَّا عَادٌ فَٱسْتَكْبَرُوا۟ فِى ٱلْأَرْضِ بِغَيْرِ ٱلْحَقِّ وَقَالُوا۟ مَنْ أَشَدُّ مِنَّا قُوَّةً أَوَلَمْ يَرَوْا۟ أَنَّ ٱللَّهَ ٱلَّذِى خَلَقَهُمْ هُوَ أَشَدُّ مِنْهُمْ قُوَّةً وَكَانُوا۟ بِـَٔايَٰتِنَا يَجْحَدُونَ ۝ فَأَرْسَلْنَا عَلَيْهِمْ رِيحًا صَرْصَرًا فِى أَيَّامٍ نَّحِسَاتٍ لِّنُذِيقَهُمْ عَذَابَ ٱلْخِزْىِ فِى ٱلْحَيَوٰةِ ٱلدُّنْيَا وَلَعَذَابُ ٱلْءَاخِرَةِ أَخْزَىٰ وَهُمْ لَا يُنصَرُونَ ۝ ﴾

"As for 'Ād, they were arrogant in the land without right, and they said: 'Who is mightier than us in strength?' See they not that Allâh, Who created them was mightier in strength than them. And they used to deny Our Ayât (proofs, evidences, verses, lessons, revelations, etc.)! So We sent upon them furious wind in days of evil omen (for them) that We might give them a taste of disgracing torment in this present worldly life, but surely the torment of the Hereafter will be more disgracing, and they will never be helped." [Fussilat: 15-16]

Pharaoh was boastful of the Egyptian Kingdom and the rivers which flowed beneath his castle. So as a result he was drowned in water, similar to the (water) which he used to boast over. And (Allâh) made Mûsâ, along with his people, inherit Pharaoh's kingdom the same one who Pharaoh mocked at, accusing him of being insignificant and not being able to speak clearly.

Likewise the tribe of **Quraysh** was boastful of their position and power. They left their homes with their leaders behaving arrogantly and showing off with what they possessed of wealth and power while saying: **"We will not return until we arrive at Badr, slaughter our cattle, drink alcohol, and let our songstress sing for us, so that the Arabs will hear about us and will continue to be afraid of us."** However, they were defeated severely at the hands of the Prophet (ﷺ) and his companions. Their dead corpses were dragged in the river of Badr, and they have become the story of the people today, and an example of humiliation until the Day of Judgment.

If we were to hold onto the means of triumph, carry out our religious responsibilities, become an example (of people) who are followed and not the followers of others, and (if we were to) grasp the modern ammunitions of war honestly and sincerely, Allâh (ﷻ) would have given us victory over our enemies as He granted victory to our ancestors. Allâh (ﷻ) has indeed fulfilled His promise, aided His slave, and overcame the hosts.

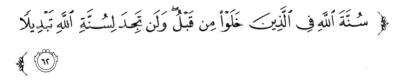

"This is Allâh's custom (ﷻ) in (dealing with) those who have proceeded and you will not see any changes in Allâh's custom." [Al-Ahzâb: 62]

O Allâh ease for us the means of triumph which will give us victory, dignity, honor, elevation of Al-Islâm, and humiliation of disbelief and sin. Verily You are the Most Generous, the Most Kind. May peace and blessings of Allâh be upon our Prophet Muhammad (ﷺ), his family members, and all his Companions.

المَجْلِسُ الحادي و العشرون
The Twenty First Sitting
The Virtues of Last Ten Days of Ramadân

All praise and thanks are due to Allâh the Almighty, the One who is Unique in His Majesty, Eternal Life, greatness, exultance and unthinkable glory. The Self-sufficient Lord, the Independent King who is not in need of any one, the One who is High above all imaginations, the Almighty, the Great, the One whom no mind can comprehend. He is self-sufficient and independent from His creatures. Everything is in constant need of His assistance. He granted success to whom He willed, who, as a result, believed and became upright. Then he tasted the sweetness of his dialogue with his Lord (at night), thus abandoning the sweetness of sleep and joined the company of those who keep their sides away from their beds seeking high rank with their Lord. If you were to see them with their caravan traveling in severe darkness, one of them asking forgiveness for his shortcomings, another complaining of his sorrow, and another forgot to ask Him because he is occupied with His remembrance. Glorified is He who woke them up while the people were sleeping. I praise Him for His lofty bounties. I thank Him and ask Him to preserve the bounty of Al-Islâm. I also testify that none has the right to be worshiped but Allâh. (He is) alone, without a partner. Whoever seeks elevation with Him will never be humiliated, and whoever is (too) arrogant to obey Him will be humiliated and punished. I also bear witness that Muhammad (ﷺ) is His slave and His Messenger, the One who clarified the lawful and the unlawful things. (May peace and blessings be upon him), Abû Bakr As-Siddîq his excellent companion in the cave, 'Umar the one who was granted success to the truth, 'Uthmân the forbearing one at times of test, the one who obtained martyrdom at the hands of his enemies, 'Alî the son of (The Prophet's) Uncle Abû Tâlib, and on all his companions and those who follow their footsteps in a proper manner till the Day of Judgment. To proceed:

O My Brothers! The last ten days of Ramadân have reached you. There are lots of good, rewards, virtues, and great distinguishing qualities within these days.

From among their distinguishing qualities is that the Prophet (ﷺ) used to strive hard in these days more than he did in any other days. It is narrated by 'Āishah (رضي الله عنها):

أن النبي صلى اللَّهُ عَلَيْهِ وَسَلَّمَ كان يجتهدُ في العَشرِ الأواخر ما لا يجتهد في غيره

"That the Prophet (ﷺ) used to strive hard in the last ten days of Ramadân more than he did in other days." [Collected by Muslim]

It is also narrated by 'Āishah (رضي الله عنها) that:

كان النبي صلى الله عليه وسلم إذا دخلَ العَشرُ شَدَّ مِئزره وأحيا ليلَه وأيقظ أهله

"The Prophet (ﷺ) used to tighten his lower garment, revive his night, and awaken his family when the last ten days of Ramadân arrived" [Collected by Al-Bukhârî and Muslim]

It is also narrated by 'Āîshah (رضي الله عنها):

كان النبي صلى الله عليه وسلم يَخْلِطُ العِشرين بصلاةٍ ونومٍ، فإذا كان العشرُ شمَّر وشدَّ المِئزرَ

"That the Prophet (ﷺ) used to blend the first twenty days of Ramadân with prayer and sleep, but when the last ten days arrived, he would prepare himself and tighten up his Izâr." [Collected by Ahmad]

The aforementioned narrations are proofs of the virtues of the last ten days of Ramadân, because the Prophet (ﷺ) worked diligently in them (even) more than he did in other days. This includes his efforts in all aspects of worship (such as) prayer, Qur'ânic recitation, remembrance of Allâh, charity and more. Also the Prophet (ﷺ) used to revive his night with prayer, Qur'ânic recitation, and remembrance of Allâh (ﷻ) with his heart, tongue, and limbs. (This was all due to) the nobility of these night and due to his eagerness to be successful (in achieving) the Night of Qadar, in which the previous sins of those who stood in prayer in this night, while seeking Allâh's pleasure, will be forgiven.

According to the apparent wording of the hadîth, the Prophet (ﷺ) used to stay up the entire night worshiping his Lord, (with various righteous deeds) including remembering Allâh, Qur'ânic recitation, prayer, preparing for Sahûr, and more.

With this we can combine between the previous narration and the narration found in <u>Sahîh Muslim</u> from 'Āishah (رضي الله عنها) who said: "I do not know the Prophet (ﷺ) to revive the whole night with prayer." Revival of the entire in prayer includes various forms of prayer. However, 'Āishah was merely negating that the Prophet (ﷺ) stood in *salâh* the entire night. And Allâh knows best.

From among the things which indicate the virtues of these ten days is that: the Prophet (ﷺ) used to wake his family up for prayer and in order to remember Allâh. This was due to his eagerness to take advantage of these blessed nights. Worshipping Allâh in them is worthwhile. For verily it is a golden opportunity for us, in our lives, as well as a precious treasure for the one Allâh grants them success to (reach these nights).

Therefore it is not befitting for the intelligent believer to waste this invaluable opportunity without him and his family benefitting from it. It is only a few days. Perhaps (Allâh) The Most Merciful's mercy may reach an individual and may be the cause for him succeeding in this world and the hereafter. It is indeed a great deprivation and a disastrous loss to see many Muslims spend these precious occasions involved in absurdities which do not benefit them. They stay up spending most of the nighttime hours engaged in pastime and falsehood. When it is time for the night prayer they go to bed, depriving themselves of abundant good, which they may not come across after that year of their (life). This is no doubt from Satan's games and plots against these people, in order to turn them away from Allâh's path, (and it is a way) to mislead them. Allâh, the Most High, said:

﴿ إِنَّ عِبَادِى لَيْسَ لَكَ عَلَيْهِمْ سُلْطَانٌ إِلَّا مَنِ ٱتَّبَعَكَ مِنَ ٱلْغَاوِينَ ﴿٤٢﴾ ﴾

"Surely, thou shall have no power over My servants, except such of the erring ones as choose to follow thee." [Al-Hijr: 42]

The intelligent person will not take the devil as his protector besides Allâh, after knowing his enmity towards him. Doing this contradicts sound intellect and true faith. Allâh, the Most High said:

﴿ أَفَتَتَّخِذُونَهُ وَذُرِّيَّتَهُ أَوْلِيَآءَ مِن دُونِى وَهُمْ لَكُمْ عَدُوٌّ بِئْسَ لِلظَّٰلِمِينَ بَدَلًا ﴿٥٠﴾ ﴾

"Will you then take him and his offspring for friends instead of Me while they are your enemies? Evil is the exchange for the wrongdoers" [Al-Kahf: 50]

Sittings During the Blessed Month of Ramaḍān رَمَضَان

He also said:

$$\text{﴿ إِنَّ ٱلشَّيْطَٰنَ لَكُمْ عَدُوٌّ فَٱتَّخِذُوهُ عَدُوًّا ۚ إِنَّمَا يَدْعُوا۟ حِزْبَهُۥ لِيَكُونُوا۟ مِنْ أَصْحَٰبِ ٱلسَّعِيرِ ۝ ﴾}$$

"Surely, the devil is an enemy to you, so (treat) him as an enemy. He only invites his (followers) that they may become the dwellers of the blazing Fire" [Fâtir: 6]

From the virtues of these ten days is that the Prophet (ﷺ) used to perform "Al-I'tikâf" in them. **Al-I'tikâf** is to dedicate your time (to be) in Allâh's service by staying in the Masjid. The proof for its legislation is mentioned in Allâh's Book and the tradition of His Messenger (ﷺ). Allâh, the Most High said:

$$\text{﴿ وَلَا تُبَٰشِرُوهُنَّ وَأَنتُمْ عَٰكِفُونَ فِى ٱلْمَسَٰجِدِ ﴾}$$

"And do not have sexual relations with them (your wives) while you are in Al-I'tikâf (i.e. confining oneself in a mosque for prayers and invocations leaving the worldly activities) in the Masjids" [Al-Baqarah: 187]

The Prophet (ﷺ) isolated himself in the Masjid, as well as his companions who followed him. As it is narrated by Abû Sa'îd Al-Khudrî (ﷺ): "The Prophet (ﷺ) isolated himself in the Masjid during the first ten days of Ramaḍân and then the middle ten days of Ramaḍân. Then he said: **'I remained in the Masjid for the first and the middle ten days of Ramaḍân looking for the night of Qadr. But then it was said to me that the Night of Qadr is in the Last ten days of Ramaḍân. Therefore anyone amongst you who wants to isolate himself in these ten days should do so.'** [Collected by Muslim]

It is also narrated by 'Āîshah (ﷺ) who said:

Sittings During the Blessed Month of Ramaḍān

كان النبي صلى الله عليه وسلم يعتكف العشرالأواخر مِنْ رمضانَ حتى توفّاه الله عزَّ وجل ثم اعتكف أزواجه من بعده

"The Prophet (ﷺ) used to remain in the Masjid during the last ten days of Ramaḍân and he continued upon that until Allâh the Most High took his soul. Then his wives performed Al-I'tikâf after his death" [Collected by Al-Bukhârî and Muslim]

It is also narrated by 'Āishah (رضي الله عنها)

كان النبيُّ صلَّى اللَّهُ عَلَيْهِ وَسَلَّمَ يعتكفُ في كلِّ رمضانَ عشرةَ أيامٍ، ؛ فلما كان العامُ الذي قُبِضَ فيه اعتكفَ عشرين يوماً

"The Prophet (ﷺ) used to isolate himself in the Masjid for ten days in every Ramaḍân, but in the following year he isolated himself in the Masjid for twenty days (to make up a previous year he missed.) [Collected by Al-Bukhârî]

It is also narrated by Anas (ﷺ):

كانَ النَّبيُّ صلَّى اللَّهُ عليهِ وسلَّمَ يعتَكفُ في العشرِ الأواخرِ من رمضانَ فلم يعتَكف عامًا فلمَّا كانَ في العامِ المقبلِ اعتَكفَ عشرينَ

"The Prophet (ﷺ) used to isolate himself in every last ten days of Ramaḍân. So there was a year that he missed and did not seclude himself. So when the next year came he performed Al-I'tikâf for twenty days." [Collected by Ahmad and At-Tirmidhî. Al-Albânî graded it to be authentic]

'Āishah, may Allâh be pleased with her, said: "The Prophet (ﷺ) used to pray the dawn prayer and then isolate himself in his tent in the Masjid. So I asked permission from him to set up my tent in the Masjid and he granted me permission. Then Hafsah asked me to seek permission for her from the Prophet (ﷺ) to set up her tent and permission was granted to her. When Zaynab saw this she also asked that a tent be erected for her. And when the Prophet (ﷺ) saw the tents in the Masjid he asked: 'What are these?' They said: 'They are tents for 'Āishah, Hafsah and Zaynab.' So the Prophet (ﷺ) said: 'Do you seek with this to be obedient to Allâh? Take them down I do not want to see them.' They then took them down. But the Prophet (ﷺ) did not make Al-I'tikâf in that Ramadân and made them up in the first ten days of Shawwal." [Collected by Al-Bukhârî and Muslim]

Al-Imâm Ahmad bin Hanbal may Allâh have mercy on him, said: "I do not know anyone from the scholars that opposed the legislation of Al-I'tikâf being a supererogatory (act of worship)."

Al-I'tikâf is when a Muslim secludes himself from the people in order to devote his time in the worship of his Lord in a Masjid seeking with that his Lord's pleasure and reward as well as seeking the Night of Qadar. This is the reason why it is highly recommended for the one performing Al-I'tikâf to keep himself busy with the remembrance of Allâh, Qur'ânic recitation, prayers, and worship. Likewise it is also recommended for him to stay away from things that do not concern him and from talking about the worldly affairs. There is nothing wrong with talking seldom about permissible things with one's family or with others if there is a need to it. And the proof for this is the narration of Safiyyah, the Mother of the Believers, may Allâh be pleased with her, who said: "The Prophet (ﷺ) was performing Al-I'tikâf in the Masjid when I came and visited him and spoke with him one night. I then stood up to return back to the house and the Prophet (ﷺ) also stood up with me and escorted me." [Collected by Al-Bukhârî and Muslim]

It is impermissible for the one performing Al-I'tikâf to have intercourse with his spouse or involve in flirtatious behavior including kissing and touching for sexual desires. This is because of Allâh's statement, The Most High:

$$\{ وَلَا تُبَاشِرُوهُنَّ وَأَنتُمْ عَاكِفُونَ فِي ٱلْمَسَاجِدِ \}$$

"And do not have sexual relations with them (your wives) while you are in Al-I'tikâf (i.e. confining oneself in a mosque for prayers and invocations leaving the worldly activities) in the Masjids" [Al-Baqarah: 187]

But as for leaving the Masjid, if only part of the body is outside the Masjid (and not the entire body) then there is nothing wrong with that. This is based on 'Âi'shah's (رضي الله عنها) statement: "The Prophet (ﷺ) used to push out his head from the Masjid to my room while he was in his seclusion. And I would wash his head while I am on my menses" [Collected by Al-Bukhârî]

In another narration it says she used to comb his head while she was on her menses and while he was in seclusion (worshipping) his Lord in the Masjid.

Leaving the Masjid in totality (with one's entire body) is of three types:

The First: To leave the Masjid for an inescapable matter religiously or naturally. For example relieving oneself, performing an obligatory ablution, (performing the) mandatory washing due to major ritual impurity, eating, drinking, or other than what are mentioned. In this case it will be permissible for him to leave the Masjid as long as those needs cannot be fulfilled inside the Masjid. However if these needs can be fulfilled in the Masjid then there is no need for him to go out. For example if there are bathrooms in the Masjid where he can relieve himself, perform the ritual ablution, and even wash up, and if there is someone who provides him with food and drink (then he is not allowed to leave the Masjid).

The Second: To leave for the purpose of worship that is not obligatory on him. This (includes) visiting the sick, following the funeral procession, and (other deeds). It is permissible for him to leave the Masjid for these acts of worship as long as he put a condition from the beginning of his Al-I'tikâf that he wants to visit a sick person that he knows who is in a critical condition, otherwise it is not permissible.

The Third: Leaving the Masjid to do something which contradicts with Al-I'tikâf. An example of this is leaving the Masjid for the purpose of buying and selling, or to have relations with one's wife, or to (behave with her in a) flirtatious manner etc. In this case, he should not leave the Masjid whether with conditions or without, because these things contradict Al-I'tikâf and the intended objective behind it.

And from among the virtues of these Last Ten Days: The Night of Al-Qadar, which is better than a thousand months, is found in these days. Therefore know the virtue of these days, may Allâh have mercy on you, and do not waste them. For verily, its time is precious and its good is crystal clear.

O Allâh! Grant us success to whatever is beneficial for us in our religion, and beautify our end and magnify our reward. Forgive us, our parents, and all the Muslims with Your mercy. You are the Most Merciful. May the peace and blessings of Allâh be upon our Prophet Muhammad, his family members, and his companions.

المَجْلِسُ الثَّانِي وَالعِشْرُونَ
The Twenty Second Sitting
Striving Hard in the Last Ten Days & in The Night of Al-Qadar

All praise is due to Allâh, the Knower of the seen and the unseen, and Exterminator of the tyrants with might and power, He completely calculated (every) drop of water as it flows in the rivers, the One who sends forth the darkness of the night which is caused to disappear by the light of the dawn, the Giver of reward to the worshipers in full, the Knower of the cheating of the eye and what is hidden in the hearts. His provisions encompass all the creatures, He did not leave out the ants in the sand and neither the chickens in the nest. He sustains and withholds, and it is from His wisdom that poverty and wealth exist. He has given preference to some of the creatures over others, even certain parts of the year: the night of Al-Qadar is better than a thousand months. I praise Him with a praise without limitation, and I thank Him with a thanks that drives in ample blessings from Him, I testify that none has the right to be worshiped but Allâh alone without a partner, a testimony of one sincere in his creed. And I also testify that Muhammad is His slave and messenger, the one whom water gushed forth from his fingers. May Allâh shower His blessings on Him, on Abû Bakr, his companion at times of ease and hardship, on 'Umar bin Al-Khattâb the cave of Islâm and its supporter, on 'Uthmân the compiler of the Book of Allâh, on 'Alî who sufficed the Muslims in their wars with his courage by himself, and on (the Prophet's) family members, and his companions who were sincere in their deeds and objectives.

O My Brothers! In these ten blessed days, there is the Night of Decree which is given preference by Allâh over other days. Allâh has blessed this ummah with its ample virtues and bounties. Allâh (ﷺ) has recognized this night in His book with His saying:

Sittings During the Blessed Month of Ramaḍān رَمَضَان

$$\{ \text{إِنَّا أَنزَلْنَٰهُ فِى لَيْلَةٍ مُّبَٰرَكَةٍ إِنَّا كُنَّا مُنذِرِينَ ۝ فِيهَا يُفْرَقُ كُلُّ أَمْرٍ حَكِيمٍ ۝ أَمْرًا مِّنْ عِندِنَآ إِنَّا كُنَّا مُرْسِلِينَ ۝ رَحْمَةً مِّن رَّبِّكَ إِنَّهُۥ هُوَ السَّمِيعُ ٱلْعَلِيمُ ۝ رَبِّ ٱلسَّمَٰوَٰتِ وَٱلْأَرْضِ وَمَا بَيْنَهُمَآ إِن كُنتُم مُّوقِنِينَ ۝ لَآ إِلَٰهَ إِلَّا هُوَ يُحْىِۦ وَيُمِيتُ رَبُّكُمْ وَرَبُّ ءَابَآئِكُمُ ٱلْأَوَّلِينَ ۝ \}$$

"We sent it (this Qur'ân) down on a blessed night (i.e. night of Qadr in the month of Ramadân.) Verily, We are ever warning [mankind that Our Torment will reach those who disbelieve in Our Oneness of Lordship and in Our Oneness of worship]. Therein (that night) is decreed every matter of ordainments. (A Command) from Us. Verily, We are ever sending (the Messengers), (As) a Mercy from your Lord. Verily! He is the All-Hearer, the All-Knower. The Lord of the heavens and the earth and all that is between them, if you (but) have a faith with certainty. (None has the right to be worshipped but He). It is He Who gives life and causes death, your Lord and the Lord of your fore-fathers" [Ad-Dukhân: 3-8]

Allâh (ﷻ) has described it with being blessed due to its abundant good and virtues.

From among (the blessings of this night) is that the Qur'ân was revealed in it. Allâh described (this Night) saying that, in it, every matter of ordainment is predecreed. This means: (Allâh) exposed to the Angels) what is predestined in the [Preserved Tablet, Book of Divine Decrees] concerning what will happen from Allâh's command, in that year pertaining to provisions, life spans, good and evil, and more of every wise affair from the affairs of Allâh which are perfect, proficient, have no faults, nor deficiency, stupidity, or falsehood. That is the determination of the Almighty the All-Knowing. Allâh said:

$$\text{﴿ إِنَّا أَنزَلْنَٰهُ فِى لَيْلَةِ ٱلْقَدْرِ ۝ وَمَآ أَدْرَىٰكَ مَا لَيْلَةُ ٱلْقَدْرِ ۝ لَيْلَةُ ٱلْقَدْرِ خَيْرٌ مِّنْ أَلْفِ شَهْرٍ ۝ تَنَزَّلُ ٱلْمَلَٰٓئِكَةُ وَٱلرُّوحُ فِيهَا بِإِذْنِ رَبِّهِم مِّن كُلِّ أَمْرٍ ۝ سَلَٰمٌ هِىَ حَتَّىٰ مَطْلَعِ ٱلْفَجْرِ ۝ ﴾}$$

"Verily! We have sent it (this Qur'ân) down in the night of Al-Qadr (Decree) And what will make you know what the night of Al-Qadr (Decree) is? The night of Al-Qadr (Decree) is better than a thousand months. Therein descend the angels and the Rûh [Jibrâ'îl (Gabriel)] by Allâh's Permission with all Decrees, Peace! (All that night, there is Peace and Goodness from Allâh to His believing slaves) until the appearance of dawn" [Al-Qadr: 1-5]

The word "Qadr" means honor and respect. It also means determined and predestined. That is because this Night is honorable and great. Allâh determines in this night what will happen in that year and the things that He will allow to occur according to His wisdom. Allâh's statement in this verse: **"The Night of Honor is better than a thousand months,"** means: in virtue, honor, and the abundant reward that we get for our deeds. This is the reason why the one who stands in prayer in this night, seeking Allâh's pleasure and reward, will have his previous sins forgiven.

His statement, **"the angels descend,"** The Angels are slaves from the slaves of Allâh. They worship Him day and night,

$$\text{﴿ وَمَنْ عِندَهُۥ لَا يَسْتَكْبِرُونَ عَنْ عِبَادَتِهِۦ وَلَا يَسْتَحْسِرُونَ ۝ يُسَبِّحُونَ ٱلَّيْلَ وَٱلنَّهَارَ لَا يَفْتُرُونَ ۝ ﴾}$$

"And those who are near Him (i.e. the angels) are not too proud to worship Him, nor are they weary (of His worship). They glorify His Praises night and day, (and) they never slacken (to do so)" [Al-Anbiyâ: 19-20]

They descend to the earth with good, mercy, and blessings in the Night of Honor. "**The Rûh**" is Jibrîl (ﷺ) he is mentioned separately because of his rank and honor.

"**It is peaceful,**" referring to the night of power. It is peaceful for the believers from all fear because of the large number of people who will be freed from the hell fire in that night and be granted salvation from it.

"**Till the rising of the dawn,**" it means the night of power ends with the rising of the dawn, because the night worship ends with the rising of the dawn.

In this Noble Qur'ânic Chapter there are a number of Virtues for the Night of Honor

The First Virtue: In this Night, Allâh the Most High revealed the Qur'ân, which is a source of guidance for humanity and a means for them to obtain happiness in this world and the hereafter.

The Second Virtue: The question in His statement: "**What will make you know what the night of honor is,**" indicates the greatness of this night and its loftiness.

The Third Virtue: It is better than a thousand months.

The Fourth Virtue: the Angels descend in that night, only descending with good, blessings, and mercy.

The Fifth Virtue: It is peaceful because of the salvation many people will have from the punishment, due to their obedience to Allâh.

The Sixth Virtue: Allâh has sent down a chapter regarding its virtues which will be recited until the Day of Judgment.

From among the virtues of the night of honor is the hadîth which is narrated by Abû Hurayrah (ﷺ) who said that the Prophet (ﷺ) said:

من قَامَ ليلةَ القدرِ إيماناً واحتساباً غُفِرَ له ما تقدَّم من ذنبِهِ

"Whoever stands the night of honor in prayer, with faith and hope will have his previous sins forgiven" [Collected by Al-Bukhârî and Muslim]

The meaning of the Prophet's (ﷺ) statement, **"With faith and hope:"** is having faith in Allâh and the reward which He has prepared for the believers who stand during the night in prayer, seeking with it Allâh's reward. The reward is obtained by the one who knows that it is the Night of Honor and the one who does not know, because the Prophet (ﷺ) did not make that as a condition for obtaining the reward.

The night of honor is in the month of Ramadân because it is in (this month) that Allâh revealed the Qur'an, as He the Most High mentioned in the Qur'an:

﴿ إِنَّآ أَنزَلْنَٰهُ فِى لَيْلَةِ ٱلْقَدْرِ ﴾ ۝

"We have indeed revealed it in the Night of Al-Qadar" [Al-Qadar: 1]

And His statement:

$$\{ \text{شَهْرُ رَمَضَانَ ٱلَّذِىٓ أُنزِلَ فِيهِ ٱلْقُرْءَانُ} \}$$

"The Month of Ramadân in which the Qur'ân was revealed" [Al-Baqarah: 185]

With these proofs it is clearly determined that the night of honor is in the month of Ramadân. It existed in the previous nations just as it exists in ours, and it will continue to exist till the Day of Judgment. The proof for this is the narration of Abû Dharr (ﷺ) who said to the Prophet (ﷺ): "O messenger of Allâh! Tell me about the Night of Honor. Is it in the month of Ramadân or in other months?' So the Prophet responded saying: "Rather it is in the month of Ramadân." He said: "Does it remain with the Prophets till they pass away or it will remain with us till the day of Judgment?" The Prophet (ﷺ) said: "Rather it will remain till the Day of Judgment" [Narrated by Ahmad, An-Nasâ'î and Al-Hâkim. He said: the hadîth is sound]

However the virtues of this month are exclusive to this nation (i.e. the nation of Muhammad ﷺ) and Allâh knows best, just as this ummah is gifted the virtue of Friday and some other virtues. And all praise belongs to Allâh.

Also the night of honor is in the last ten days of Ramadân due to the Prophet's (ﷺ) statement,

$$\text{تَحَرَّوْا ليلةَ القدرِ في العشرِ الأواخرِ من رمضان}$$

"Search for the night of honor in the last ten days of Ramadân" [Collected by Al-Bukhârî and Muslim]

رَمَضَان Sittings During the Blessed Month of Ramaḍān

It is most likely to be in the odd nights rather than the even nights, because of his statement:

$$تحروا ليلة القدر في الْوِترِ من العشرِ الأواخر من رمضان$$

"Search the night of honor during the odd nights of the last ten days of Ramaḍân" [Collected by Al-Bukhârî]

It is most likely to be in the last seven days because of the narration of 'Abdullâh bin 'Umar (ﷺ):

$$أنَّ رجالاً من أصحاب النبيِّ صلَّى اللَّهُ عَلَيْهِ وَسَلَّمَ أُرُوا ليلةَ القدرِ في المنام في السبعِ الأواخر، فقال النبيُّ صلَّى اللَّهُ عَلَيْهِ وَسَلَّمَ: " أَرَى رُؤياكُمْ قد تواطأت (يعني اتفقت) في السبعِ الأواخر، فمن كانَ مُتَحَرِّيهَا فَلْيَتَحَرَّهَا في السبعِ الأواخر$$

"A group of men from the Companions of the Prophet (ﷺ) saw the Night of Honor in their dreams in the last seven nights. So the Prophet (ﷺ) said to them: 'I can see that your dreams confirm one another that it is in the last seven. Therefore whoever is searching for it should do so in the last seven nights.'" [Reported by Al-Bukhârî and Muslim]

It is also narrated that the Prophet (ﷺ) said: **"Seek the night of honor during the last ten days, and if one of you becomes weak or is unable, then he should not miss the last seven."** [Collected by Muslim]

From the odd nights (the Night of Honor) is most likely to be the twenty seventh night, which is supported by the narration of Ubayy bin Ka'b (ﷺ) who said: "By Allâh I know in which night is the night of Honor. It is the night in which the Prophet (ﷺ)

commanded us to stand in prayer. It is the twenty seventh night." [Collected by Muslim]

The Night of Honor is not exclusive to one specific night every year. Rather it moves from one day to another. For example if it is the twenty seventh night in this year, it may be in the twenty fifth night the following year based on Allâh's Will and His wisdom. This is supported by the Prophet's Statement (ﷺ):

اِلْتَمِسُوهَا فِي تَاسِعَةٍ تَبْقَى فِي سَابِعَةٍ تَبْقَى فِي خَامِسَةٍ تَبْقَى

"Seek the night of honor in the last ninth or the last seventh or the last fifth." [Narrated by Al-Bukhârî]

Ibn Hajar mentioned in Fath Al-Bârî: "The closest opinion to the truth is that it is in the odd nights of the last ten and that it moves from one odd to another."

Allâh has hidden the knowledge of this night from the slaves as a mercy for them, in order that they will increase in their deeds pursuing this night, striving with prayer, remembrance of Allâh, and supplication. This is a means of them gaining nearness to their Lord and an increased reward.

Likewise Allâh hid it as a trial and a test for slaves, in order to distinguish between the one who is serious in seeking it, eager to acquire it, and the one who is lazy and neglectful of it. This is because the one who is eager to obtain something will be serious in seeking it and he will overlook (the trials) and bear the hardships in the way.

Perhaps Allâh may expose the knowledge of the night of honor to some people by (allowing them to) see some of the signs which the Prophet (ﷺ) saw. He saw himself in a dream prostrating in water and mud. In that night it rained and he prostrated, while praying Fajr, in water and mud.

O My Brothers! In the night of honor, the doors are opened, the beloved ones are drawn near, their call is heard, (their supplications are accepted) and the laborers of this night receive great rewards. The night of honor is better than a thousand months! Therefore strive hard in seeking it. For verily this is the time to seek it and beware of negligence for verily negligence is perdition.

> The age has passed in negligence, pastime and a loss
> Alas! How much have I wasted of the days of my life
> I do not have any excuse for what I have wasted of my years
> How negligent are we of the duties of praise and thanks
> Indeed Allâh has favored us with a great month
> The month in which the Most Gracious revealed His Book
> How can there be a month comparable to it, while the Night of Honor is in it?
> How many authentic narrations are there about its virtues?
> We have narrated from trustworthy people that it is searched for during the odd nights
> Therefore blessed is the individual who searches for it in these ten nights
> It is in it that the Angels descend with light and much good
> Indeed (Allâh) said: 'Peace is that night until the rising of the dawn'
> Therefore save it for verily it is from the most precious treasures
> How many are freed from the hell fire in that night without even knowing [From Ibn Rajab's Latâif Al-Mâ'rif page 351,352]

O Allâh make us amongst those who fast the month and reach the Night of Honor. (O Allâh make us) successful with the great reward. O Allâh! Make us amongst those who compete with one another in good, who flee from evil deeds, who will be safe in the abode of paradise along with those whom You have bestowed Your favor unto, and those who You have granted them security from shortcomings. O Allāh! Grant us protection from the misguiding temptations and distance us from licentiousness, both the open and the hidden ones. O Allāh! Sustain us with gratefulness of Your bounties, perfection in our worship, and make us among those slaves who are obedient to You, and those who are Your friends. Give us the good of this world and the good of the Hereafter and grant us protection from the punishment of the Hell Fire. With Your mercy forgive us, our parents, and all the Muslims. For verily You are the Most Merciful.

May the peace and blessings of Allāh be upon our Prophet Muhammad (ﷺ), his family members, and all his Companions.

المَجْلِسُ الثَّالِثُ و العِشْرُونَ
The Twenty Third Sitting
The Description of the Paradise (May Allâh Make Us Amongst from its Dwellers)

All praise is due to Allâh, the One Who allows the hopeful person to reach beyond his goal, the One Who gives more than what He is asked; the One Who is Bounteous to the repentant by accepting his repentance. He created the human being and made the hereafter his abode, and made this world as a path towards His destination. However, those who do not know the value of the perpetual abode (which awaits them) have taken this world as their home due to their intellectual deficiency. They took from this world unlawfully before reaching their goal, but their wealth and children did not save them from being destroyed. Do you not see the crows mourning over its ruins? But as for the one who is granted success, he recognizes the deceitfulness (of this worldly life), therefore he is not deceived by its mirage. He competes towards seeking his Lord's forgiveness, and obtaining the Paradise which is more spacious than the heavens and the earth, (and it has been) prepared for those who believe in Allâh and His Messenger.

I further bear witness that none has the right to be worshiped but Allâh alone without a partner, a testimony of the one who knows the proof and its principles. And I also bear witness, as long as the gentle breeze continues to blow from all directions, that Muhammad is His slave and His Messenger. May Allâh shower His blessings on him, on Abû Bakr his companion in his journeys and residency, on 'Umar the one who defended Al-Islâm with a sword without the fear of failure, on 'Uthmân the one who was patient upon his test when it descended, on 'Alî the one who proceeded with his bravery before proceeding with his arrowhead, on his family members, his companions, and whoever follow their footsteps till the Day of Judgment.

Sittings During the Blessed Month of Ramaḍān رَمَضَان

O My Brothers! Hasten towards seeking your Lord's forgiveness and (hasten to) a Paradise which is more spacious than the heavens and the earth. In paradise there is that which the eye has never seen, the ear has never heard, and the heart has never even imagined. Allâh, the Most High, said:

﴿ ۞ مَّثَلُ ٱلۡجَنَّةِ ٱلَّتِي وُعِدَ ٱلۡمُتَّقُونَۖ تَجۡرِي مِن تَحۡتِهَا ٱلۡأَنۡهَٰرُۖ أُكُلُهَا دَآئِمٞ وَظِلُّهَاۚ تِلۡكَ عُقۡبَى ٱلَّذِينَ ٱتَّقَواْۚ وَّعُقۡبَى ٱلۡكَٰفِرِينَ ٱلنَّارُ ﴿٣٥﴾ ﴾

"The example of Paradise, which the righteous have been promised, is [that] beneath it rivers flow. Its fruit is lasting, and its shade. That is the consequence for the righteous." [Ar-Ra'd: 35]

And Allâh's statement:

﴿ مَّثَلُ ٱلۡجَنَّةِ ٱلَّتِي وُعِدَ ٱلۡمُتَّقُونَۖ فِيهَآ أَنۡهَٰرٞ مِّن مَّآءٍ غَيۡرِ ءَاسِنٖ وَأَنۡهَٰرٞ مِّن لَّبَنٖ لَّمۡ يَتَغَيَّرۡ طَعۡمُهُۥ وَأَنۡهَٰرٞ مِّنۡ خَمۡرٖ لَّذَّةٖ لِّلشَّٰرِبِينَ وَأَنۡهَٰرٞ مِّنۡ عَسَلٖ مُّصَفّٗىۖ وَلَهُمۡ فِيهَا مِن كُلِّ ٱلثَّمَرَٰتِ وَمَغۡفِرَةٞ مِّن رَّبِّهِمۡ ﴾

"The description of Paradise, which the righteous are promised, is that wherein are rivers of water unaltered, rivers of milk the taste of which never changes, rivers of wine delicious to those who drink, and rivers of purified honey, in which they will have from all [kinds of] fruits and forgiveness from their Lord." [Muhammad: 15]

And Allâh's statement:

رَمَضَان Sittings During the Blessed Month of Ramaḍān

﴿ وَبَشِّرِ ٱلَّذِينَ ءَامَنُوا۟ وَعَمِلُوا۟ ٱلصَّٰلِحَٰتِ أَنَّ لَهُمْ جَنَّٰتٍ تَجْرِى مِن تَحْتِهَا ٱلْأَنْهَٰرُ كُلَّمَا رُزِقُوا۟ مِنْهَا مِن ثَمَرَةٍ رِّزْقًا قَالُوا۟ هَٰذَا ٱلَّذِى رُزِقْنَا مِن قَبْلُ وَأُتُوا۟ بِهِۦ مُتَشَٰبِهًا وَلَهُمْ فِيهَآ أَزْوَٰجٌ مُّطَهَّرَةٌ وَهُمْ فِيهَا خَٰلِدُونَ ۞ ﴾

"And give good tidings to those who believe and do righteous deeds that they will have gardens [in Paradise] beneath which rivers flow. Whenever they are provided with a provision of fruit therefrom, they will say, 'This is what we were provided with before.' And it is given to them in likeness. And they will have therein purified spouses, and they will abide therein eternally."
[Al-Baqarah: 25]

And Allâh's statement:

﴿ وَدَانِيَةً عَلَيْهِمْ ظِلَٰلُهَا وَذُلِّلَتْ قُطُوفُهَا تَذْلِيلًا ۞ وَيُطَافُ عَلَيْهِم بِـَٔانِيَةٍ مِّن فِضَّةٍ وَأَكْوَابٍ كَانَتْ قَوَارِيرَا۠ ۞ قَوَارِيرَا۟ مِن فِضَّةٍ قَدَّرُوهَا تَقْدِيرًا ۞ وَيُسْقَوْنَ فِيهَا كَأْسًا كَانَ مِزَاجُهَا زَنجَبِيلًا ۞ عَيْنًا فِيهَا تُسَمَّىٰ سَلْسَبِيلًا ۞ وَيَطُوفُ عَلَيْهِمْ وِلْدَٰنٌ مُّخَلَّدُونَ إِذَا رَأَيْتَهُمْ حَسِبْتَهُمْ لُؤْلُؤًا مَّنثُورًا ۞ وَإِذَا رَأَيْتَ ثَمَّ رَأَيْتَ نَعِيمًا وَمُلْكًا كَبِيرًا ۞ ﴾

"And near above them are its shades, and its [fruit] to be picked will be lowered in compliance. And there will be circulated among them vessels of silver and cups having been [created] clear [as glass], clear glasses [made] from silver of which they have determined the measure. And they will be given to drink a cup [of wine] whose mixture is of ginger [From] a fountain within Paradise named Salsabîl. And round about them will (serve) boys of everlasting youth. If you see them, you would think them [as beautiful as] scattered pearls. And when you look there [in

Paradise], you will see pleasure and great dominion." [Al-Insân: 14-20]

And Allâh's statement:

﴿ فِى جَنَّةٍ عَالِيَةٍ ۝ لَّا تَسْمَعُ فِيهَا لَٰغِيَةً ۝ فِيهَا عَيْنٌ جَارِيَةٌ ۝ فِيهَا سُرُرٌ مَّرْفُوعَةٌ ۝ وَأَكْوَابٌ مَّوْضُوعَةٌ ۝ وَنَمَارِقُ مَصْفُوفَةٌ ۝ وَزَرَابِيُّ مَبْثُوثَةٌ ۝ ﴾

"In an elevated garden wherein they will hear no unsuitable speech. Within it is a flowing spring; within it are couches raised high and cups put in place, and cushions lined up, and carpets spread around." [Al-Ghâshiyah: 10-16]

And Allâh's statement:

﴿ إِنَّ ٱللَّهَ يُدْخِلُ ٱلَّذِينَ ءَامَنُوا۟ وَعَمِلُوا۟ ٱلصَّٰلِحَٰتِ جَنَّٰتٍ تَجْرِى مِن تَحْتِهَا ٱلْأَنْهَٰرُ يُحَلَّوْنَ فِيهَا مِنْ أَسَاوِرَ مِن ذَهَبٍ وَلُؤْلُؤًا وَلِبَاسُهُمْ فِيهَا حَرِيرٌ ۝ ﴾

"Indeed, Allâh will admit those who believe and do righteous deeds to gardens beneath which rivers flow. They will be adorned therein with bracelets of gold and pearl, and their garments therein will be silk." [Al-Hajj: 23]

And Allâh's statement:

﴿ مُّتَّكِئِينَ فِيهَا عَلَى ٱلْأَرَآئِكِ لَا يَرَوْنَ فِيهَا شَمْسًا وَلَا زَمْهَرِيرًا ۝ ﴾

"[They will be] reclining therein on adorned couches. They will not see therein any [burning] sun or [freezing] cold." [Al-Insân: 13]

And Allâh's statement:

$$﴿ عَلِيَهُمْ ثِيَابُ سُندُسٍ خُضْرٌ وَإِسْتَبْرَقٌ وَحُلُّوٓا۟ أَسَاوِرَ مِن فِضَّةٍ وَسَقَىٰهُمْ رَبُّهُمْ شَرَابًا طَهُورًا ﴾$$

"Upon the inhabitants will be green garments of fine silk and brocade. And they will be adorned with bracelets of silver, and their Lord will give them a purifying drink." [Al-Insân: 21]

And Allâh's statement:

$$﴿ مُتَّكِـِٔينَ عَلَىٰ رَفْرَفٍ خُضْرٍ وَعَبْقَرِيٍّ حِسَانٍ ﴾$$

"Reclining on green cushions and beautiful fine carpets." [Ar-Rahmân: 76]

And Allâh's statement:

$$﴿ إِنَّ ٱلْمُتَّقِينَ فِى مَقَامٍ أَمِينٍ ۝ فِى جَنَّـٰتٍ وَعُيُونٍ ۝ يَلْبَسُونَ مِن سُندُسٍ وَإِسْتَبْرَقٍ مُّتَقَـٰبِلِينَ ۝ كَذَٰلِكَ وَزَوَّجْنَـٰهُم بِحُورٍ عِينٍ ۝ يَدْعُونَ فِيهَا بِكُلِّ فَـٰكِهَةٍ ءَامِنِينَ ۝ ﴾$$

"Indeed, the righteous will be in a secure place; Within gardens and springs, Wearing [garments of] fine silk and brocade, facing each other. Thus, and We will marry them to fair women with large, [beautiful] eyes. They will call therein for every [kind of] fruit, safe and secure." [Ad-Dukhân: 51-55]

And Allâh's statement:

$$\{ ادْخُلُوا الْجَنَّةَ أَنتُمْ وَأَزْوَاجُكُمْ تُحْبَرُونَ ۝ \}$$

"Enter Paradise, you and your kinds, delighted." [Az-Zukhruf: 70]

And Allâh's statement:

$$\{ فِيهِنَّ قَاصِرَاتُ الطَّرْفِ لَمْ يَطْمِثْهُنَّ إِنسٌ قَبْلَهُمْ وَلَا جَانٌّ ۝ فَبِأَيِّ آلَاءِ رَبِّكُمَا تُكَذِّبَانِ ۝ كَأَنَّهُنَّ الْيَاقُوتُ وَالْمَرْجَانُ ۝ \}$$

"In them are women limiting [their] glances, untouched before them by man or jinni. So which of the favors of your Lord would you deny? As if they were rubies and coral" [Ar-Rahmân: 56-58]

And Allâh's statement:

$$\{ فِيهِنَّ خَيْرَاتٌ حِسَانٌ ۝ فَبِأَيِّ آلَاءِ رَبِّكُمَا تُكَذِّبَانِ ۝ حُورٌ مَّقْصُورَاتٌ فِي الْخِيَامِ ۝ \}$$

"In them are good and beautiful women. So which of the favors of your Lord would you deny? Fair ones reserved in pavilions." [Ar-Rahmân: 70-72]

And Allâh's statement:

﴿ فَلَا تَعْلَمُ نَفْسٌ مَّآ أُخْفِيَ لَهُم مِّن قُرَّةِ أَعْيُنٍ جَزَآءً بِمَا كَانُوا۟ يَعْمَلُونَ ۝ ﴾

"And no soul knows what has been hidden for them, of comfort for eyes, as reward for what they used to do." [As-Sajdah: 17]

And Allâh's statement:

﴿ ۞ لِّلَّذِينَ أَحْسَنُوا۟ الْحُسْنَىٰ وَزِيَادَةٌ ۖ وَلَا يَرْهَقُ وُجُوهَهُمْ قَتَرٌ وَلَا ذِلَّةٌ ۚ أُو۟لَـٰٓئِكَ أَصْحَـٰبُ الْجَنَّةِ ۖ هُمْ فِيهَا خَـٰلِدُونَ ۝ ﴾

"For them who have done good is Al-Husnâ and Ziyâdah. No darkness will cover their faces, nor humiliation. Those are companions of Paradise; they will abide therein eternally." [Yûnus: 26]

The word Al-Husnâ (i.e. the best) means paradise because there is no home better than it. As for the word ziyâdah (i.e. more) it means: looking at the Honorable Face of Allâh, the Most High. May Allâh provide us, out of His Bounty and Kindness, with the honor of looking at His Face. The Qur'ânic verses about Paradise's description, its favors, its joyfulness, and pleasures are many.

As for the prophetic narrations which mention the description of Paradise:

It is narrated by Abû Hurayrah (ﷺ), he said, we said, "O Messenger of Allâh! Inform us about the Paradise. What is it built of? He replied: 'Brick of gold, brick of silver, its mortar is musk, its pebbles are pearls and rubies, its sand is saffron. Whoever enters it will be blessed and will not be wretched, and will remain forever and will never perish. His garment will never get faded and his youthfulness will remain forever.'" [Collected by At-Tirmidhî. This narration is Hasan. See Sahîh Al-Jâmi' No. 2111]

It is also narrated by 'Utbah bin Ghazwân (ﷺ) who said that the Prophet (ﷺ) gave a speech. He (ﷺ) thanked and praised Allâh and then said:

أمَّا بعدُ فإن الدنيا قد آذَنَتْ بِصُرْمٍ ووَلَّتْ حَذَّاءَ ولم يَبْقَ منها إلا صُبابةٌ كصُبابةِ الإناءِ يصطبُّها صاحبُها، وإنَّكُمْ منتقِلونَ منها إلى دارٍ لا زوالَ لها فانتقلوا بخيرٍ ما يَحْضُرُنكُمْ، ولَقَدْ ذُكِرَ لنا أنَّ مِصراعينِ منْ مصاريعِ الجنةِ بيْنَهما مسيرةُ أربعينَ سَنَةً، وليأتينَّ عليه يومٌ وهو كَظيظٌ مِنَ الزحام

"And to proceed: Indeed the world has announced its departure and it is departing quickly. What is left from this world is like the little amount of water that is left in the bottom of a cup which is quickly drank by its owner. And you will soon depart from it to a home that remains forever, therefore proceed with the good that comes to you, for indeed we were informed that the distance between its two doors is a journey of forty years, and a day will come to it when it will be filled from crowding." [Collected by Muslim]

It is narrated by Sahl bin Sa'd (ﷺ) who said that the Prophet (ﷺ) said:

في الجنةِ ثمانيةُ أبوابٍ فيها بابٌ يسمَّى الريان لا يدخله إلا الصائمون

"In Paradise there are eight doors, one of these doors is named Rayyân, only the fasting people will enter it." [Collected by Al-Bukhârî and Muslim]

رَمَضَان Sittings During the Blessed Month of Ramaḍān

On the authority of Usâmah bin Zayd (ﷺ) who said that the Messenger (ﷺ) said: "Is there anyone who desires Paradise? For verily, there is nothing like Paradise? By the Lord of the Ka'bah it is an illuminating light, in it is swinging basil, fortress castles, running rivers, ripened fruits, beautiful wives, many ornaments, eternal abode, there are fruits and vegetables. It is a place of jubilation full of bounty with overwhelming glory. They said: 'O Messenger of Allâh we long for that Paradise.' He said to them 'Say: Inshâ Allâh' and they said: 'Inshâ Allâh.'" [Graded weak by Al-Albânî in Daî'f At-Targhîb]

It is narrated by Abû Hurayrah (ﷺ) who said that the Prophet (ﷺ) said:

إن في الجنة مائة درجةٍ أعَدَّها الله للمجاهدين في سبيله، بينَ كلِّ درجتين كما بينَ السماءِ والأرض، فإذا سألتُمُ الله فأسألُوه الفِرْدوسَ فإنَّه وسطُ الجنة وأعلى الجنة، ومنه تفجَّرُ أنهار الجنة وفوقه عرش الرحمن

"There are indeed hundred ranks in paradise that are prepared by Allâh for those who fight for His sake. Between every rank is like the distance between the heaven and the earth. And if you ask Allâh, then ask Him for Al-Firdaws, for verily it is the middle of paradise and the highest level of paradise. And the spring of Paradise gushes forth from it. And above it is the Throne of the Most Beneficent." [Collected by Al-Bukhârî]

It is also narrated by Abû Sa'îd Al-Khudrî (ﷺ) that the Messenger of Allâh (ﷺ) said:

إن أهل الجنةِ يتراءَوْن أهل الغُرَف فوقَهم كما تتراءوْن الكوكبَ الدُّرِّيَّ الغابرَ في الأفُقِ من المشرق أو المغرب لتفاضلِ ما بيْنَهم ". قالوا: يا رسولَ الله تلك مَنازلُ الأنبياء لا يبلغُها غيرُهم. قال: " بَلى والَّذي نَفْسي بِيَدهِ رجالٌ آمنوا بالله وصدَّقوا المرسلينَ

"The People of Paradise will see the preferences in their castles from above them based on the virtuous of their deeds, just as you can see the glittering of the elapsing star in the horizons of the east or west. They said: 'O messenger of Allâh! Are those castles the abodes of the Prophets which none can reach but they alone?' He said: 'Nay! I swear by Him in Whose Hand is my soul! They are for men who believe in Allâh and believe in the Messengers.'" [Collected by Al-Bukhârî]

It is narrated by Abû Mâlik Al-Ash'arî (﷜) that the Prophet (ﷺ) said:

إن في الجنة غُرَفاً يُرَى ظاهرُها من باطِنها وباطنُها مِن ظاهرها، أعَدَّها الله لَمَنْ أطْعَمَ الطعامَ وأدامَ الصيامَ وصلى بالليل والناس نيام

"Surely in Paradise there are houses which the inside could be seen from the outside, and the outside could be seen from the inside. Allâh prepared them for the one who fed the (poor), fasted constantly, and prayed in the night while the people were asleep." [Collected by At-Tabarânî. Al-Albânî graded it to be authentic due to other corroborating narrations, as is found in his checking of Mishkât Al-Masâbîh]

It is also narrated by Abû Mûsâ Al-Ash'arî (﷜) that the Prophet (ﷺ) said:

﷽ Sittings During the Blessed Month of Ramaḍān

إِنَّ لِلْمُؤْمِنِ فِي الجنةِ لَخَيْمَةً مِنْ لُؤْلُؤَةٍ وَاحِدَةٍ مُجَوَّفَةٍ، طُولُهَا فِي السَّمَاءِ سِتُّونَ مِيلاً، لِلْمُؤْمِنِ فِيهَا أَهْلُونَ يَطُوفُ عَلَيْهِمْ فَلَا يَرَى بَعْضُهُمْ بَعْضًا

"The believer has a boat-shaped tent in Paradise which is made of pearls. Its height is sixty miles. The believer has wives in it, and he will be with them one after the other without them seeing one-another." [Collected by Al-Bukhârî and Muslim]

It is narrated by Abû Hurayrah (ﷺ) that the Prophet (ﷺ) said: "The first badges of believers who will enter paradise resemble the full moon (in their beauty), and then the ones that follow them will resemble the brightest star in the sky (in beauty). Then they will end up in houses where they will not defecate, urinate, blow their nose, or spit. Their combs are made of gold, their grills are aloes, their sweat smells like musk, all of them have the same built, like the built of their father Ādam, he was sixty cubits tall." [Collected by Muslim]

In other narrations it says: "There is no disagreement amongst them or hatred. Their hearts are united, they glorify Allâh every morning and evening" [Collected by Muslim]

In other narration it says: "their wives are the women with lovely eyes." [Collected by Al-Bukhârî]

It is also narrated by Jâbir (ﷺ) that the Messenger of Allâh (ﷺ) said:

إِنَّ أَهْلَ الجَنَّةِ يَأْكُلُونَ فِيهَا وَيَشْرَبُونَ وَلَا يَتْفُلُونَ وَلَا يَبُولُونَ وَلَا يَتَغَوَّطُونَ وَلَا يَمْتَخِطُونَ " قَالُوا: فَمَا بَالُ الطَّعَامِ؟ قَالَ: " جُشَاءٌ وَرَشْحٌ كَرَشْحِ المِسْكِ، يُلْهَمُونَ التَّسْبِيحَ وَالتَّحْمِيدَ كَمَا يُلْهَمُونَ النَّفَسَ

"The people of paradise will eat and drink in it. However they will not spit, urinate, defecate, or blow their nose. They said: 'O Messenger of Allâh how do we excrete the food?' He said: 'It will ooze out of our body like the spray of musk. And they will be inspired with glorification and the praise of their Lord just as they breathe." [Collected by Muslim]

It is narrated by Zayd bin Arqam (ﷺ) that the Prophet (ﷺ) said:

والذي نفسُ محمدٍ بيدِه إن أحدَهُمْ (يعني أهل الجنةِ) لَيُعْطَى قوة مائة رجلٍ في الأكلِ والشربِ والجماعِ والشهوةِ، تكون حاجةُ أحدِهم رَشْحاً يفيض مِنْ جلودهم كرشْحِ المسكِ فَيَضْمُرُ بطنه

"I swear by Him in Whose Hand is the soul of Muhammad, a man will be given the strength of a hundred men in eating, drinking, having sex, and desires. The excretion of one of them will be sweat of musk which will ooze out of their skin and cause his belly to atrophy" [Narrated by Ahmad and An-Nasâî' with an authentic chain. Muqbil declared it to be authentic in As-Sahîh Al-Musnad as well as Al-Albânî in Sahîh At-Targhîb]

It is narrated by Anas (ﷺ) that the Prophet (ﷺ) said:

لَقَابُ قوسٍ أحدِكم أو موضعِ قدمٍ في الجنة خيرٌ من الدنيا وما فيهَا، ولَوْ أنَّ امرأةً من نساءِ أهلِ الجنةِ اطلعتْ إلى الأرضِ لأضاءتْ ما بَيْنَهُمَا ولملأتْ ما بينهما ريحاً وَلَنَصِيفُهَا (يعني الخمارَ) خيرٌ من الدنيا وما فيها

"The space of a bow of one of you or a space of his footstep in paradise is better than the world and what so ever is in it. And if a woman from the women of the people of paradise appear on this earth she will illuminate whatsoever is between the heaven and earth and fill them up with a good smell. Her veil is better than the world and whatsoever is in them." [Collected by Al-Bukhârî].

It is narrated by Anas (؈) that the Prophet (ﷺ) said:

إنَّ في الجنة لسُوقا يأتونَها كُلَّ جمعةٍ فتهب رياح الشمال فتحثوا في وجوهِهِم وثيابهم، فيزدادُونَ حُسناً وجَمَالاً فيرجعونَ إلى أهلِيْهِمْ فيقولُونَ لهم: والله لقد ازددتم بعدنا حسناً وجمالاً، فيقولون: وأنتم والله لقد ازددتم بعدنا حسنا وجمالا

"In Paradise there is a market where the people of Paradise gather every Friday. Then the north breeze of Paradise will blow on their faces and garments causing them to increase in beauty. They will then return back to their wives, and their wives will say to them: 'By Allâh you have increased in beauty after you have left us and came back,' and they will also say to their families, 'By Allâh you have also increased in beauty.'" [Collected by Muslim]

It is narrated by Abû Sa'îd (؈) who said that the Prophet (ﷺ) said:

إذا دخل أهلُ الجنةِ الجنةَ ينادِي منادٍ: إن لكمْ أنْ تَصِحُّوا فلا تَسْقموا أبداً، وإن لكم أن تَحْيَوْا فلا تموتوا أبداً، وإنَّ لكم أن تَشِبُّوا فلا تَهرموا أبداً، وإن لكم أن تنعموا فلا تيأسوا أبداً، وذلك قولُ الله عز وجل:

﴿ وَنُودُوٓاْ أَن تِلْكُمُ ٱلْجَنَّةُ أُورِثْتُمُوهَا بِمَا كُنتُمْ تَعْمَلُونَ ﴾ ﴿٤٣﴾

"When the people of paradise enter paradise, a caller will proclaim saying: 'Indeed yours is to live healthy and never fall sick, and to live forever without dying, and to remain young without growing old, and to enjoy ceaselessly without wretchedness.' And this is the interpretation of Allâh's statement:

$$\left\{ وَنُودُوٓاْ أَن تِلْكُمُ ٱلْجَنَّةُ أُورِثْتُمُوهَا بِمَا كُنتُمْ تَعْمَلُونَ ۝ \right\}$$

"And they will be called, 'This is Paradise, which you have been made to inherit for what you used to do.'" [Al-A'râf:43]

It is narrated by Abû Hurayrah (ﷺ) who said that the Prophet (ﷺ) said:

$$قال الله عزَّ وجلَّ: أَعْدَدْتُ لعبادي الصالحينَ مَا لا عينَ رأتْ ولا أذنَ سمعت ولا خطرَ على قلبِ بشر، واقرؤوا إن شئتُم:$$

$$\left\{ فَلَا تَعْلَمُ نَفْسٌ مَّآ أُخْفِىَ لَهُم مِّن قُرَّةِ أَعْيُنٍ جَزَآءًۢ بِمَا كَانُوا۟ يَعْمَلُونَ ۝ \right\}$$

"Allâh (ﷻ) said: I have prepared for my pious slaves in paradise that which the eye has never seen, the ear has never heard, and has never come across the heart of any mortal.' Then he said, 'recite if you will:

$$\left\{ فَلَا تَعْلَمُ نَفْسٌ مَّآ أُخْفِىَ لَهُم مِّن قُرَّةِ أَعْيُنٍ جَزَآءًۢ بِمَا كَانُوا۟ يَعْمَلُونَ ۝ \right\}$$

"And no soul knows what has been hidden for them of comfort for eyes as a reward for what they used to do." (As-Sajdah: 17) [Collected by Al-Bukhârî and Muslim]

It is narrated by Suhayb (ﷺ) that the Messenger of Allâh (ﷺ) said:

إذا دخلَ أهلُ الجنةِ الجنةَ نادىَ منادٍ: يا أهلَ الجنةِ إن لكم عندَ الله مَوْعِداً يريدُ أن يُنْجِزَكُموهُ، فيقولونَ: ما هُوَ؟ أَلَمْ يُثَقِّلْ موازينَنا ويبيِّضْ وجوهَنا ويدخلْنا الجنةَ ويزحْزحْنا عن النار؟ فيكشفُ لهم الحجَابَ فينظرون إليه، فواللهِ ما أعطاهم الله شيئاً أحبَّ إليهمْ من النظرِ إليه، ولا أقرّ لأعينهم منه

"When the people of Paradise enter paradise, a caller will proclaim saying: 'O people of paradise you have with your Lord a promise which He wants to fulfill for you.' So they will say: 'What is the promise? Has he not made our scales heavy? Has he not made our faces delighted? Has he not placed us in Paradise and distanced us from the Hell-Fire?' Then Allâh will remove the veil and they will look at Him. By Allâh! Allâh has not given them anything that is more beloved to them and more pleasant for their eyes than them looking at Him" [Collected by Muslim]

It is narrated by Abû Sa'îd Al-Khudrî (ﷺ) who said:

أنَّ اللهَ يقولُ لأهلِ الجنةِ: " أحِلُّ عليكم رضواني فلا أسخطُ عليكم بعدَه أبداً

"Allâh will say to the people of Paradise: 'I will send down my pleasure upon you and never will I be angry at you afterwards.'" [Collected by Muslim]

O Allâh grant us eternity in Your Paradise, send down on us Your pleasure, and sustain us with the sweetness of looking at Your face and the aspiration of meeting with You, without any harm or misleading temptation. O Allâh! Send peace and salutation to Your slave and Prophet Muhammad, his family members, and all his companions.

Sittings During the Blessed Month of Ramaḍān رَمَضَان

المجلس الرابع و العشرون
The Twenty Fourth Sitting

The Description of the People of Paradise (May Allâh make us among them, with His Bounty and Kindness)

All praise is due to Allâh, the One who made everything with perfection. He divided the Heavens and the earth, although they were once a united piece. With His Wisdom, He separated the slaves, some of them He made successful and others wretched. He placed the means for success, so the pious ones have taken the means and looked at the consequences with insight. As a result (they) chose that which is more lasting (over that which perishes). I praise Him even though I do not give Him His right due of praise. And I thank Him (although) His worthiness of being thanked is ageless. I bear witness that none has the right to be worshipped but Him alone, without a partner. (He is) the Owner of all that exist. I also bear witness that Muhammad is His slave and Messenger, the most complete of mankind in his nature and manners. May Allâh's blessings be upon him, his companion Abû Bakr As-Siddîq, the one who grasped the virtue of precedence in fellowship, upon 'Umar, the just, who has never taken sides with any creature, upon 'Uthmân the one who submitted to martyrdom and did not try to avoid it, upon 'Ali, the one who sold what perishes (i.e. the worldly life) and purchased what remains forever (i.e. the paradise and that which is with Allâh), and upon (the Prophet's) family, and the Companions, the true helpers of the religion.

O My Brothers! You have heard the description of Paradise, its bounties, and what is in it of happiness, jubilation, and fun. By Allâh, this Paradise is worthy of being labored after and competed for. It is (precious) enough for a man to spend all his life seeking it while renouncing the inferior world.

If you asked about the deeds (one must do in order to obtain it), or the path to take (in order to reach it), then Allâh (ﷻ) has indeed clarified it in what He has revealed to His most honorable creature. Allâh (ﷻ) said:

$$\text{﴿ ۞ وَسَارِعُوٓا۟ إِلَىٰ مَغْفِرَةٍ مِّن رَّبِّكُمْ وَجَنَّةٍ عَرْضُهَا ٱلسَّمَٰوَٰتُ وَٱلْأَرْضُ أُعِدَّتْ لِلْمُتَّقِينَ ۝ ٱلَّذِينَ يُنفِقُونَ فِى ٱلسَّرَّآءِ وَٱلضَّرَّآءِ وَٱلْكَٰظِمِينَ ٱلْغَيْظَ وَٱلْعَافِينَ عَنِ ٱلنَّاسِ ۗ وَٱللَّهُ يُحِبُّ ٱلْمُحْسِنِينَ ۝ وَٱلَّذِينَ إِذَا فَعَلُوا۟ فَٰحِشَةً أَوْ ظَلَمُوٓا۟ أَنفُسَهُمْ ذَكَرُوا۟ ٱللَّهَ فَٱسْتَغْفَرُوا۟ لِذُنُوبِهِمْ وَمَن يَغْفِرُ ٱلذُّنُوبَ إِلَّا ٱللَّهُ وَلَمْ يُصِرُّوا۟ عَلَىٰ مَا فَعَلُوا۟ وَهُمْ يَعْلَمُونَ ۝ ﴾}$$

"And hasten to forgiveness from your Lord and a garden as wide as the heavens and earth, prepared for the pious. Who spend [in the cause of Allâh] during ease and hardship and who restrain anger and who pardon the people, and Allâh loves the doers of good; And those who, when they commit an immorality or wrong themselves [by transgression], remember Allâh and seek forgiveness for their sins , and who can forgive sins except Allâh? and [who] do not persist in what they have done while they know" [Āli Imrân: 133-135]

This is the Description of the People of Paradise:

The First Description: "The Pious." They are those who feared their Lord by placing a barrier between them and His punishment, by adhering to His Commandments while hoping for His reward and abstaining from His prohibitions out of obedience to Him and out of fear of His punishment.

The Second Description: "Those who spend at times of ease and at times of hardship." They spend whatever they are commanded to spend as it is required from them, including the obligatory alms giving, charities, and spending on whomever they are financially responsible for. Likewise (they) spend in the path of Allâh and in all paths of good. They (spend) at times of ease and hardship. (Times of) comfort and happiness does not lead them to greed and selfishness. Likewise difficulty and hardship does not cause them to become stingy due to fear of poverty.

The Third Description: "Those who suppress their anger." These are those who control their anger when they are enraged. As a result they do not envy or hate others due to this anger of theirs.

The Fourth Description: "Those who forgive the people." They forgive those who wrong them and transgress upon their rights. They do not seek revenge for themselves even though they have the ability to do so. And in His statement, the Most High:

$$وَٱللَّهُ يُحِبُّ ٱلْمُحْسِنِينَ$$

"**Allâh loves those who are kind,**" this is an indication that "forgiveness" will be considered praiseworthy if it results in 'Al-Ihsân' [i.e. a positive outcome and reformation]. The forgiveness that increases the transgressor in his transgression, will not be considered praiseworthy and the individual will not be rewarded for it. For indeed Allâh (ﷺ) said:

$$﴿ فَمَنْ عَفَا وَأَصْلَحَ فَأَجْرُهُ عَلَى ٱللَّهِ ﴾$$

"**Whoever forgave and reformed then his reward is with Allâh.**" [Ash-Shûrâ: 40]

The Fifth Description: "**And those who, when they commit a Fâhishah (i.e. immorality) or wrong themselves [by transgression], they remember Allâh and seek forgiveness for their sins.**" The word "Al-Fâhishah" refers to sins that are considered to be atrocities and immorality. These are major sins. (Examples of these sins include): committing murder, being undutiful to your parents, consuming interest, consuming the wealth of the orphan, running away from the battle field, fornication, robbery, and their likes from among the major sins. Wronging oneself is more general, it includes both the major and the minor sins. Whenever the believers commit any of the abovementioned sins they remember the greatness of the One they disobeyed. As a result they will be afraid of Him, leading them to remember His forgiveness and mercy. Thus they will hasten to it. They ask forgiveness of their sins by asking Allâh to cover their sins and to overlook them and not punishment them for it.

In His statement: "**None forgives sins but Allâh**" is an indication that (the believers) do not seek forgiveness from anyone but Allâh, because none forgives sins except Him.

The Sixth Description: "**They do not persist on their sins and they acknowledge that it is a sin**" meaning they do not continue to commit the sin while acknowledging that it is a sin, while knowing the Greatness of the One they disobeyed, and while knowing the closeness of His Forgiveness. Rather they hasten to free themselves from sins, repenting from them. This is because persisting upon committing sins, with this awareness, turns the minor sins into major sins. And it leads the (sinner) to difficult and dangerous situations.

Also Allâh (ﷻ) said:

﴿ قَدْ أَفْلَحَ ٱلْمُؤْمِنُونَ ۝ ٱلَّذِينَ هُمْ فِى صَلَاتِهِمْ خَٰشِعُونَ ۝ وَٱلَّذِينَ هُمْ عَنِ ٱللَّغْوِ مُعْرِضُونَ ۝ وَٱلَّذِينَ هُمْ لِلزَّكَوٰةِ فَٰعِلُونَ ۝ وَٱلَّذِينَ هُمْ لِفُرُوجِهِمْ حَٰفِظُونَ ۝ إِلَّا عَلَىٰٓ أَزْوَٰجِهِمْ أَوْ مَا مَلَكَتْ أَيْمَٰنُهُمْ فَإِنَّهُمْ غَيْرُ مَلُومِينَ ۝ فَمَنِ ٱبْتَغَىٰ وَرَآءَ ذَٰلِكَ فَأُو۟لَٰٓئِكَ هُمُ ٱلْعَادُونَ ۝ وَٱلَّذِينَ هُمْ لِأَمَٰنَٰتِهِمْ وَعَهْدِهِمْ رَٰعُونَ ۝ وَٱلَّذِينَ هُمْ عَلَىٰ صَلَوَٰتِهِمْ يُحَافِظُونَ ۝ أُو۟لَٰٓئِكَ هُمُ ٱلْوَٰرِثُونَ ۝ ٱلَّذِينَ يَرِثُونَ ٱلْفِرْدَوْسَ هُمْ فِيهَا خَٰلِدُونَ ۝ ﴾

"Successful indeed are the believers, who are humble in their prayers, and who shun all that which is vain, and who are prompt and regular in paying the Zakât, and who guard their chastity except from their wives or what their right hands possess, for then they are not to be blamed. But those, who seek anything beyond that are the transgressors. (Successful are the believers who) are watchful of their trusts and their covenants, and who are strict in the observance of their Prayers. These are the heirs, who will inherit Paradise. They will abide therein forever". [Al-Mu'minûn:1-11]

These Noble Verses Gathered Many Qualities of the People of Paradise:

The First Quality: "The Believers." They are those who believe in Allâh and all the things that are necessary upon them to believe, including belief in Allâh's Angels, His Books, His Messengers, the Last Day, and the belief in the divine decree, the good and bad of it. They believe in (these pillars) with the belief that necessitates acceptance and submission with statements and actions.

The Second Quality: "Those who are humble in their prayers." They focus with their hearts while keeping their limbs tranquil. They recall that they are standing before their Lord, addressing Him in their prayer with His speech, and seeking closeness to Him with His remembrance. And they rely on Him with their invocation. They are humble to Him inwardly and outwardly.

The Third Quality: "Those who shun laghw (i.e. all that which is vain). The term "laghw" refers to anything that is void of good or benefit, whether it is a statement or action. (So the believers are those who) turn away from it because of their strong determination. They only spend their precious time engaged in that which will bring benefit to them. Just as they preserve their prayers with tranquility, they also preserve their time from being wasted. And if turning away from vanity is part of their qualities then it is more deserving of them to turn away from things that are harmful to them.

The Fourth Quality: "Those who pay their Zakât." The term "zakât" could mean the percentage from your money that must be paid to the poor, or it could carry the general meaning which is every statement or action that purifies the soul.

The Fifth Quality: "Those who preserve their chastity, except from their wives or that which their right hand possesses. They are not to be blamed." They preserve their chastity from fornication and homosexuality, because these acts are disobedience to Allâh, social deterioration, and inferiority in character.

And even more general than the abovementioned, (is also) the obligation of preserving oneself from touching and looking (at that which is not permissible to touch or look at). As for the statement, **"they are not to be blamed,"** this is an indication that the origin of this act is blameworthy except if it is done with the wife or the possession of the right hand, because of the need to that in order to fulfill the natural need for the production of babies and other benefits.

The generality of the statement, **"But those, who seek anything beyond that are the transgressors,"** is a proof for the impermissibility of masturbation, also known as العادة السرية "the Secret habit," (that is) because (masturbation) is ejaculation but not by way of the legal spouse or the possession of the right hand.

The Sixth Quality: "And who are watchful of their trusts and their covenants." "Trusts" includes statements, actions, and items. Therefore if someone informed you of a secret, he has entrusted you. Whoever does an action in your presence but does not want it to be exposed, has entrusted you. And if someone gave you his wealth to preserve it, he has entrusted you. But "covenant" is whatever an individual imposes on himself to do for someone else. An example of that is to make a vow to Allâh (to do a particular deed), or (even) the promises (which take place) between the people. The people of paradise (are those who) fulfill their trusts and keep their promises with Allâh and with the people. This also includes fulfilling the contracts and the lawful conditions between the people.

The Seventh Quality: "Those who establish their prayers." They are consistent in preserving their prayers as to not neglect them. They carry them out in a complete manner fulfilling their conditions, pillars, and obligations.

Allâh has mentioned in the Qur'ân many qualities of the people of Paradise besides what we have transmitted here. Allâh the Glorified mentioned these qualities so that those who want to enter paradise will adorn themselves with these characteristics. Likewise, many of these qualities are mentioned in a number of prophetic narrations. Abû Hurayrah (ﷺ) said that the Prophet (ﷺ) said:

$$\text{مَنْ سَلَكَ طريقاً يلتمس فيه عِلْمَاً سَهَّلَ الله له به طريقا إلى الجنة}$$

"Whoever treads a path, in which he seeks knowledge, Allâh will ease for him a path to Paradise." [Collected by Muslim]

It is also narrated by Abû Hurayrah, that the Prophet (ﷺ) said:

$$\text{ألا أدلُّكم على ما يمحُو الله به الخطايَا ويرفعُ به الدرجاتِ؟ " قالوا: بَلَى يا رسول الله. قال: " إسباغُ الوضوءِ على المَكارِهِ وكثرةُ الخُطَا إلى المساجدِ وانتظارُ الصلاةِ بعد الصلاة}$$

"Shall I not guide you to what Allâh expiates the sins with and elevates the ranks? They said: 'Yes O Messenger of Allâh!' He said: 'Performing the ablution in the perfect manner at times of discomfort, taking many steps to the Masjid, and waiting for the next prayer after the previous prayer.'" [Collected by Muslim]

It is narrated by 'Umar (ﷺ) that the Prophet (ﷺ) said:

$$\text{ما مِنْكم مِنْ أحدٍ يتوضَّأُ فيُسْبِغُ الوضوءَ ثم يقولُ: أشهد أنْ لا إله إلا الله وحده لا شريك له وأشهد أن محمداً عبدُه ورسولُه إلا فُتِحَت له أبوابُ الجنةِ الثمانيةُ يدخلُ من أيِّها شاءَ}$$

"None of you who will perform ablution in the perfect manner and then say: 'I testify that none has the right to be worshipped but Allâh Alone without a partner and I testify that Muhammad is His slave and His Messenger,' except that the eight doors of

Paradise will be opened for him to enter from whichever door he wants." [Collected by Muslim]

It is also narrated by 'Umar bin Al-Khattâb (رضي الله عنه) that the Prophet (ﷺ) said, **"Whoever repeats the call to prayer in his hearts will enter paradise."** [Collected by Muslim]

'Uthmân bin 'Affân (رضي الله عنه) said that the Prophet (ﷺ) said,

مَنْ بَنَى مسجداً يَبْتَغِي به وجهَ الله بنى الله له بيتا في الجنة

"Whoever built a Masjid, sincerely seeking the Face of Allâh, Allâh will build for him a house in Paradise" [Collected by Al-Bukhârî and Muslim]

It is narrated by 'Ubâdah bin Sâmit (رضي الله عنه) that the Messenger of Allâh (ﷺ) said:

خمسُ صلواتٍ كتبهنَّ الله على العبادِ، فمن جاء بهنَّ ولم يُضَيِّعْ منهن شيئاً استخفافاً بحقِّهن كان له عندَ الله عهد أن يدخله الجنة

"There are five daily prayers that Allâh prescribed on the slaves, whoever establishes them without being neglectful of them and belittling their obligation, will have with his Lord the promise to admit him into paradise." [Collected by Al-Imâm Ahmad, Abû Dâwûd and An-Nasâî'. Some of its chains of narration strengthen others. Al-Albânî graded it authentic in Sahîh Abî Dâwûd]

It is narrated by Thawbân (رضي الله عنه) that he asked the Prophet (ﷺ) about a deed by which Allâh will admit him into Paradise. So the Prophet (ﷺ) said to him: **"You must perform a lot of prostration. Because whenever you prostrate to Allâh, He elevates your rank with it and expiates your sins."** [Collected by Muslim]

It is narrated by Umm Habîbah, may Allâh be pleased with her, that the Prophet (ﷺ) said:

ما مِنْ عبدٍ مسلمٍ يصلِّي لله تعالى في كلِّ يومٍ ثِنْتَيْ عَشْرَةَ ركعة تطوعاً غير فريضة إلا بنى الله له بيتا في الجنة

"There is no Muslim slave of Allâh who prays twelve voluntary rak'ahs (sincerely) for Allâh, other than the compulsory prayers, except that Allâh will build for him a house in Paradise." [Collected by Muslim]

(These twelve units are as follows): Four before Ath-Thuhr, two after it, two after Al-Maghrib, two after Al-'Ishâ, and two before the Fajr prayer.

It is narrated by Mu'âdh bin Jabal (ﷺ) that he asked the Prophet (ﷺ) saying:

أخبرني بعملٍ يدخلُني الجنةَ ويباعدُني عن النار قال: " لقد سَأَلْتَ عن عظيمٍ وإنه لَيَسيرٌ على مَنْ يسَّرَهُ الله عليه: تعبدُ الله ولا تشركُ به شيئاً، وتقيمُ الصلاةَ، وتؤتي الزكاةَ، وتصومُ رمضانَ، وتحجُّ البيت

"Inform me about a deed that will allow me to enter into Paradise and distance me from the Hell-Fire. The Prophet (ﷺ) said to him: 'You have indeed asked about a great matter, but it is easy for whomever Allâh makes it easy. Worship Allâh and do not associate partners with Him, establish the prayer, pay the zakât, fast the month of Ramadân, and perform pilgrimage to the sacred house of Allâh.'" [Collected by Ahmad and At-Tirmidhî. Al-Albânî graded it to be authentic in Sahîh At-Tirmidhî]

It is narrated by Sahl bin Sa'd (ﷺ) that the Prophet (ﷺ) said:

إنَّ في الجنةِ باباً يقالُ له الرَّيَّانُ يدخلُ منه الصائمون يومَ القيامةِ لا يدخل منه أحد غيرهم

"Indeed in Paradise there is a door called Ar-Rayyân. Only those who fast will enter it. No one else besides them will enter it." [Collected by Al-Bukhârî and Muslim]

It is narrated by Abû Hurayrah (ﷺ) that the Messenger of Allâh (ﷺ) said:

مَن كان له ثلاثُ بناتٍ يُؤْوِيهنَّ ويرحمهنَّ ويَكفَلُهنَّ وَجَبَتْ له الجنةُ الْبَتَّة

"'Whoever has three daughters who he takes good care of, shows mercy to, and nurtures them, the paradise will be obligatory for him.' It was said: 'O Messenger of Allâh! What if they are only two?' He said: 'Even if they are only two.'" (The Narrator said: So some of them thought if they were to ask him about one daughter he would have said yes.) [Ahmad narrated this hadîth and its chains of narration are weak. However there are other authentic narrations that support this narration]: From among these narrations is the statement of the Prophet (ﷺ):

من ابْتُلِيَ من البنات بشيءٍ فأحسنَ إليهم كُنَّ له سترا من النار

"Whoever is tested with having daughters, but took good care of them, they will be a veil for him against the Hell-Fire" [Collected by Muslim]

It is narrated by Abû Hurayrah (ﷺ) that the Prophet (ﷺ) was asked about the most common thing which leads an individual to Paradise. He said: **"The Fear of Allâh and good character."**

[Collected by At-Tirmidhî and Ibn Hibbân. Al-Arna'ût graded it to be sound.]

It is also narrated by Iyâd bin Al-Himâr Al-Mujâshi' that the Prophet (ﷺ) said:

أهلُ الجنةِ ثلاثةٌ: ذو سلطانٍ مُقْسِط متصدِّق موفقٌ، ورجلٌ رحيمٌ رقيقُ القلبِ لكل ذِي قُرْبَى، ومُسْلِمٌ عفيف متعفّف ذو عيال

"The People of Paradise are three: a just ruler, who is generous and successful, a man who is merciful and softhearted to every kin, and every content Muslim who has a large family but adopts abstinence." [Collected by Muslim]

O Brothers! This is a compilation of some prophetic narrations which clarify many of the deeds of the people of Paradise for whoever wants to enter it.

I ask Allâh (to make the path to paradise easy for us) and for you (o reader). (I ask Him) to keep us firm upon (this path). Indeed He is the Most Generous, the Most Kind. May the peace and blessings be upon our Prophet Muhammad, his family members, and all his Companions.

المجلس الخامس و العشرون
The Twenty Fifth Sitting
The Description of the Hell-Fire (May Allâh Protect Us From It)

All praises and thanks are due to Allâh, The Ever-Living, the Self-Sufficient, The Only One who will remain after everything else has perished. He raised up the sky and beautified it with the stars. He stabilized the earth with firm mountains. He fashioned the (human) body with His ability and then caused them to die and wiped out their form. Then the trumpet will be blown, and behold, these dead bodies will rise up. Some of them will end up in the abode of bliss and others will end up in the blazing fire. Its doors will be opened for them in categories, and then the doors will be closed on them in buildings of high pillars filled with sorrow and grief. On the day when they will be overshadowed with torment from above them and from beneath them, none of them will receive mercy.

I testify that none has the right to be worshipped except Allâh alone without a partner, the testimony of the one who desires salvation. I testify that Muhammad (ﷺ) is His slave and Messenger, the one whom Allâh conquered, with his religion, the Persian and Roman Empires. May the peace and blessings of Allâh be upon him, his family members, his companions and whoever follows their footsteps in a good manner as long as the clouds continue to pour down rain.

O My Brothers! Allâh the Most High has warned us, in His Book, against the punishment of the Hell-Fire. He has informed us of the different kinds of punishment which cause livers to split and hearts to explode. Out of His Mercy, He has informed us so that (perhaps) we will take caution and be afraid of it. Therefore listen to some of what has been mentioned in the Book of Allâh and the Sunnah of His Messenger (ﷺ) regarding the different kinds of punishments of the Hell-Fire, so that perhaps you will reflect. Turn to your Lord in repentance and submit to His Will before the punishment comes to you and you will not have any one to help. Allâh said:

$$\text{﴿ وَٱتَّقُوا۟ ٱلنَّارَ ٱلَّتِىٓ أُعِدَّتْ لِلْكَٰفِرِينَ ۝ ﴾}$$

"And fear the Fire which has been prepared for the disbelievers" [Āli Imrân: 131]

Likewise Allâh said:

$$\text{﴿ إِنَّآ أَعْتَدْنَا لِلْكَٰفِرِينَ سَلَٰسِلَا۟ وَأَغْلَٰلًا وَسَعِيرًا ۝ ﴾}$$

"Verily, We have prepared for the disbelievers chains and iron-collars and blazing Fire" [Al-Insân: 4]

The Most High also said:

$$\text{﴿ إِنَّآ أَعْتَدْنَا لِلظَّٰلِمِينَ نَارًا أَحَاطَ بِهِمْ سُرَادِقُهَا ۝ ﴾}$$

"We have prepared for the wrongdoers a fire whose flaming canopy shall enclose them" [Al-Kahf: 29]

Allâh (ﷻ) said while addressing the devil:

$$\text{﴿ إِنَّ عِبَادِى لَيْسَ لَكَ عَلَيْهِمْ سُلْطَٰنٌ إِلَّا مَنِ ٱتَّبَعَكَ مِنَ ٱلْغَاوِينَ ۝ وَإِنَّ جَهَنَّمَ لَمَوْعِدُهُمْ أَجْمَعِينَ ۝ لَهَا سَبْعَةُ أَبْوَٰبٍ لِكُلِّ بَابٍ مِّنْهُمْ جُزْءٌ مَّقْسُومٌ ۝ ﴾}$$

"Surely, thou shall have no power over My servants, except such of the erring ones as choose to follow thee. And, surely, Hell is the promised place for them all. It has seven gates, and each gate has a portion of them allotted to it." [Al-Hijr: 42-44]

Allâh, the Most High, said:

﴿ وَسِيقَ ٱلَّذِينَ كَفَرُوٓا۟ إِلَىٰ جَهَنَّمَ زُمَرًا حَتَّىٰٓ إِذَا جَآءُوهَا فُتِحَتْ أَبْوَٰبُهَا ﴾

"And those who disbelieve will be driven to Hell in troops until, when they arrive there, its gates will be opened" [Az-Zumar: 71]

Allâh, the Most High, also said:

﴿ وَلِلَّذِينَ كَفَرُوا۟ بِرَبِّهِمْ عَذَابُ جَهَنَّمَ وَبِئْسَ ٱلْمَصِيرُ ۝ إِذَآ أُلْقُوا۟ فِيهَا سَمِعُوا۟ لَهَا شَهِيقًا وَهِيَ تَفُورُ ۝ ﴾

"And for those who disbelieve in their Lord, is the punishment of Hell, and an evil resort it is. When they are cast therein, they will hear it roaring as it boils up." [Al-Mulk 6-7]

Likewise, the Most High, said:

﴿ يَوْمَ يَغْشَىٰهُمُ ٱلْعَذَابُ مِن فَوْقِهِمْ وَمِن تَحْتِ أَرْجُلِهِمْ وَيَقُولُ ذُوقُوا۟ مَا كُنتُمْ تَعْمَلُونَ ۝ ﴾

"On the day when the punishment will overwhelm them from above them and from underneath their feet, and He will say, 'Taste ye the fruit of your actions.'" [Al-'Ankabût: 55]

Allâh, the Most High, said:

{ لَهُم مِّن فَوْقِهِمْ ظُلَلٌ مِّنَ ٱلنَّارِ وَمِن تَحْتِهِمْ ظُلَلٌ ذَٰلِكَ يُخَوِّفُ ٱللَّهُ بِهِۦ عِبَادَهُۥ يَٰعِبَادِ فَٱتَّقُونِ ۝ }

"They will have over them coverings of fire, and beneath them similar coverings. It is this against which Allâh warns His servant. 'O My servants, Fear Me.'" [Az-Zumar:16]

Allâh, the Most High, also said:

{ وَأَصْحَٰبُ ٱلشِّمَالِ مَآ أَصْحَٰبُ ٱلشِّمَالِ ۝ فِى سَمُومٍ وَحَمِيمٍ ۝ وَظِلٍّ مِّن يَحْمُومٍ ۝ لَّا بَارِدٍ وَلَا كَرِيمٍ ۝ }

"And those on the left hand - how unfortunate are those on the left hand! They will be in the midst of scorching winds and scalding water, And under the shadow of pitch-black smoke; neither cool nor wholesome." [Al-Wâqi'ah: 42-44]

Allâh, the Most High, said:

{ وَقَالُواْ لَا تَنفِرُواْ فِى ٱلْحَرِّ قُلْ نَارُ جَهَنَّمَ أَشَدُّ حَرًّا }

"They said, 'Go not forth in the heat.' Say, 'The fire of Hell is more intense in heat.' If only they could understand." [At-Tawbah: 81]

And His statement, the Most High:

$$﴿ وَمَآ أَدْرَىٰكَ مَا هِيَهْ ۝ نَارٌ حَامِيَةٌ ۝ ﴾$$

"And what should make thee know what that is? It is a blazing Fire." [Al-Qâri'ah: 10-11]

And His statement, the Most High:

$$﴿ إِنَّ ٱلْمُجْرِمِينَ فِي ضَلَٰلٍ وَسُعُرٍ ۝ يَوْمَ يُسْحَبُونَ فِي ٱلنَّارِ عَلَىٰ وُجُوهِهِمْ ذُوقُوا۟ مَسَّ سَقَرَ ۝ ﴾$$

"Surely, the guilty are in manifest error and suffer from madness. On the day when they will be dragged into the Fire on their faces, it will be said to them, 'Taste ye the touch of Hell.'" [Al-Qamar: 47-48]

The Most High said:

$$﴿ سَأُصْلِيهِ سَقَرَ ۝ وَمَآ أَدْرَىٰكَ مَا سَقَرُ ۝ لَا تُبْقِى وَلَا تَذَرُ ۝ ﴾$$

"Soon shall I cast him into the fire of Hell. And what will make thee know what Hell-fire is? It spares not and it leaves naught." [Al-Mudathir: 26-28]

Allâh, the Most High, says:

$$﴿ يَٰٓأَيُّهَا ٱلَّذِينَ ءَامَنُوا۟ قُوٓا۟ أَنفُسَكُمْ وَأَهْلِيكُمْ نَارًا وَقُودُهَا ٱلنَّاسُ وَٱلْحِجَارَةُ عَلَيْهَا مَلَٰٓئِكَةٌ غِلَاظٌ شِدَادٌ لَّا يَعْصُونَ ٱللَّهَ مَآ أَمَرَهُمْ وَيَفْعَلُونَ مَا يُؤْمَرُونَ ۝ ﴾$$

"O ye who believe ! Save yourselves and your families from a Fire whose fuel is men and stones over which are appointed angels, stern and severe, who disobey not Allâh in what He commands them and do as they are commanded" [At-Tahrîm: 6]

Allâh, the Most High, says:

$$\{ إِنَّهَا تَرْمِي بِشَرَرٍ كَالْقَصْرِ ۝ كَأَنَّهُ جِمَالَتٌ صُفْرٌ ۝ \}$$

"It throws up sparks like huge castles, As if they were tawny camels" [Al-Mursalât: 32-33]

And His statement, the Most High:

$$\{ وَتَرَى الْمُجْرِمِينَ يَوْمَئِذٍ مُّقَرَّنِينَ فِي الْأَصْفَادِ ۝ سَرَابِيلُهُم مِّن قَطِرَانٍ وَتَغْشَىٰ وُجُوهَهُمُ النَّارُ ۝ \}$$

"And thou wilt see the guilty on that day bound in chains. Their garments will be, of pitch and fire shall envelop their faces" [Ibrâhîm: 49-50]

And His statement, the Most High:

$$\{ إِذِ الْأَغْلَالُ فِي أَعْنَاقِهِمْ وَالسَّلَاسِلُ يُسْحَبُونَ ۝ فِي الْحَمِيمِ ثُمَّ فِي النَّارِ يُسْجَرُونَ ۝ \}$$

"When the iron-collars will be round their necks and chains as well; and they will be dragged into boiling water; then in the Fire will they be burnt" [Ghâfir: 71-72]

The Most High said:

Sittings During the Blessed Month of Ramaḍān رَمَضَان

﴿ ۞ هَٰذَانِ خَصْمَانِ ٱخْتَصَمُوا۟ فِى رَبِّهِمْ ۖ فَٱلَّذِينَ كَفَرُوا۟ قُطِّعَتْ لَهُمْ ثِيَابٌ مِّن نَّارٍ يُصَبُّ مِن فَوْقِ رُءُوسِهِمُ ٱلْحَمِيمُ ﴿١٩﴾ يُصْهَرُ بِهِۦ مَا فِى بُطُونِهِمْ وَٱلْجُلُودُ ﴿٢٠﴾ وَلَهُم مَّقَٰمِعُ مِنْ حَدِيدٍ ﴿٢١﴾ كُلَّمَآ أَرَادُوٓا۟ أَن يَخْرُجُوا۟ مِنْهَا مِنْ غَمٍّ أُعِيدُوا۟ فِيهَا وَذُوقُوا۟ عَذَابَ ٱلْحَرِيقِ ﴿٢٢﴾ ﴾

"These two opponents (believers and disbelievers) dispute with each other about their Lord. As for those who disbelieve, garments of fire will be cut out for them; and boiling water will be poured down over their heads, whereby that which is in their bellies, and their skins too, will be melted; And for them are hooked rods of iron (to punish them). Every time they seek to get away therefrom, from anguish, they will be driven back therein; and it will be said to them, 'taste ye the torment of burning.'"
[Al-Hajj: 19-22]

The Most High says:

﴿ إِنَّ ٱلَّذِينَ كَفَرُوا۟ بِـَٔايَٰتِنَا سَوْفَ نُصْلِيهِمْ نَارًا كُلَّمَا نَضِجَتْ جُلُودُهُم بَدَّلْنَٰهُمْ جُلُودًا غَيْرَهَا لِيَذُوقُوا۟ ٱلْعَذَابَ ۗ إِنَّ ٱللَّهَ كَانَ عَزِيزًا حَكِيمًا ﴿٥٦﴾ ﴾

"Those who disbelieve in Our Signs, We shall soon cause them to enter Fire. As often as their skins are burnt up, We shall give them in exchange other skins that they may continue to taste the punishment. Surely, Allâh is Mighty and Wise" [An-Nisâ: 56]

Also the Most High said:

﴿ إِنَّ شَجَرَتَ ٱلزَّقُّومِ ﴿٤٣﴾ طَعَامُ ٱلْأَثِيمِ ﴿٤٤﴾ كَٱلْمُهْلِ يَغْلِى فِى ٱلْبُطُونِ ﴿٤٥﴾ كَغَلْىِ ٱلْحَمِيمِ ﴿٤٦﴾ ﴾

"Indeed, the tree of zaqqûm is food for the sinful, like murky oil, it boils within bellies, like the boiling of scalding water" [Ad-Dukhân: 43-46]

Allâh, the Most High, said about the Tree (of Az-Zaqqûm):

﴿ إِنَّهَا شَجَرَةٌ تَخْرُجُ فِى أَصْلِ ٱلْجَحِيمِ ۝ طَلْعُهَا كَأَنَّهُۥ رُءُوسُ ٱلشَّيَٰطِينِ ۝ ﴾

"Verily, it is a tree that springs out of the bottom of Hell-fire. The shoots of its fruit-stalks are like the heads of Devils." [As-Sâffât: 64-65]

Allâh, the Most High, mentioned about the tree in another Qur'ânic chapter:

﴿ ثُمَّ إِنَّكُمْ أَيُّهَا ٱلضَّآلُّونَ ٱلْمُكَذِّبُونَ ۝ لَآكِلُونَ مِن شَجَرٍ مِّن زَقُّومٍ ۝ فَمَالِئُونَ مِنْهَا ٱلْبُطُونَ ۝ فَشَٰرِبُونَ عَلَيْهِ مِنَ ٱلْحَمِيمِ ۝ فَشَٰرِبُونَ شُرْبَ ٱلْهِيمِ ۝ هَٰذَا نُزُلُهُمْ يَوْمَ ٱلدِّينِ ۝ ﴾

"Then moreover, verily, you the erring-ones, the deniers (of Resurrection)! You will eat of the tree of Zaqqûm. Then you will fill your bellies therewith, and drink boiling water on top of it, so you will drink (that) like thirsty camels! That will be their entertainment on the Day of Recompense!" [Al-Wâqi'ah: 51-56]

Allâh, the Most High, said:

﴿ وَإِن يَسْتَغِيثُوا۟ يُغَاثُوا۟ بِمَآءٍ كَٱلْمُهْلِ يَشْوِى ٱلْوُجُوهَ بِئْسَ ٱلشَّرَابُ وَسَآءَتْ مُرْتَفَقًا ۝ ﴾

"And if they ask for help (relief, water, etc.) they will be granted water like boiling oil which will scald their faces. Terrible the drink, and what an evil (dwelling, resting place, etc.)!" [Al-Kahf: 29]

The Most High said:

$$\text{﴿ وَسُقُوا۟ مَآءً حَمِيمًا فَقَطَّعَ أَمْعَآءَهُمْ ۝ ﴾}$$

"And be given, to drink, boiling water, so that it cuts up their intestines?" [Muhammad: 15]

The Most High said:

$$\text{﴿ مِّن وَرَآئِهِۦ جَهَنَّمُ وَيُسْقَىٰ مِن مَّآءٍ صَدِيدٍ ۝ يَتَجَرَّعُهُۥ وَلَا يَكَادُ يُسِيغُهُۥ وَيَأْتِيهِ ٱلْمَوْتُ مِن كُلِّ مَكَانٍ وَمَا هُوَ بِمَيِّتٍ ۖ وَمِن وَرَآئِهِۦ عَذَابٌ غَلِيظٌ ۝ ﴾}$$

"In front of him (every obstinate, arrogant dictator) is Hell, and he will be made to drink boiling, festering water. He will sip it unwillingly, and he will find a great difficulty to swallow it down his throat, and death will come to him from every side, yet he will not die and in front of him, will be a great torment." [Ibrâhîm: 16-17]

Allâh, the Most High, said:

$$\text{﴿ إِنَّ ٱلْمُجْرِمِينَ فِى عَذَابِ جَهَنَّمَ خَٰلِدُونَ ۝ لَا يُفَتَّرُ عَنْهُمْ وَهُمْ فِيهِ مُبْلِسُونَ ۝ وَمَا ظَلَمْنَٰهُمْ وَلَٰكِن كَانُوا۟ هُمُ ٱلظَّٰلِمِينَ ۝ وَنَادَوْا۟ يَٰمَٰلِكُ لِيَقْضِ عَلَيْنَا رَبُّكَ ۖ قَالَ إِنَّكُم مَّٰكِثُونَ ۝ ﴾}$$

"Verily, the Mujrimûn (criminals, sinners, disbelievers, etc.) will be in the torment of Hell to abide therein forever. (The torment) will not be lightened for them, and they will be plunged into destruction with deep regrets, sorrows and in despair therein. We wronged them not, but they were the Thâlimûn (polytheists, wrong-doers, etc.). And they will cry: 'O Mâlik (Keeper of Hell)! Let your Lord make an end of us.' He will say: 'Verily you shall abide forever.'" [Az-Zukhruf: 74-77]

The Most High said:

$$﴿ وَنَحْشُرُهُمْ يَوْمَ ٱلْقِيَٰمَةِ عَلَىٰ وُجُوهِهِمْ عُمْيًا وَبُكْمًا وَصُمًّا ۖ مَّأْوَىٰهُمْ جَهَنَّمُ ۖ كُلَّمَا خَبَتْ زِدْنَٰهُمْ سَعِيرًا ۝ ﴾$$

"And We shall gather them together on the Day of Resurrection on their faces, blind, dumb and deaf, their abode will be Hell; whenever it abates, We shall increase for them the fierceness of the Fire" [Al-Isrâ: 97]

Allâh, the Most High, said:

$$﴿ إِنَّ ٱلَّذِينَ كَفَرُوا۟ وَظَلَمُوا۟ لَمْ يَكُنِ ٱللَّهُ لِيَغْفِرَ لَهُمْ وَلَا لِيَهْدِيَهُمْ طَرِيقًا ۝ إِلَّا طَرِيقَ جَهَنَّمَ خَٰلِدِينَ فِيهَآ أَبَدًا ۚ وَكَانَ ذَٰلِكَ عَلَى ٱللَّهِ يَسِيرًا ۝ ﴾$$

"Verily, those who disbelieve and did wrong, Allâh will not forgive them, nor will He guide them to anyway, except the way of Hell, to dwell therein forever, and this is ever easy for Allâh." [An-Nisâ: 168-169]

The Most High said:

$$﴿ إِنَّ ٱللَّهَ لَعَنَ ٱلْكَٰفِرِينَ وَأَعَدَّ لَهُمْ سَعِيرًا ۝ ﴾$$

"Allâh has cursed the disbelievers and prepared for them a blazing fire." [Al-Ahzâb: 64]

Sittings During the Blessed Month of Ramaḍān رَمَضَان

The Most High said:

﴿ إِلَّا بَلَاغًا مِّنَ ٱللَّهِ وَرِسَالَٰتِهِۦ ۚ وَمَن يَعْصِ ٱللَّهَ وَرَسُولَهُۥ فَإِنَّ لَهُۥ نَارَ جَهَنَّمَ خَٰلِدِينَ فِيهَآ أَبَدًا ﴿٢٣﴾ ﴾

"My responsibility is only to convey what is revealed to me from Allâh and His Messages. And those who disobey Allâh and His Messenger, surely, for them is the Fire of Hell, wherein they will abide for a long period." [Al-Jinn: 23]

The Most High said:

﴿ كَلَّا لَيُنۢبَذَنَّ فِى ٱلْحُطَمَةِ ﴿٤﴾ وَمَآ أَدْرَىٰكَ مَا ٱلْحُطَمَةُ ﴿٥﴾ نَارُ ٱللَّهِ ٱلْمُوقَدَةُ ﴿٦﴾ ٱلَّتِى تَطَّلِعُ عَلَى ٱلْأَفْـِٔدَةِ ﴿٧﴾ إِنَّهَا عَلَيْهِم مُّؤْصَدَةٌ ﴿٨﴾ ﴾

"Nay! Verily, he will be thrown into the crushing Fire. And what will make you know what the crushing Fire is? The fire of Allâh, kindled, Which leaps up over the hearts, Verily, it shall be closed in on them, In pillars stretched forth (i.e. they will be punished in the Fire with pillars, etc)." [Al-Humazah: 4-8]

(There are many verses in the Qur'ân) regarding the description of the Hell-Fire and its painful punishments.

(What follows are some) prophetic narrations about the description of the Hell-Fire and its severe torments.

It is narrated by 'Abdullâh bin Mas'ûd (ﷺ) that the Messenger of Allâh (ﷺ) said:

يُؤْتَى بِالنَّارِ يَوْمَ القيامةِ لها سبعونَ ألفَ زمامٍ، مع كلِّ زمامٍ سبعونَ ألفَ مَلَكٍ يجرُّونها

"The Hell-Fire will brought on the Day of Judgment with seventy-thousand reins with each rein there are seventy thousand Angels pulling it." [Collected by Muslim]

It is also narrated by Abû Hurayrah (ﷺ) that the Prophet (ﷺ) said:

نَارُكم هذِه ما يُوقد بَنُو آدَمَ جُزْءٌ واحِدٌ من سبعين جزءاً من نار جهنَّم "، قالوا: يا رسولَ الله إنَّها لَكَافِيةٌ؟ قال: " إِنَّها فُضِّلَت عليها بِتِسْعَةٍ وستينَ جزءاً كلُّهن مثلُ حرِّها

"This fire of yours which the sons of Ādam light is a single part from the seventy parts of the Hell-Fire. They said: 'O Messenger of Allâh! Indeed this fire is hot enough for us.' The Prophet (ﷺ) said: 'The Fire of the Hell is sixty-nine times hotter than this fire." [Collected by Al-Bukhârî and Muslim]

It is narrated by Abû Hurayrah (ﷺ) that he said:

كنَّا عندَ النبيِّ صَلَّى اللَّهُ عَلَيْهِ وَسَلَّمَ فسَمِعنَا وَجْبَة فقال النبيُّ صَلَّى اللَّهُ عَلَيْهِ وَسَلَّمَ: " أَتَدْرُونَ ما هَذَا؟ " قلْنَا: الله ورسولُه أعلمُ. قال: " هذا حجرٌ أَرْسَلَه الله في جهنَّمَ مُنْذُ سبعينَ خَرِيفاً (يَعْني سبعينَ سنةً) فالان حين انتهى إلى قعرها

"We were with the Prophet (ﷺ) one day when we heard a booming sound. So the Prophet (ﷺ) said: 'Do you know what this sound is?' We said: 'Allâh and His Messenger know best.' He said: 'This is a rock which Allâh sent in the Hell-Fire from seventy autumns ago (i.e seventy years). It has just landed to the bottom of the Hell Fire.'" [Collected by Muslim]

'Utbah bin Ghazwân (﷠) said: "Certainly it has been mentioned to us that a rock will be thrown from the edge of the Hell-Fire and it will tumble in it for seventy years before reaching its bottom. By Allâh (the Hell-Fire) will be filled up, are you all amazed?" [Collected by Muslim]

It is also narrated by Ibn Abbâs (﷠) who said that the Prophet (ﷺ) said:

لَوْ أَنَّ قَطْرَةً مِن الزَّقُّومِ قَطَرَت في دار الدنيا لأفسدت على أهل الدنيا معايشهم

"If a tiny piece from the tree of zaqqûm dropped in this world, it would destroy the livelihood of the inhabitants of the earth." [Graded authentic by Al-Albânî in <u>Sahîh Al-Jâmi'</u>]

It is narrated by Nu'mân bin Bashîr (﷠) the Prophet (ﷺ) said:

إنَّ أَهْوَنَ أهل النارِ عذاباً مَنْ لَهُ نَعْلانٍ وشِراكان من نارٍ يَغلي منهما دماغُه كما يغلي المِرْجَل ما يَرَى أنَّ أحداً أشد منه عذابا، وإنه لأهونهم عذابا

"The one who will receive the least punishment of the hell fire will have two sandals from fire that will cause his brain to boil like the boiling of hot water in a pot. He will think that he is receiving the worst punishment even though he is receiving the least punishment" [Collected by Al-Bukhârî and Muslim]

Anas bin Mâlik (﷠) said the Messenger of Allâh (ﷺ) said:

يُؤْتَى بأَنْعَم أهل الدنيا مِنْ أهل النار فيُصْبَغ في النار صَبْغَةً ثم يُقَال: يا بن آدمَ هل رأيتَ خيراً قط؟ هل مَرَّ بكَ نعيمٌ قط؟ فيقولُ: لا والله يا ربِّ، ويُؤْتَى بأشَدِّ الناسِ بؤساً في الدنيا مِنْ أهل الجنة فيصبغ صبغةً في

الجنة فيقال: يا بن آدمَ هل رأيتَ بؤساً قط؟ هل مَرَّ بك من شدة قط؟ فيقولُ: لا والله يا ربِّ ما رأيتُ بؤساً ولا مرّ بي من شدة

"The most comfortable person in this world from the disbelievers will be brought on the Day of Judgment and will be dipped in the Hell and then it will be said to him: 'Did you ever see good? Did you ever experience comfort before?' And he will reply saying: 'No, by Allâh, O my Lord!' And the most uncomfortable person in this world from the people of Paradise will be brought and will be dipped in paradise. And it will be said to him: ' Have you ever seen any hardship or experienced any adversities?' He will say: 'By Allâh, no O my Lord!" [Collected by Muslim]

This means that the people of Hell will forget all of the bounties they had in this world. While the people of paradise will forget all of the hardships they underwent in this life.

It is also narrated by (Anas bin Mâlik) that the Prophet (ﷺ) said:

يُقَالُ للرجلِ من أهل النار يومَ القيامةِ: أرأيْتَ لو كانَ لكَ ما على الأرض من شيءٍ أكنتَ تفتدي به؟ قال: فيقول: نعم. قال: فيقول: قد أردتُ منكَ ما هُو أهْونُ من ذلكَ، قد أخذتُ عَلَيْك في ظهرِ آدم أن لا تُشْرِكَ بي شيئاً، فأبيتَ إلاَّ أنْ تشركَ بي

"It will be said to a man from the people of the Hell-Fire on the Day of Judgment: 'If you possessed all that is on the earth, would you ransom yourself with it?' He will say 'yes.' Then Allâh will say to him: 'I asked you for what is less than that. I have taken the covenant with you from the back of Ādam that you will not associate partners with Me, but you refused except but to associate partners with Me.'" [Narrated by Ahmad, and Al-Bukhârî. Muslim also has a similar narration]

Ibn Mardawayih narrated that Yahyah bin Munyah, the son of Umayyah and Munyah is his mother. He said: "**Allâh will send a cloud above the people of Hell.** When the cloud approaches them, He will call them and say: 'O people of the Hell! What is it that you are seeking? What is it that you are asking?' And they will remember that when they were in the world, they used to get rain from the clouds, so they will say: 'O our Lord! We are asking you for drinking water.' So He will send upon them collars and chains in addition to the ones they already have, and coals of fire which increase the blazing of the fire." [A Weak Narration. Collected by Al-Haythamî in Majma' Az-Zawâid]

It is narrated by Abû Mûsâ (ﷺ) that the Prophet (ﷺ) said: "There are three people who will not enter the Paradise: the alcoholic, the one who severs the family ties, and the one who affirms Magic. The one who dies while addicted to alcohol will be given to drink from the river of ghûtah. It was asked: 'What is the river of ghûtah?' He said: 'it is a river in hell made from the discharge of the prostitutes, the smell of their private parts harms the people of the hell-Fire." [Al-Albânî graded it weak in Daî'f Al-Jâmi']

It is narrated by Jâbir bin 'Abdullâh that the Prophet (ﷺ) said:

إن على الله عهداً لمنْ شربَ الْمُسْكِراتِ لَيَسْقِيه من طِينةِ الْخَبَالِ ". قالوا: يا رسولَ الله وما طينةُ الْخَبَالِ؟ قال: " عَرق أهل النار أو عصارة أهل النار

"Allâh has taken a covenant with those who consume intoxicants, that He will make them drink from the mud of khabâl. They said: 'O Messenger of Allâh! What is the mud of khabâl?' He said: 'it is the sweat of the people of the Hell-Fire or the excrement of the people of the Hell-Fire.'" [Collected by Muslim]

It is also reported by the Prophet (ﷺ) that he said:

يُقَالُ لليهودِ والنصارى: ماذا تَبْغُونَ؟ فيقولونَ: عَطِشنا رَبَّنا فاسْقِنَا. فيُشار إليهم: ألا تَرِدُونَ؟ فيُحْشَرونَ إلى جهنَم كأنها سرابٌ يحطِمُ بعضُها بعضاً فيتساقطونَ في النار

"It will be said to the Jews and the Christians: 'What do you want?' And they will say in reply: 'O our Lord we are thirsty so give us some drink.' Then (the Hell-Fire) will be pointed at, and it will be said to them: 'Will you not go and get some drink from there.' Then all of them will be gathered and dragged to the hell-fire as if they are a mirage; they will be crushing on one another till they fall in to the Hell-Fire." [Collected by Al-Bukhârî and Muslim]

Al-Hasan said: "What do you think of the people who stand on their feet for fifty thousand years. They did not eat any food or drink any water, to the point that their necks starts to split due to thirst, and their bellies start to burn due to hunger, then they will, after wards, be taken to the hellfire and be giving to drink from a boiling water!"

Ibn Al-Jawzî, may Allâh have mercy on him, said in his description of the hellfire: "It is an abode in which its dwellers are outcast. (They) are deprived of life's sweetness and happiness. The brightness of their faces is replaced with dimness, and they will be hit with whips stronger than mountains. Its guards are Angels who are stern and severe.

If you were to see (one of these people) being dragged in the boiling water and flung in to the severe frost, you will see them in constant grief. Their spots in the hellfire are inescapable. Its guards are Angels who are stern and severe.

Their scolding is more severe than the actual punishment, their regret is more intense than the calamity that has befallen them. They cry for not taking advantage of their (years when they were) youth, and whenever they increase in their mourning the stern Angels will increase in their punishment. (It is) very unfortunate for them that the anger of the Creator is over them. (How very unfortunate is it for them) to be in the midst of this test, filled with enormous catastrophes, very embarrassing for them amongst all the creatures to be disgraced in their presence.

Where is their earning of the (worthless) debris (of the worldly life)? Where is their effort in the disobedience of the Lord? It is as if it all was nothing more than mixed up false dreams? Then these bodies will be burnt, and whenever they are burnt, their skins will be replaced for them. Its guards are stern and severe Angels."

O Allāh grant us protection from the hellfire, and protection from the home of disgrace and destruction. (O Allāh) admit us, with Your mercy, into the abode of the pious and the righteous ones. With Your Mercy, forgive us, our parents, and all the Muslims. You are the Most Merciful.

We ask Allāh to shower His blessings and mercy on our Prophet Muhammad, his family members, and all his Companions.

المجلس السادس و العشرون
The Twenty Sixth Sitting
Things that lead to the Hellfire

All praises are due to Allâh, the Strong, the Powerful, the Omnipotent, the Vanquisher. The slightest whimper is not hidden from His hearing and the movement of the fetus in the womb is not hidden from His sight. The tyrannical rulers humble themselves to His glory and the conspiring of the plotters is rendered worthless (in front of) His Might and Power. He made His decision on the sinners as He wills, and His decision to choose whom He will from amongst the creatures has already proceeded. The first ones are the people of the left hand and the second are the people of the right hand. The destiny has already been written before the deeds of the doers, and had it not been because of this separation, then the efforts of those who strive would have been a waste, and there would not have been any difference between the believers and the disbelievers, between those who have certainty and those who are in doubt. Had it not been because of this division, the Hell-Fire would have been filled up with the criminals. Allâh said:

﴿ وَلَوْ شِئْنَا لَآتَيْنَا كُلَّ نَفْسٍ هُدَىٰهَا وَلَٰكِنْ حَقَّ ٱلْقَوْلُ مِنِّى لَأَمْلَأَنَّ جَهَنَّمَ مِنَ ٱلْجِنَّةِ وَٱلنَّاسِ أَجْمَعِينَ ۝ ﴾

"And if We had enforced Our will, We could have given every soul its appropriate guidance, but the word from Me has come true that I will fill Hell with jinn and men all together." [As-Sajdah: 13]

O my Brother, that indeed is the wisdom of Allâh and He is the Most Just of judges. I thank Him, Glorified is He, the thanks of the grateful ones, and I ask Him to grant me the support of those who are patient. I seek His refuge from the humiliating punishment. I further bear witness that none has the right to be worshiped but Allâh alone, the Only True King. And I further bear witness that Muhammad (ﷺ) is His slave and His chosen Messenger, the trustworthy. May the peace and blessings of Allâh be upon him, his companion Abû Bakr, the first follower of this religion amongst men, 'Umar the one who was strong and firm with the command of Allâh, 'Uthmân the husband of the two daughters of the Prophet (ﷺ) how excellent is his companionship, upon 'Alî, the Ocean of knowledge, upon all the righteous family members of the Prophet (ﷺ), upon his pious Companions, and upon all of those who follow him in his religion until the Day of Resurrection.

O My Brothers! Know (O reader) that entering the Hell-Fire has many causes which Allâh has clarified in His Book and on the tongue of His Messenger (ﷺ) in order that the people will be cautious of them and abstain from them. These causes are of two types.

The First Type are causes that actually take a person outside of Islâm into disbelief. These causes necessitate that if a person commits them (and does not repent) he will abide in the Hell-Fire forever.

The Second Type are causes that make an individual lose the eligibility of being considered just (and truthful). Rather, he will be considered a wicked sinner. They make him deserving of being entered into the hellfire without abiding therein forever.

As for the First type: We will mention categories from it

The First Category: Associating partners with Allâh, by ascribing partners to Allâh in His Lordship, His right to be worshipped alone, or in His Names and Attributes. Whoever believes that there is another creator along with Allâh who participated with

Him in the creation or has his own creation, or the one who believes that there is another deity who is worthy of being worshiped besides Allâh, or worships other deities along with Allâh by directing some of the acts of worship to him, or the one who believes that there is someone who has knowledge like that of Allâh, power like Allâh's power, might like Allâh's might, or other attributes similar to this, such an individual has indeed associated partners with Allâh and has committed major polytheism. This person (if he does not repent) will abide in the hellfire forever. Allâh (ﷻ) states:

$$\text{﴿ إِنَّهُۥ مَن يُشْرِكْ بِٱللَّهِ فَقَدْ حَرَّمَ ٱللَّهُ عَلَيْهِ ٱلْجَنَّةَ وَمَأْوَىٰهُ ٱلنَّارُۖ وَمَا لِلظَّٰلِمِينَ مِنْ أَنصَارٍ ﴾ (٧٢)}$$

"Indeed whosoever associates partners with Allâh the Almighty, Allâh will make the paradise forbidden on him, and his abode will be in the hellfire, and for the evil doers there will be no helpers." [Al-Mâi'dah: 72]

The Second Category: To disbelieve in Allâh, or His Angels, His Books, His Messengers, the Last Day, or Allâh's Divine Decree and Pre-ordainment. Whoever rejects any of the above mentioned (pillars of faith) by denying them or having doubts in them is indeed a disbeliever who will abide in the hellfire forever (if he does not repent before he dies). Allâh the Most High said:

$$\text{﴿ إِنَّ ٱلَّذِينَ يَكْفُرُونَ بِٱللَّهِ وَرُسُلِهِۦ وَيُرِيدُونَ أَن يُفَرِّقُوا۟ بَيْنَ ٱللَّهِ وَرُسُلِهِۦ وَيَقُولُونَ نُؤْمِنُ بِبَعْضٍ وَنَكْفُرُ بِبَعْضٍ وَيُرِيدُونَ أَن يَتَّخِذُوا۟ بَيْنَ ذَٰلِكَ سَبِيلًا (١٥٠) أُو۟لَٰٓئِكَ هُمُ ٱلْكَٰفِرُونَ حَقًّاۚ وَأَعْتَدْنَا لِلْكَٰفِرِينَ عَذَابًا مُّهِينًا (١٥١) ﴾}$$

"Surely, those who disbelieve in Allâh and His Messengers and seek to make a distinction between Allâh and His Messengers, and say, 'We believe in some and disbelieve in others,' and seek to take a way between; These really are the disbelievers, and We have prepared for the disbelievers a humiliating punishment." [An-Nisa: 150-151]

The Most High also says:

﴿ إِنَّ ٱللَّهَ لَعَنَ ٱلْكَٰفِرِينَ وَأَعَدَّ لَهُمْ سَعِيرًا ۝ خَٰلِدِينَ فِيهَآ أَبَدًا لَّا يَجِدُونَ وَلِيًّا وَلَا نَصِيرًا ۝ يَوْمَ تُقَلَّبُ وُجُوهُهُمْ فِى ٱلنَّارِ يَقُولُونَ يَٰلَيْتَنَآ أَطَعْنَا ٱللَّهَ وَأَطَعْنَا ٱلرَّسُولَا۠ ۝ وَقَالُوا۟ رَبَّنَآ إِنَّآ أَطَعْنَا سَادَتَنَا وَكُبَرَآءَنَا فَأَضَلُّونَا ٱلسَّبِيلَا۠ ۝ رَبَّنَآ ءَاتِهِمْ ضِعْفَيْنِ مِنَ ٱلْعَذَابِ وَٱلْعَنْهُمْ لَعْنًا كَبِيرًا ۝ ﴾

"Allâh has, surely, cursed the disbelievers, and has prepared for them a blazing fire, Wherein they will abide forever; they will find therein no friend, nor helper. On the day when their faces are turned over into the fire they will say, 'O, would that we had obeyed Allâh and obeyed the Messenger!' And they will say, 'Our Lord, we obeyed our chiefs and our great ones and they led us astray from the way, Our Lord, give them double punishment and curse them with a mighty curse." [Al-Ahzâb: 64-68]

The Third Category: Denying the obligation of any of the five pillars of Al-Islâm. Whoever rejects the obligation of the two testimonies of Al-Islâm (i.e. that none has the right to be worshipped but Allâh and that Muhammad is the Messenger of Allâh) or denies that it is required to be said by all of mankind, or denies the obligation of the five daily prayers, the (obligation of) paying the alms, the fast during the month of Ramadân, or performing pilgrimage to the sacred house of Allâh, that individual will be considered a disbeliever, because he is belying

Allâh, His Messenger (ﷺ), and the consensus of the Muslims. Likewise, whoever denies the impermissibility of polytheism, murder, fornication, homosexuality, alcohol, or their likes from among the things that are clearly declared impermissible according to the Book of Allâh and the Sunnah of His Messenger (ﷺ). This is because he is rejecting Allâh and His Messenger. However if the one who rejected the abovementioned is a new convert, who (only denied these things) out of ignorance, he will not become a disbeliever until he is taught. If he rejects them after being taught, then in this case he will become a disbeliever as well.

The Fourth Category: Mocking Allâh, His Religion, or His Messenger (ﷺ). Allâh the Most High said:

$$\text{﴿ وَلَئِن سَأَلْتَهُمْ لَيَقُولُنَّ إِنَّمَا كُنَّا نَخُوضُ وَنَلْعَبُ قُلْ أَبِٱللَّهِ وَءَايَٰتِهِۦ وَرَسُولِهِۦ كُنتُمْ تَسْتَهْزِءُونَ ۝ لَا تَعْتَذِرُوا۟ قَدْ كَفَرْتُم بَعْدَ إِيمَٰنِكُمْ ﴾}$$

"And if thou question them, they will most surely say, 'We were only talking idly and jesting.' Say, 'Was it Allâh and His Signs and His Messenger that you mocked at? Make ye no excuses. You certainly disbelieved after believing.'" [At-Tawbah: 65-66]

Mocking is one of the worst ways of degrading Allâh, His religion, and His Messenger (ﷺ). It is the worst form of belittling and scorning. Glorified is Allâh from that.

The Fifth Category: Insulting Allâh, the Most High, or insulting His religion, His Messenger by defaming and denigrating them, mentioning them with malicious intent in order to attack their reputation by way of cursing, distorting, and the likes. Sheikh Al-Islâm Ibn Taymiyyah, may Allâh have mercy on him, said: "Whoever insults Allâh and His Messenger, has become a disbeliever inwardly and outwardly, whether he believes that it is forbidden for him or not and whether he is unmindful of the creed or not. Our companions, (i.e. the scholars of the Hanbalî School of Thought) say: 'Whoever insults Allâh disbelieves, whether he is serious or joking. This is the correct opinion in this subject matter.

It is also reported from Ishâq bin Râhûyah that: 'The Muslims have agreed that whoever insults Allâh or His Messenger or denies anything from the revelations of Allâh, he disbelieves even if he believes in what Allâh (ﷻ) has revealed." [The Unsheathed Sword against the One who Insults the Messenger page 512, 513]

Likewise the Sheikh said: "Insulting other Messengers takes the same ruling as insulting our Prophet (ﷺ). Therefore whoever insults any Messenger from among the Messengers that are mentioned by name in the Qur'ân or described in the prophetic tradition by their actions or statements has disbelieved." [Previous Source page 565]

But as for insulting other than the Prophets, if the intention behind it is to insult the Prophet (ﷺ) then it is disbelief, such as insulting the Prophet's (ﷺ) Companions. (This is) because the Companions imitate and follow the Prophet (ﷺ). (The same applies to) to anyone who accuses one of the wives of the Prophet (ﷺ) of adultery (he has disbelieved). That is because insulting them is insulting the Prophet (ﷺ). Allâh the Most High said:

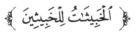

"The Evil women are for the Evil men" [An-Nûr: 26]

The Sixth Category: Judging by other than what Allâh has revealed, believing that it is the closest to the truth, that it is more beneficial to the people than judging with what Allâh has revealed, believing that it is equal to Allâh's Judgment, or even that it is permissible to judge by. Such individuals have disbelieved, based on Allâh's statement:

$$\{ وَمَن لَّمْ يَحْكُم بِمَآ أَنزَلَ ٱللَّهُ فَأُو۟لَٰٓئِكَ هُمُ ٱلْكَٰفِرُونَ ۝ \}$$

"Whoever did not judge by what Allâh revealed are indeed the disbelievers" [Al-Mâidah: 44]

If (an individual) believes that judging by other than what Allâh has revealed is better than Allâh's Judgment, he has disbelieved. That is because he has rejected Allâh's statement:

$$\{ وَمَنْ أَحْسَنُ مِنَ ٱللَّهِ حُكْمًا لِّقَوْمٍ يُوقِنُونَ ۝ \}$$

"Who is better than Allâh in Judgment for a people who have firm faith" [Al-Mâidah: 50]

And His statement:

$$\{ وَمَن لَّمْ يَحْكُم بِمَآ أَنزَلَ ٱللَّهُ فَأُو۟لَٰٓئِكَ هُمُ ٱلْكَٰفِرُونَ ۝ \}$$

"Whoever did not judge by what Allâh has revealed, then they are the disbelievers" [Al-Mâidah: 44]

The Seventh Category-Hypocrisy: When a person pretends in front of the people with his actions and statements, proclaiming that he is a Muslim, while concealing disbelief in his heart. Allâh said:

$$\{ إِنَّ ٱلْمُنَٰفِقِينَ فِى ٱلدَّرْكِ ٱلْأَسْفَلِ مِنَ ٱلنَّارِ وَلَن تَجِدَ لَهُمْ نَصِيرًا ۝ \}$$

Sittings During the Blessed Month of Ramaḍān رَمَضَان

"Indeed the hypocrites shall be in the lowest depths of the Fire; and thou shalt find no helper for them" [An-Nisâ: 145]

Hypocrisy is worse than the previously mentioned (categories). This is why the punishment of hypocrisy is the worst punishment. They will be in the lowest depths of the hellfire, because their disbelief combines between disbelief, deceit, and making mockery of Allâh, His verses, and His Messengers.

Allâh (ﷻ) said about the hypocrites:

﴿ وَمِنَ ٱلنَّاسِ مَن يَقُولُ ءَامَنَّا بِٱللَّهِ وَبِٱلْيَوْمِ ٱلْأَخِرِ وَمَا هُم بِمُؤْمِنِينَ ۝ يُخَٰدِعُونَ ٱللَّهَ وَٱلَّذِينَ ءَامَنُوا۟ وَمَا يَخْدَعُونَ إِلَّا أَنفُسَهُمْ وَمَا يَشْعُرُونَ ۝ فِى قُلُوبِهِم مَّرَضٌ فَزَادَهُمُ ٱللَّهُ مَرَضًا ۖ وَلَهُمْ عَذَابٌ أَلِيمٌۢ بِمَا كَانُوا۟ يَكْذِبُونَ ۝ وَإِذَا قِيلَ لَهُمْ لَا تُفْسِدُوا۟ فِى ٱلْأَرْضِ قَالُوٓا۟ إِنَّمَا نَحْنُ مُصْلِحُونَ ۝ أَلَآ إِنَّهُمْ هُمُ ٱلْمُفْسِدُونَ وَلَٰكِن لَّا يَشْعُرُونَ ۝ وَإِذَا قِيلَ لَهُمْ ءَامِنُوا۟ كَمَآ ءَامَنَ ٱلنَّاسُ قَالُوٓا۟ أَنُؤْمِنُ كَمَآ ءَامَنَ ٱلسُّفَهَآءُ ۗ أَلَآ إِنَّهُمْ هُمُ ٱلسُّفَهَآءُ وَلَٰكِن لَّا يَعْلَمُونَ ۝ وَإِذَا لَقُوا۟ ٱلَّذِينَ ءَامَنُوا۟ قَالُوٓا۟ ءَامَنَّا وَإِذَا خَلَوْا۟ إِلَىٰ شَيَٰطِينِهِمْ قَالُوٓا۟ إِنَّا مَعَكُمْ إِنَّمَا نَحْنُ مُسْتَهْزِءُونَ ۝ ٱللَّهُ يَسْتَهْزِئُ بِهِمْ وَيَمُدُّهُمْ فِى طُغْيَٰنِهِمْ يَعْمَهُونَ ۝ ﴾

"And of the people there are some who say, 'We believe in Allâh, and the Last Day' while they are not believers at all. They think to deceive Allâh and those who believe, but they deceive none but themselves; only they perceive it not. In their hearts is a disease, so Allâh has increased their disease, and for them is a grievous punishment because they lied. And when it is said to them, 'Create not disorder in the earth,' they say 'We are only promoters of peace.' Beware! It is surely they who create disorder, but they do not perceive it. And when it is said to them, 'Believe as other people have believed,' they say, 'Shall we believe as the fools have believed?'. Remember! It is surely they that are the fools, but they do not know. And when they meet those who believe, they say, 'We believe;' but when they are alone with their devils they say, 'We are with you, We were only mocking.' Allâh mocks at them and gives them increase in their transgression, wandering blindly." [Al-Baqarah: 8-15]

Hypocrisy Has Many Signs:

From the signs of hypocrisy is having doubt in what Allâh revealed, even if this person pretends to be a believer in front of the people. Allâh the Most High said:

$$\text{﴿ إِنَّمَا يَسْتَـٔذِنُكَ ٱلَّذِينَ لَا يُؤْمِنُونَ بِٱللَّهِ وَٱلْيَوْمِ ٱلْءَاخِرِ وَٱرْتَابَتْ قُلُوبُهُمْ فَهُمْ فِى رَيْبِهِمْ يَتَرَدَّدُونَ ۝ ﴾}$$

"Only those will ask leave of you to be exempted who do not believe in Allâh and the Last Day, and whose hearts are full of doubt, and in their doubt they waver" [At-Tawbah: 45]

From the signs of hypocrisy is to dislike Allâh and His Messenger's Judgment. Allâh states:

$$\text{﴿ أَلَمْ تَرَ إِلَى ٱلَّذِينَ يَزْعُمُونَ أَنَّهُمْ ءَامَنُوا۟ بِمَآ أُنزِلَ إِلَيْكَ وَمَآ أُنزِلَ مِن قَبْلِكَ يُرِيدُونَ أَن يَتَحَاكَمُوٓا۟ إِلَى ٱلطَّـٰغُوتِ وَقَدْ أُمِرُوٓا۟ أَن يَكْفُرُوا۟ بِهِۦ وَيُرِيدُ ٱلشَّيْطَـٰنُ أَن يُضِلَّهُمْ ضَلَـٰلًۢا بَعِيدًا ۝ وَإِذَا قِيلَ لَهُمْ تَعَالَوْا۟ إِلَىٰ مَآ أَنزَلَ ٱللَّهُ وَإِلَى ٱلرَّسُولِ رَأَيْتَ ٱلْمُنَـٰفِقِينَ يَصُدُّونَ عَنكَ صُدُودًا ۝ ﴾}$$

Sittings During the Blessed Month of Ramaḍān رَمَضَان

"Hast thou not seen those who assert that they believe in what has been revealed to you and what has been revealed before you? They desire to seek judgment from the Evil One, although they were commanded not to obey him. And Satan desires to lead them far astray. And when it is said to them, 'Come you to what Allâh has sent down and to His Messenger,' you see the hypocrites turn away from you with aversion" [An-Nisâ: 60-61]

From the signs of hypocrisy is to dislike seeing the Muslims victorious, but rather being happy at (news of their) defeat. Allâh said:

$$\text{إِن تُصِبْكَ حَسَنَةٌ تَسُؤْهُمْ وَإِن تُصِبْكَ مُصِيبَةٌ يَقُولُواْ قَدْ أَخَذْنَآ أَمْرَنَا مِن قَبْلُ وَيَتَوَلَّواْ وَّهُمْ فَرِحُونَ ۝}$$

"If good befalls you, it grieves you, but if a misfortune befalls you, they say, 'We had indeed taken our precaution beforehand.' And they turn away rejoicing" [At-Tawbah: 50]

And His statement:

$$\text{هَٰٓأَنتُمْ أُوْلَآءِ تُحِبُّونَهُمْ وَلَا يُحِبُّونَكُمْ وَتُؤْمِنُونَ بِٱلْكِتَٰبِ كُلِّهِۦ وَإِذَا لَقُوكُمْ قَالُوٓاْ ءَامَنَّا وَإِذَا خَلَوْاْ عَضُّواْ عَلَيْكُمُ ٱلْأَنَامِلَ مِنَ ٱلْغَيْظِ قُلْ مُوتُواْ بِغَيْظِكُمْ إِنَّ ٱللَّهَ عَلِيمٌۢ بِذَاتِ ٱلصُّدُورِ ۝ إِن تَمْسَسْكُمْ حَسَنَةٌ تَسُؤْهُمْ وَإِن تُصِبْكُمْ سَيِّئَةٌ يَفْرَحُواْ بِهَا وَإِن تَصْبِرُواْ وَتَتَّقُواْ لَا يَضُرُّكُمْ كَيْدُهُمْ شَيْـًٔا إِنَّ ٱللَّهَ بِمَا يَعْمَلُونَ مُحِيطٌ ۝}$$

"Behold! You are those who love them, but they love you not. And you believe in the Book, all of it. When they meet you, they say, 'We believe;' but when they are alone, they bite their fingertips at you for rage. Say, 'Perish in your rage. Surely Allâh has full knowledge of what is hidden in your breast.' If anything good befalls you, it grieves them; and if an evil afflicts you, they rejoice thereat. But if you be steadfast and righteous, their designs will not harm you at all; surely Allâh encompasses all that they do" [Āli 'Imrân: 119-120]

From the signs of hypocrisy: creating turmoil between the Muslims, dividing their unity, and desiring to see them in that state. Allâh, the Most High, states:

$$\{ لَوْ خَرَجُواْ فِيكُم مَّا زَادُوكُمْ إِلَّا خَبَالًا وَلَأَوْضَعُواْ خِلَٰلَكُمْ يَبْغُونَكُمُ ٱلْفِتْنَةَ وَفِيكُمْ سَمَّٰعُونَ لَهُمْ ۗ وَٱللَّهُ عَلِيمٌۢ بِٱلظَّٰلِمِينَ ٤٧ \}$$

"Had they gone forth with you, they would have added to you naught but trouble, and would have hurried to and fro in your midst, seeking to sow discord among you. And there are among you those who would listen to you so as to convey information to them. And Allâh well knows the wrongdoers" [At-Tawbah: 47]

From the signs of hypocrisy: is to show love to the enemies of Al-Islâm and the leaders of disbelief, praising them and spreading their opinions which oppose the teachings of Al-Islâm. Allâh, the Most High, said:

$$\{ ۞ أَلَمْ تَرَ إِلَى ٱلَّذِينَ تَوَلَّوْاْ قَوْمًا غَضِبَ ٱللَّهُ عَلَيْهِم مَّا هُم مِّنكُمْ وَلَا مِنْهُمْ وَيَحْلِفُونَ عَلَى ٱلْكَذِبِ وَهُمْ يَعْلَمُونَ ١٤ \}$$

"Do you not see those who take for friends a people with whom Allâh is angry? They are neither of you nor of them, and they swear to falsehood knowingly" [Al-Mujâdilah: 14]

From the signs of hypocrisy is carping at the believers and defaming them in their acts of worship. Allâh, the Most High, said:

﴿ ٱلَّذِينَ يَلْمِزُونَ ٱلْمُطَّوِّعِينَ مِنَ ٱلْمُؤْمِنِينَ فِى ٱلصَّدَقَٰتِ وَٱلَّذِينَ لَا يَجِدُونَ إِلَّا جُهْدَهُمْ فَيَسْخَرُونَ مِنْهُمْ سَخِرَ ٱللَّهُ مِنْهُمْ وَلَهُمْ عَذَابٌ أَلِيمٌ ۝ ﴾

"These hypocrites are those who find fault with such of the believers as give freely in charity and with such as find nothing to give except the earnings of their toil. So they deride them. Allâh shall punish them for their derision, and for them is a grievous punishment" [At-Tawbah: 79]

They criticize the believers who strive hard in their worship and accuse them of not being sincerity. They criticize the believers who are unable to strive hard [due to poverty or sickness] and accuse them of remissness.

From the signs of hypocrisy: is arrogance towards answering the call of the believers due to them belittling (and looking down upon) them and having doubt in them. Allâh said:

﴿ وَإِذَا قِيلَ لَهُمْ تَعَالَوْا۟ يَسْتَغْفِرْ لَكُمْ رَسُولُ ٱللَّهِ لَوَّوْا۟ رُءُوسَهُمْ وَرَأَيْتَهُمْ يَصُدُّونَ وَهُم مُّسْتَكْبِرُونَ ۝ ﴾

"And when it is said to them 'Come, that the Messenger of Allâh ask forgiveness for you,' they turn their heads aside, and you see them holding back disdainfully while they are big with pride." [Al-Munâfiqûn: 5]

From the signs of hypocrisy: is being lazy in carrying out the prayers. Allâh said:

﴿ إِنَّ ٱلْمُنَٰفِقِينَ يُخَٰدِعُونَ ٱللَّهَ وَهُوَ خَٰدِعُهُمْ وَإِذَا قَامُوٓا۟ إِلَى ٱلصَّلَوٰةِ قَامُوا۟ كُسَالَىٰ يُرَآءُونَ ٱلنَّاسَ وَلَا يَذْكُرُونَ ٱللَّهَ إِلَّا قَلِيلًا ﴾ (١٤٢)

"The hypocrites seek to deceive Allâh, but it is Allâh who deceives them for their deception. And when they stand up for Prayer, they stand up lazily and to be seen of men and they don't remember Allâh but little" [An-Nisâ: 142]

The Prophet (ﷺ) said:

أثقلُ الصلاةِ على المنافقينَ صلاةُ العشاءِ وصلاةُ الفجرِ

"The most difficult prayers for the hypocrite are the 'Ishâ and Fajr Prayer." [Collected by Al-Bukhârî and Muslim]

From the signs of hypocrisy is to harm Allâh, His Messenger, and the believers. Allâh, the Most High, said:

﴿ وَمِنْهُمُ ٱلَّذِينَ يُؤْذُونَ ٱلنَّبِيَّ وَيَقُولُونَ هُوَ أُذُنٌ قُلْ أُذُنُ خَيْرٍ لَّكُمْ يُؤْمِنُ بِٱللَّهِ وَيُؤْمِنُ لِلْمُؤْمِنِينَ وَرَحْمَةٌ لِّلَّذِينَ ءَامَنُوا۟ مِنكُمْ وَٱلَّذِينَ يُؤْذُونَ رَسُولَ ٱللَّهِ لَهُمْ عَذَابٌ أَلِيمٌ ﴾ (٦١)

"And among them are those who annoy the Prophet and say, 'He is all ears.' Say, 'His giving ear to all is for your good; he believes in Allâh and is true to the Faithful, and is a mercy for those of you who believe.' And those who annoy the Messenger of Allâh shall have a grievous punishment" [At-Tawbah: 61]

Likewise His statement the Most High:

﴿ إِنَّ ٱلَّذِينَ يُؤْذُونَ ٱللَّهَ وَرَسُولَهُۥ لَعَنَهُمُ ٱللَّهُ فِى ٱلدُّنْيَا وَٱلْءَاخِرَةِ وَأَعَدَّ لَهُمْ عَذَابًا مُّهِينًا ۝ وَٱلَّذِينَ يُؤْذُونَ ٱلْمُؤْمِنِينَ وَٱلْمُؤْمِنَٰتِ بِغَيْرِ مَا ٱكْتَسَبُوا۟ فَقَدِ ٱحْتَمَلُوا۟ بُهْتَٰنًا وَإِثْمًا مُّبِينًا ۝ ﴾

"Verily, those who malign Allâh and His Messenger Allâh has cursed them in this world and in the Hereafter, and has prepared for them an abasing punishment. And those, who malign believing men and believing women for what they have not earned, shall bear the guilt of a calumny and a manifest sin" [Al-Ahzâb: 57-58]

The above-mentioned are some of the signs of hypocrisy. We mentioned them in order that we will be cautious (as to not be described by any of these characteristics) and (so that we will) purify our souls from them.

O Allâh! Grant us refuge from hypocrisy, and sustain us with actualizing faith in the manner that pleases You. Forgive us, our parents, and all the Muslims. O Lord of the worlds.

May Allâh shower His blessings on our Prophet Muhammad (ﷺ), His family, and all his Companions.

المجلس السابع و العشرون
The Twenty Seventh Sitting
The Second Category of Things which Lead an Individual to Enter the Hell-Fire (Temporarily)

All praise and thanks are due to Allâh, the One Who, with His ability, created the creatures, showed them the wonders of His wisdom within themselves, and proves His oneness with His signs. He decreed punishment on the sinner because of his disobedience, and then invites him to repent and is graceful to him by accepting his repentance. Therefore respond to Allâh's Call and compete with one another towards His Paradise, He will forgive you your sins and will give you double reward from His mercy. I praise Him for the magnificence of His Attributes and the perfection of His Names. I thank Him for granting us success and bestowing His bounties on us. I further bear witness that none has the right to be worshipped but Allâh. (He is Alone) without a partner in His right to worshipped and and He is (alone) in His Lordship.

I also bear witness that Muhammad is His slave and His Messenger, the one who was sent to Allâh's creatures as a bringer of glad tidings of paradise to the believers and as a warner of the hellfire to the disbelievers. May Allâh shower His blessings on him and on his successor Abû Bakr, 'Umar the one who is famous for his strength and sternness against the disbelievers, 'Uthmân the one who has passed away in his test, 'Alî, the Prophet's Cousin and son-in-law, on the rest of his family, Companions, and whoever follows his footsteps and his tradition.

O My Brothers! In the previous class we mentioned many things that lead an individual to enter the hellfire and abide in it forever. And here we are, in this lecture, by Allâh's grace, we will mention a few reasons from the second category of things which cause a person to enter the hellfire temporarily:

The First Cause-Violating the rights of the parents: the father and the mother, by not fulfilling their rights which they have over you. For example, being disobedient to them, severing the ties between you and them, or harming them with statements or actions. Allâh, the Most High, said:

﴿ ۞ وَقَضَىٰ رَبُّكَ أَلَّا تَعْبُدُوٓا۟ إِلَّآ إِيَّاهُ وَبِٱلْوَٰلِدَيْنِ إِحْسَٰنًا ۚ إِمَّا يَبْلُغَنَّ عِندَكَ ٱلْكِبَرَ أَحَدُهُمَآ أَوْ كِلَاهُمَا فَلَا تَقُل لَّهُمَآ أُفٍّ وَلَا تَنْهَرْهُمَا وَقُل لَّهُمَا قَوْلًا كَرِيمًا ۝ وَٱخْفِضْ لَهُمَا جَنَاحَ ٱلذُّلِّ مِنَ ٱلرَّحْمَةِ وَقُل رَّبِّ ٱرْحَمْهُمَا كَمَا رَبَّيَانِى صَغِيرًا ۝ ﴾

"And your Lord has decreed that you worship none but Him. And that you be dutiful to your parents. If one of them or both of them attain old age in your life, say not to them a word of disrespect, nor shout at them but address them in terms of honor. And lower unto them the wing of submission and humility through mercy, and say: 'My Lord! Bestow on them Your Mercy as they did bring me up when I was small.'" [Al- Isrâ: 23-24]

The Prophet (ﷺ) said:

ثلاثةٌ قد حرَّمَ اللهُ عليهم الجنَّةَ: مدمنُ الخمرِ والعاقُّ لوالديهِ والدَّيُّوثُ الَّذي يُقِرُّ الخُبْثَ في أهلهِ

"There are three on whom Allâh forbade paradise: the alcoholic, the one who is undutiful to his parents, and the pimp, the one who allows his wife to do illicit (and evil) behavior." [Collected by Ahmad. Al-Albânî graded it Hasan, due to other narrations]

The Second Cause-severing the ties of kinship: This is when a man boycotts his family and stops giving them their financial and physical rights.

It is narrated by Jubayr bin Mut'im (ﷺ) that the Prophet (ﷺ) said:

لا يدخلُ الجنَّةَ قاطعٌ

"The one who severs (the family ties) will not enter paradise."
[Collected by Al-Bukhârî and Muslim]

It is also narrated by Abu Hurayrah (ﷺ) that the Prophet (ﷺ) said:

إنَّ الرَّحِمَ قامتْ فقالتْ لله عزَّ وجلَّ: هذا مقامُ العائذِ بكَ من القطيعةِ. قال: نَعَمْ أما ترضَيْنَ أن أَصِلَ مَن وَصَلَكِ، وأقطعَ مَنْ قطعكِ؟ قالت: بَلَى. قال: فذلِكَ لكِ"، ثمَّ قال رسولُ الله صلَّى اللهُ عَلَيْهِ وَسَلَّمَ: "اقرؤوا إن شئتُمْ

﴿ فَهَلْ عَسَيْتُمْ إِن تَوَلَّيْتُمْ أَن تُفْسِدُوا۟ فِى ٱلْأَرْضِ وَتُقَطِّعُوٓا۟ أَرْحَامَكُمْ ۝ أُو۟لَٰٓئِكَ ٱلَّذِينَ لَعَنَهُمُ ٱللَّهُ فَأَصَمَّهُمْ وَأَعْمَىٰٓ أَبْصَٰرَهُمْ ۝ ﴾

"The womb said to Allâh (ﷺ): '(O Allâh) at this place I seek refuge with you from all those who sever me (i.e. sever the ties of Kith and kin).' Allâh said, 'Yes, won't you be pleased that I will keep good relations with the one who will keep good relations with you, and I will sever the relation with the one who will sever the relations with you?' It said, 'Yes, O my Lord.' Allâh said, 'Then that is for you.' Allâh's Messenger (ﷺ) added: "Read (in the Qur'an) if you wish, Allâh's statement: 'Would you then, if you were given the authority, do mischief in the land and sever your ties of kinship?' (Muhammad: 22-23)" [Collected by Al-Bukhârî and Muslim]

It is very unfortunate that today many Muslims have neglected to fulfill their parents' rights and the family ties. (Rather they) sever the ties. Some of them justify this act by saying that their families do not keep *their* ties. However this excuse is unacceptable, because if we only keep the ties of those who keep their ties with us then we are not doing it for the sake of Allâh, rather it is only us paying them back (i.e. reciprocating the good they did). As it is narrated by 'Abdullâh bin 'Amr bin 'Âs (ﷺ) that the Prophet (ﷺ) said:

ليس الواصل بالمكافئ، ولكنَّ الواصل الَّذي إذا قُطِعَت رَحِمُه وَصَلَها

"The one who keeps the ties is not the one who only does it in return of what is done to him. Rather the one who keeps the ties is the one who when the people sever their ties with him he keeps (ties with them)." [Collected by Al-Bukhârî]

It is also narrated by Abû Hurayrah (ﷺ) that a man said: "O Messenger of Allâh I have family members whom I keep ties with them, but they sever the ties with me. I treat them with kindness but they harm me, and I am patient with them but they are mean to me. So the Prophet (ﷺ) said: 'If you are what you say you are to them, then it is as if you are filling up their mouths with hot ashes and Allâh will help you against them as long as you remain consistent upon that.'" [Collected by Muslim]

If he keeps his ties with them while they sever (ties with him), then for him will be a good end, and they will return back to keeping their ties with him if Allâh wants good for them.

The Third Cause-Consuming Interest. Allâh, the Most High said:

$$\text{﴿ يَٰٓأَيُّهَا ٱلَّذِينَ ءَامَنُواْ لَا تَأْكُلُواْ ٱلرِّبَوٰٓاْ أَضْعَٰفًا مُّضَٰعَفَةً وَٱتَّقُواْ ٱللَّهَ لَعَلَّكُمْ تُفْلِحُونَ ۝ وَٱتَّقُواْ ٱلنَّارَ ٱلَّتِيٓ أُعِدَّتْ لِلْكَٰفِرِينَ ۝ ﴾}$$

"O you who believe! Devour not interest involving multiple additions, and fear Allâh that you may prosper. And fear the Fire which has been prepared for the disbelievers" [Āli 'Imrân: 130-131]

As for those who persist upon consuming interest after Allâh's warning and His admonition has reached them, He has threatened to put them in the Hell-Fire.

$$\text{﴿ ٱلَّذِينَ يَأْكُلُونَ ٱلرِّبَوٰاْ لَا يَقُومُونَ إِلَّا كَمَا يَقُومُ ٱلَّذِى يَتَخَبَّطُهُ ٱلشَّيْطَٰنُ مِنَ ٱلْمَسِّ ذَٰلِكَ بِأَنَّهُمْ قَالُوٓاْ إِنَّمَا ٱلْبَيْعُ مِثْلُ ٱلرِّبَوٰاْ وَأَحَلَّ ٱللَّهُ ٱلْبَيْعَ وَحَرَّمَ ٱلرِّبَوٰاْ فَمَن جَآءَهُۥ مَوْعِظَةٌ مِّن رَّبِّهِۦ فَٱنتَهَىٰ فَلَهُۥ مَا سَلَفَ وَأَمْرُهُۥٓ إِلَى ٱللَّهِ وَمَنْ عَادَ فَأُوْلَٰٓئِكَ أَصْحَٰبُ ٱلنَّارِ هُمْ فِيهَا خَٰلِدُونَ ۝ ﴾}$$

"Those who devour interest do not rise except as rises one whom Satan has smitten with insanity. That is because they say, 'Trade also is like interest;' whereas Allâh has made trade lawful and has made interest unlawful. So he to whom an admonition comes from his Lord and he desist, then will that which he received in the pass be his; and his affair rests with Allâh. And those who revert to it, they are the inmates of the Fire; therein shall they abide" [Al-Baqarah: 275]

The Fourth Cause-Devouring the wealth of the orphans whether they are males or females and misusing it. Allâh, the Most High said:

﴿ إِنَّ ٱلَّذِينَ يَأْكُلُونَ أَمْوَٰلَ ٱلْيَتَٰمَىٰ ظُلْمًا إِنَّمَا يَأْكُلُونَ فِى بُطُونِهِمْ نَارًا ۖ وَسَيَصْلَوْنَ سَعِيرًا ۝ ﴾

"Surely they who devour the property of the orphans unjustly, only swallow fire into their bellies, and they shall burn in a blazing fire" [An-Nisâ: 10]

An orphan is the one who lost his father before reaching puberty.

The Fifth Cause-False witness. ('Abdullâh) bin 'Umar (ﷺ) narrated that the Prophet (ﷺ) said: **"The bearer of false witness will not take a step until Allâh necessitates on him that he enters the Hell-Fire"** [Ibn Mâjah narrated this hadîth, likewise Al-Hâkim. **Important Note:** Al-Albânî graded this narration to be fabricated in Ad-Da'îfah no.1259]

False witness is to testify concerning what you do not know, or to testify concerning something while knowing that the truth is the opposite of what you are saying. Testimony is not permissible except if the testifier knows what he is testifying to. And in another narration, he (ﷺ) said to a man: **"Can you see the sun? He said: 'yes.' He then said to him: 'Let your testimony be like the way you can witness the sun, otherwise do not testify at all.'"** [Collected by Al-Bayhaqî and Al-Hâkim with another wording]

The Sixth Cause-Taking bribes when judging between the people. It is narrated by 'Abdullâh bin 'Amr (ﷺ) that the Prophet (ﷺ) said: **"The Râshî (i.e. the giver of bribery) and the Murtashî (i.e. the receiver of bribery) are both in the Hell-Fire."** [Collected by At-Tabarânî and others. Al-Albânî graded it to be weak in Daî'f Al-Jâmi']

He (i.e. Ibn Athîr) said in An-Nihâyah: "The "Râshî" which means the briber, is the one who gives to whoever helps him upon his falsehood, and the "Murtashî" is the one who takes the bribe. They are those intended in the hadîth, but as for whatever (money) is given to help receive your due right or repel oppression, this will not be considered bribery."

The Seventh Cause-The Ghamûs Oath (i.e. False oath or Perjury) It is narrated by Al-Hârith bin Mâlik (ﷺ) who said, I heard the Prophet (ﷺ) saying:

مَنَ اقتطعَ مالَ أخيهِ بيمينٍ فاجرةٍ فلْيَتَبَوَّأَ مقعدَه من النارِ لِيُبَلِّغْ شاهدُكم غائبَكم " مرَّتَيْنِ أو ثلاثاً

"'Whoever swears falsely in order to oppressively take the wealth of his brother, should take his sitting place in the hell-fire. Let those who are present convey the message to those who are absent.' He repeated it twice or three times." [Collected by Ahmad and Hâkim. Al-Albânî graded it to be authentic in Sahîh At-Targhîb]

It is called ghamûs (i.e. literally means plunging or sinking) because it plunges the one who took the oath in to sin and plunges him into the Hell-Fire. And there is no difference between him swearing falsely on his claim in order to receive judgment on his side or swearing falsely on something that he denies in order to be judged for his innocence.

The Eighth Cause-Oppressively judging between the people without knowledge, while taking sides: It is narrated by Buraydah bin Al-Husayn (ﷺ) that the Prophet (ﷺ) said:

القضاةُ ثلاثةٌ: واحدٌ في الجنّةِ واثنانِ في النارِ، فأمَّا الَّذي في الجنةِ فرجلٌ عرفَ الحقَ وقضى به، ورجلٌ عرفَ الحقَّ فجارَ في الحكمِ فهو في النارِ، ورجلٌ قضَى للناسِ على جهلٍ فهو في النارِ

"There are three types of judges. One of them will be in paradise and two will be in the hellfire. As for the one who will be in Paradise, it is a man who knows the truth and judges by it. And the two who will go to the hell-fire are a man who knows the truth but is wrongful in his judgment; he will be in the hellfire. And a man who judges between the people upon ignorance, he will also be in the hell-fire." [Collected by Abû Dâwûd, At-Tirmidhî and Ibn Mâjah. Al-Albânî graded it to be authentic in Sahîh Abî Dâwûd]

The Ninth Cause-Cheating the subjects (i.e. the citizens) and not putting their interest in to consideration, in such a way that the leader does things which are not beneficial to the subjects and not in their interest. The proof for this is the narration of Ma'qal bin Yasâr (ﷺ) who said, "I heard the Prophet (ﷺ) saying:

مَا مِنْ عبدٍ يسترْعِيه الله على رعيةٍ يموتُ يوم يموت وهو غاشٌ لِرَعيَّته إلاَّ حرَّمَ الله عليه الجنَّةَ

"There is no slave whom Allâh will put to be in charge of subjects and then dies while cheating them, except that Allâh will make the Paradise forbidden for him." [Collected by Al-Bukhârî and Muslim]

This includes the responsibility of a man over his family, a ruler over his subjects, and other than them. The proof for this is the narration of 'Abdullâh bin 'Umar who said, "I heard the Messenger of Allâh (ﷺ) saying:

كُلُّكُمْ راعٍ ومسؤولٌ عن رعيَّته، الإمامُ راعٍ ومسؤولٌ عن رعيَّته، والرجلُ راعٍ في أهلِه ومسؤولٌ عن رعيَّته، والمرأةُ راعية في بيتزوجها

وَمَسْؤُولَةٌ عَنْ رَعِيَّتِهَا، وَالْخَادِمُ رَاعٍ فِي مَالِ سَيِّدِهِ وَمَسْؤُولٌ عَنْ رَعِيَّتِهِ،
وَكُلُّكُمْ رَاعٍ وَمَسْؤُولٌ عَنْ رَعِيَّتِهِ

"All of you are shepherds and all of you are responsible for your flocks. The ruler is a shepherd and is responsible for his flock. A man is a shepherd over his family and is responsible for his flock. A woman is a shepherd in her husband's home and is responsible for her flock. A servant is a shepherd over the wealth of his master and is responsible for his flock. All of you are shepherds and all of you are responsible (i.e. you will be questioned on the Day of Judgment about these responsibility) for your flocks." [Collected by Al-Bukhârî and Muslim]

The Tenth Cause-Making pictures of living things, including humans and animals: The proof for this is the narration of 'Abdullâh bin 'Abbâs (ﷺ) who said, "I heard the Prophet (ﷺ) saying:

كُلُّ مُصَوِّرٍ فِي النَّارِ يَجْعَلُ لَهُ بِكُلِّ صُورَةٍ صَوَّرَهَا نَفْسًا فَتُعَذِّبُهُ فِي جَهَنَّمَ

"All picture makers will be in the Hell-Fire. For each picture that he made, a soul will be made for him and it will punish him in the Hell-Fire." [Collected by Al-Bukhârî and Muslim]

In the narration of Al-Bukhârî it says:

مَنْ صَوَّرَ صُورَةً فَإِنَّ اللهَ مُعَذِّبُهُ حَتَّى يَنْفُخَ فِيهَا الرُّوحَ وَلَيْسَ بِنَافِخٍ فِيهَا أَبَدًا

"Whoever made a picture, Allâh will punish him till he blows a spirit in it, but he will not be able to do so." [Collected by Al-Bukhârî]

As for making pictures of trees, plants, grains and their likes from among the things which Allâh created, there is nothing wrong with that, according to the statement of the majority of the scholars. However some of the scholars also prohibited that as well. This is based on the narration of Abû Hurayrah (ﷺ), (where he said), "I heard the Messenger of Allâh (ﷺ) saying: "Allâh said:

ومَنْ أَظْلَمُ مِمَّن ذهبَ يَخلقُ كخلقي فَلْيَخْلُقوا ذرَّةً أَوْ لِيخلقوا حبةً أو شَعِيرةً

"Who is more sinful than the one who tries to create like my creation? Let them create an atom, let them create a seed, or let them create barley." [Collected by Al-Bukhârî]

The Eleventh Cause: What is narrated by Hârithah bin Wahb who said that the Prophet (ﷺ) said:

ألا أخبركُم بأهل النارِ؟ كلُّ عُتُلٍّ جَوَّاظٍ مستكبرٍ

"Shall I not inform you of the people of the Hell-Fire? It is every stonehearted (who does not lean to the truth and is not lenient to the creatures), and every selfish and stingy person (who takes but does not give), and every arrogant individual (who rejects the truth, belittles the people and thinks he is better than others and that his opinion is more correct than the truth). [Collected by Al-Bukhârî and Muslim]

The Twelfth Cause-Using the utensils of gold and silver for eating and drinking, for both men and women. It is narrated from Umm Salamah, May Allâh be pleased with her, that the Prophet (ﷺ) said:

الذي يشربُ في آنية الفضة إنما تُجَرْجِرُ في بطنه نارَ جهنم

"The one who drinks from silver utensils is only dragging the Hell-Fire in his stomach." [Collected by Al-Bukhârî]

In the narration of Muslim it says: "The one who *eats* or drinks from the gold and silver utensils is only dragging the hell-fire in his stomach." [Collected by Muslim]

And on the authority of 'Abdullâh bin 'Abbâs (ﷺ), who reported: "That the Messenger (ﷺ) saw a man wearing a gold ring on his hand. The Prophet (ﷺ) pulled it off and threw it away, saying: 'One of you is aiming for live coal from Hell, and wearing it on his hand.' It was said to the man after the Prophet (ﷺ) departed, 'Take your ring and get some type of benefit from it.' At that point (the man) said, 'I would never take this ring, when the Messenger has thrown it away.'" [Collected by Muslim, Hadith 5209]

Be careful My Brothers of everything that leads to the hellfire. Take the means that will keep you far away from the hellfire, in order that you can be successful (in obtaining) the home of perpetuity. And know that this world is a little enjoyment which will quickly vanish and be over. So pray to your Lord to keep you firm upon the truth until death reaches you. (Ask Allâh) to resurrect you amongst those whom He has bestowed His favor upon, from among the believing men and women.

O Allâh keep us firm upon the truth and take our lives while we are (firmly) established upon it. (O Allâh), with Your mercy, forgive us, our parents, and all the Muslims. You are the Most Merciful. May Allâh shower His mercy and blessings on our Prophet Muhammad (ﷺ), his family, and all his companions.

المجلس الثامن و العشرون
The Twenty Eighth Sitting:
The Zakât of Fitr

All praise are due to Allâh, the All-Knowing, the All-Wise, the Most High, The Great. He created everything and determined its proper measure. He perfected His legislations with His infinite wisdom as a clarification to His slaves and as an enlightenment for them. I praise Him for His Perfect Attributes, and I thank Him for His out flowing bounties. I bear witness that none has the right to be worshipped but Allâh Alone without a partner. To Him belongs the sovereignty and to Him belongs the praise. He is able to do all things. I further bear witness that Muhammad (ﷺ) is His slave and His Messenger, the giver of glad tidings and a warner. May Allâh shower His blessings and mercy on him, his family members, his companions, and whoever follows their footstep till the Day of Return.

O My Brothers: Indeed your blessed month is bidding you farewell, and it is not left from it but a short period of time. Therefore whoever finds himself upon good; he should be grateful to Allâh. And whoever finds himself to be neglectful; he should repent to Allâh and ask forgiveness from his Lord for his negligence. For indeed seeking forgiveness before death is acceptable.

O my brothers! Allâh (ﷺ) has legislated that you give the Zakâtul-fitr (i.e. **the charity that you give to the poor upon completing the month of Ramadân.**) (It should be given) before the 'Eîd prayer at the conclusion of this month of yours. Therefore (in this sitting) we shall address its ruling, wisdom, what to give, its quantity, when is it obligatory to give out the zakât, and where do you give it.

Beginning with its ruling: it is obligatory. The Prophet (ﷺ) prescribed it on the Muslims, and whatever the Prophet (ﷺ) prescribed or commanded us with is similar to whatever Allâh prescribed and commanded us with. The proof for this is Allâh's statement:

$$﴿ مَّن يُطِعِ ٱلرَّسُولَ فَقَدْ أَطَاعَ ٱللَّهَ ۖ وَمَن تَوَلَّىٰ فَمَا أَرْسَلْنَاكَ عَلَيْهِمْ حَفِيظًا ۝ ﴾$$

"Whoever obeys the Messenger has indeed obeyed Allâh, but whoever turns away, then We have not sent you as a watcher over them" [An-Nisâ: 90]

Likewise His statement:

$$﴿ وَمَن يُشَاقِقِ ٱلرَّسُولَ مِنۢ بَعْدِ مَا تَبَيَّنَ لَهُ ٱلْهُدَىٰ وَيَتَّبِعْ غَيْرَ سَبِيلِ ٱلْمُؤْمِنِينَ نُوَلِّهِۦ مَا تَوَلَّىٰ وَنُصْلِهِۦ جَهَنَّمَ ۖ وَسَآءَتْ مَصِيرًا ۝ ﴾$$

"And whoso opposes the Messenger after guidance has become manifest to him, and follows a way other than that of the believers, We shall let him pursue the way he is pursuing and shall cast him into Hell, and an evil destination it is" [An-Nisâ: 115]

Likewise Allâh's statement:

$$﴿ وَمَآ ءَاتَىٰكُمُ ٱلرَّسُولُ فَخُذُوهُ وَمَا نَهَىٰكُمْ عَنْهُ فَٱنتَهُوا۟ ﴾$$

"And whatsoever the Messenger gives you take it, and whatsoever he forbids you, abstain from it." [Al-Hashr: 7]

Zakâtul-Fitr is obligatory upon the adult, the young, the male and female, the free, and enslaved from the Muslims. 'Abdullâh bin 'Umar (ﷺ) said:

Sittings During the Blessed Month of Ramaḍân ﷺ

فرض رسول الله صلى الله عليه وسلم زكاة الفطر من رمضان صاعاً من تمرٍ أو صاعاً من شعيرٍ على العبدِ والحرِّ والذكر والأنثى والصغير والكبير من المسلمين

"The Prophet (ﷺ) has obligated the giving of Zakâtul-fitr of Ramadân, a sâ' of dates, or barley, on every slave and free male and female, adult and young from the Muslims" [Collected by Al-Bukhârî and Muslim]

Zakâtul-fitr is not obligatory (to be given on behalf of) the fetus, except if you choose to do so voluntarily. The Commander of the Believers, 'Uthmân (ﷺ) used to give out the zakâtul-fitr on behalf of the fetus inside the womb. Every Muslim must give it on behalf of himself and those whom he is responsible for, including his wife and relatives if they cannot give it out on their own. But if they can, then it is preferable for them to give it out on behalf of themselves because the command is directed to them.

It is obligatory only on those who have enough to cover their needs for the feast day and extra. If whatever was left after covering his needs of that day is less than a sâ' he can still give it away to the needy. This is based on Allâh's statement:

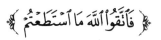

"Fear Allâh to the best of your ability" [At-Taghâbun: 16]

The Prophet (ﷺ)'s statement: **"If I command you with anything, do it to the best of your ability."** [Collected by Al-Bukhârî and Muslim]

But as for the wisdom behind its legislation, it is crystal clear. Giving away the charity is (way of) being kind to the poor and a (way of) preventing them from begging, in order that they may also participate with the rich in the celebration of that day with joy and happiness. Also giving the charity of that day is a sign of good character; it proves our love for consolation. Also it is purification for the fasting person from the shortcomings he committed during his fasting. It also proves our appreciation of Allâh's Bounties upon us by allowing us to complete the fasting of Ramadân, the standing in prayer at night, and carrying out whatever we could of righteous deeds in that blessed month.

It is narrated by Ibn Abbâs (ﷺ) that:

فرضَ رسولُ الله صلَّى اللهُ عليه وسلم زكاة الفطر طُهْرة للصائم من اللغوِ والرفثِ وطعمةً للمساكين، فمن أدَّاها قبل الصلاةِ فهي زكاةٌ مقبولة، ومن أداها بعد الصلاة فهي صدقة من الصدقات

"The Prophet (ﷺ) has prescribed the giving of the zakâtul-fitr as a purification for the fasting person from vanity and flirtation, as well as a nourishment for the poor. Therefore whoever gives it before the feast prayer it will be accepted from him as zakâtul-fitr. But whoever gives it after the prayer then it will be accepted from him as the regular charities." [Collected by Abû Dâwûd, Ibn Mâjah and Ad-Daraqutnî. Al-Albânî graded it to be Hasan in Sahîh Abî Dâwûd].

As for what (exactly) should be given for the zakât, it is whatever the sons of Âdam consume including dates, wheat, rice, barley, raisins, cheese, or other than the above-mentioned. It is narrated by Ibn Abbâs that:

فرضَ رسول الله صلى الله عليه وسلم زكاة الفطر من رمضان صاعا من تمر أو صاعاً من شعيرٍ

"The Prophet (ﷺ) has prescribed the giving of the zakâtul-fitr for the month of Ramadân from a sâ' of date or barley." [Collected by Al-Bukhârî and Muslim]

Barley was their food then. As Abû Sa'îd Al-Khudrî (ﷺ) used to say:

كنا نُخرِج يومَ الفطر في عهدِ النبيِّ صَلَّى اللَّهُ عَلَيْهِ وَسَلَّمَ صاعاً من طعامٍ وكان طعامُنَا الشعيرَ والزبيبَ والأقِطَ والتمر

"During the time of the Prophet (ﷺ) we used to give a sâ' of food, and our food then was barley, raisins, cheese, and dates." [Collected by Al-Bukhârî]

Therefore giving the food which is consumed by the cattle is not accepted, because (zakâtul-fitr should be) nourishment for the poor Muslims, and is not that which is given to cattle. Likewise if you give clothes, utensils, furniture, or anything besides the food (which is consumed by humans) it will not be accepted. This is because the Prophet (ﷺ) legislated on us to give from the food of the people. Therefore do not go beyond where the Messenger of Allâh has placed us.

Likewise giving cash instead of food will not be accepted, because it is contrary to what the Prophet (ﷺ) commanded us with. It is narrated that the Prophet (ﷺ) said:

مَنْ عَمِلَ عملاً ليس عليه أمرُنا فهو رَدٌّ

"Whoever does a deed which is not according to this affair of ours, it is rejected." [Collected by Muslim]

In another narration he (ﷺ) said:

مَنْ أَحْدَثَ فِي أَمْرِنَا هَذَا مَا لَيْسَ مِنْهُ فَهُوَ رَدٌّ

"Whoever innovates into this affair of ours, that which is not from it, it is rejected." [Collected by Al-Bukhârî]

This is because giving cash contradicts what the Companions (ﷺ) used to do. They used to give a sâ' of food. The Prophet (ﷺ) said:

عليكم بسُنَّتِي وسنةِ الخلفاءِ الراشدينَ المهديينَ من بعْدِي

"Hold on to my guidance and the guidance of the rightly guided successors after me" [Collected by Ahmad, Abû Dâwûd, Ibn Mâjah, and At-Tirmidhî. Al-Albânî graded it to be authentic in Sahîh Abî Dâwûd]

This is because zakâtul-fitr is a specified act of worship. Therefore it is not permissible to give other than what is specified, just us giving it before or after its specified times is also not accepted. The Prophet (ﷺ) has specified certain kinds of food that vary in their prices; if it were allowed to give cash instead of food, the Prophet (ﷺ) would have obligated on us a specific kind of food and whatever equals its price from the other kinds of food. Giving (the charity) in cash takes (zakâtul-Fitr) out of it being an open religious symbol seen by the people. Instead, it becomes a hidden charity. Giving a sâ' of food makes (this charity) open (i.e. public) and seen by the Muslims young and adult.

They will see it being measured, weighed, and distributed to the needy. It will become known amongst them, contrary to giving cash which remains hidden between the giver and the receiver.

As for the quantity of zakâtul-fitr, it is equal to the Prophetic sâ', whose measurement reaches 480 mithqâl of the pure barley and in grams it is equal to 2.04 kilos of the pure barley. That is because one mithqâl is equal to 4.25 grams. Therefore 480 mithqâl is equal to 2040 grams. [4]

(**An Important Rule of Thumb**): If a person wants to know the sâ' of the Prophet (ﷺ) he should measure 2.04 kilograms (i.e. 2040 grams) of barley and then place it in a bowl that fits it (such that the bowl is filled to the top with the barley). (After that) he can use the bowl as a tool of measuring (an accurate sâ' of other items as well).[5]

---

[4] The Measures of Zakât Al-Fitr based on various items

Semolina	2000 grams	Raisins	1640 grams
Flour	1400 grams	Couscous	1800 grams
Lentils	2100 grams	Couscous with big grains	2000 grams
Dried beans	2060 grams	Dates	1800 grams
Crushed peas	2240 grams	Chickpeas	2000 grams
Wheat	2040 grams	Rice	2300 grams

(Source: http://www.ferkous.com/site/eng/Zakat_fitr.php)

[5] **Editor's Note about the Prophetic Sâ'**: During the time of the Prophet (ﷺ) the sâ' was a specific means of measuring volume, known to the people. Similar to how in our times we know exactly what a 500ml measuring cup looks like; we use this measurement in our kitchens, restaurants, schools etc. A sâ' is a measure of volume, not weight. It equals approximately 3L (i.e. six 500ml measuring cups). So if a person were to fill up a 500 ml measuring cup with beans, rice, soup, cheese, cereal, barley, seeds, dates, ramen noodles, and then do that six times, it would come out to be 3liters or 1 sâ. Depending on the food item, the weight will be different, because all food has different weight. So instead of worrying about weight, focus on volume (i.e 3Liters of food for each person). Also, if a person has a 3liter bottle of soda and empties it out then fills it up with whatever item he is giving for zakât al-fitr, this would also suffice. **In Summary:** a

The mandatory time of giving the zakâtul-fitr is from sunset (the night before the 'Eîd prayer). Therefore, when the sun sets the night before the day of the 'Eîd it becomes obligatory on whoever fits the criteria, to give the zakâtul-fitr. Based on this, if a person passes away a minute before sunset, zakâtul-fitr will not be obligatory upon him. And if he dies a few minutes after sunset, he is required to pay the zakâtul-fitr because it has become obligatory upon him.

If a child is delivered a few minutes after the sunset, zakâtul-fitr will not be obligatory upon him. However there is nothing wrong with giving it out. On the other hand, if a child is born a few minutes before sunset, the night before the 'Eîd, zakâtul-fitr is obligatory on his behalf.

The obligatory time of giving out the zakâtul-fitr is after the sunset the night before the 'Eîd. This is because it is the time in which fasting the month of Ramadân ends and breaking the fast begins from that time. This is the reason why it is said, "zakâtul-fitr" (i.e the charity of breaking the fast of Ramadân), therefore the ruling of when to give the zakâtul-fitr is connected with that time.

There are two times in which a person can pay Zakâtul Fitr: the preferable time and the permissible time.

The preferable time begins the morning of the 'Eîd prayer, before the prayer (itself). The proof for this is the narration of Abû Sa'îd Al-Khudrî (ﷺ) who said:

كُنَّا نُخْرِجُ في عهدِ النبي صَلَّى اللَّهُ عَلَيْهِ وَسَلَّمَ يومَ الفطرِ صاعاً من طعامٍ

---

sâ' equals 3liters. A Mudd equals .75L. For more on this topic visit: (http://www.bakkah.net/en/zakat-fitr-measurements-saa-three-litres-mudd.htm)

"We used to give a sâ' of food at the time of the Prophet (ﷺ) on the 'Eîd day" [Collected by Al-Bukhârî].

It is also narrated by Ibn 'Umar (؆) that:

أن النبي صلَّى اللّهُ عَلَيْهِ وَسَلَّمَ أَمَرَ بزكاةِ الفطر أن تؤدَّى قبل خروج الناس إلى الصلاةِ

"The Prophet (ﷺ) commanded that the zakâtul-fitr should be given before the people go out for the prayer." [Collected by Al-Bukhârî and Muslim]

This is the reason why it is preferable to delay the 'Eîd prayer in order to allow people some time to give out the zakâtul-fitr.

As for the permissible time (to give Zakâtul Fitr), it begins a day or two before the day of the 'Eîd. It is narrated by Nâfi' who said: "Ibn 'Umar used to pay the zakât for every young and adult of his wards, even my children. And he used to give it to those who would take it, and they used to receive it a day or two before the 'Eîd."

It is not permissible to delay it until after the 'Eîd prayer. If a person delays it until after the 'Eîd prayer without a valid excuse, it will not be accepted from him because it is contrary to what the Prophet (ﷺ) commanded us with. The hadîth of Ibn Abbâs (؆) has been mentioned already regarding this, indicating that whoever gave it before the 'Eîd prayer it will be accepted from him as a zakât but whoever gives it after the prayer it will be written for him as a regular charity.

However if it is delayed for a valid excuse, there is nothing wrong with that. Examples of this is when the 'Eîd reaches a person while he is out of his home (land) and does not have with him the zakât or he (maybe) in a place where there is no one to take (the zakât). (Other valid excuses include the person) who receives sudden news about the arrival of the 'Eîd, and does not have enough time to give it before the 'Eîd prayer. (Another example) is the one who was depending on someone to give it on his behalf and then realized afterwards that the person did not pay his zakât due to forgetfulness. Then it will be permissible for these people to give their zakât after the 'Eîd and it will be accepted from them because they are excused. The obligation is to pay it to those who deserve it on time or to give it to those who are in charge of distributing it to the poor before the 'Eîd prayer.

If you intended to give it to a specific person but could not find him or the one who will take it on his behalf, then you should give it to another person who deserves it and not delay it till after its time is over.

As for where to give the zakâtul-fitr, you are to pay it to the poor people of your land, where you are residing, whether you are residing there permanently or temporarily. Especially if the place is virtuous, like Mecca and Al-Madînah, or if the poor people of that country are in desperate need. If you are in a land where there is no one to take (the zakât Al-Fitr) because everyone is well off, you should entrust someone who lives in a place where there are poor people, in order that they may pay on your behalf.

Those who deserve the zakâtul-fitr are the poor and those who have debt that they cannot pay. They should be given the zakâtul-fitr according to their need.

Also, a box of zakâtul-fitr can be distributed to more than one poor man, and it can also be given to one poor man. This is because the Prophet (ﷺ) has specified the amount to be given, but did not portion out what to be given to the receivers. Based on this, it is permissible for a group of people to gather their zakâtul-fitr in one container and distribute it to the people without measuring it again. However, they should inform the receivers that they do not know the amount of the food that they gave them, because some of them may be deceived and then pay *their* zakât al-fitr with (what was given to them) without knowing its quantity (it may be less than a sâ).

It *is* permissible for the poor man to give zakâtul-fitr out of what he has received for himself or his family members after measuring it or being informed by the giver, whom he trusts, that it is (indeed) the right amount.

O Allāh grant us success to be obedient to You in a manner that will make You pleased with us. O Allāh, purify our souls, statements, and actions. O Allāh purify us from evil creed, statements, and actions. Verily You are the Most Generous, the Most Bounteous. O Allāh! Shower Your mercy and blessings on our Prophet Muhammad (*), his family members, and all his Companions.*

المجلس التاسع و الشرون
The Twenty Ninth Sitting
Repentance

All praises are due to Allâh, the One who placed in every creature a proof indicating Allâh's Oneness. He deals with His creatures as He wills out of His Might and Sovereignty. He chose the pious ones and bestowed on them security and faith. Due to His Forbearance and Mercy He immersed the sinners with pardon and forgiveness, not cutting off the provision of those who disobey Him out of His generosity and kindness. He relieves the sincere people with the breeze of closeness to Him, and He warned about the tremendous grief of the Day of Reckoning. He preserves the one who takes the path toward His pleasure (as he traverses within) his passageway. He honored the believer when He inscribed (pure) faith in his heart. He made the decision in His creatures so He commanded and prohibited. He strengthens with His support whatever becomes weak and He revives with His admonition the one who forgets and is neglectful. He invited the sinful person to repent for the forgiveness of his sins; a Great Lord who does not resemble the creatures. He is Independent and Bounteous. He does not need food or drink. The creatures are in constant need of Him, and are in dire need of His Mercy day and night. I praise Him the praise of one who truly worships His Lord, who confesses to his Creator, while asking forgiveness for his remissness and sin. I bear witness that none has the right to be worshipped but He alone, without a partner, the testimony of the one who is sincere from the bottom of his heart.

I also bear witness that Muhammad is His slave and His chosen Messenger, may peace and blessings of Allâh be upon him, Abû Bakr, his best companion, 'Umar the one whom the devil does not walk near, 'Uthmân the one who attained martyrdom, but not while in the rows (of a battlefield), 'Alî, his helper in battle, and

Sittings During the Blessed Month of Ramaḍān رَمَضَان

upon the Prophet's (ﷺ) family, his Companions, and whoever follows their guidance.

O My Brothers! Complete the month of Ramadân by repenting to Allâh from your sins and turn to Him by doing things that pleases Him. For indeed man is not free from error and remissness. All the children of Ādam are fallible, and the best of them are those who repent from their sins constantly. Allâh has indeed urged the people in His Book, likewise the Messenger (ﷺ) in his speeches to seek Allâh's forgiveness and repent to Him. As He (ﷻ) said:

$$﴿ وَأَنِ ٱسْتَغْفِرُوا۟ رَبَّكُمْ ثُمَّ تُوبُوٓا۟ إِلَيْهِ يُمَتِّعْكُم مَّتَٰعًا حَسَنًا إِلَىٰٓ أَجَلٍ مُّسَمًّى وَيُؤْتِ كُلَّ ذِى فَضْلٍ فَضْلَهُۥ ۖ وَإِن تَوَلَّوْا۟ فَإِنِّىٓ أَخَافُ عَلَيْكُمْ عَذَابَ يَوْمٍ كَبِيرٍ ﴾ (٣)$$

"And that you seek forgiveness of your Lord, and then turn to Him. He will provide for you a goodly provision until an appointed term. And He will grant His grace to everyone possessed of merit. And if you turn away, then surely I fear for you the punishment of a dreadful day" [Hûd: 3]

And His Statement, the Most High:

$$﴿ قُلْ إِنَّمَآ أَنَا۠ بَشَرٌ مِّثْلُكُمْ يُوحَىٰٓ إِلَىَّ أَنَّمَآ إِلَٰهُكُمْ إِلَٰهٌ وَٰحِدٌ فَٱسْتَقِيمُوٓا۟ إِلَيْهِ وَٱسْتَغْفِرُوهُ ۗ وَوَيْلٌ لِّلْمُشْرِكِينَ ﴾ (٦)$$

"Say, 'I am only a mortal like you. It is revealed to me that your god is One God; so go ye straight to Him without deviating, and ask forgiveness of Him.' And woe to the idolaters" [Fussilat: 6]

Likewise His Statement, the Most High:

﴿ وَتُوبُوٓا۟ إِلَى ٱللَّهِ جَمِيعًا أَيُّهَ ٱلْمُؤْمِنُونَ لَعَلَّكُمْ تُفْلِحُونَ ﴾ (٣١)

"And turn you to Allâh all together, O believers that you may prosper" [An-Nûr: 31]

And His statement (ﷺ):

﴿ يَٰٓأَيُّهَا ٱلَّذِينَ ءَامَنُوا۟ تُوبُوٓا۟ إِلَى ٱللَّهِ تَوْبَةً نَّصُوحًا عَسَىٰ رَبُّكُمْ أَن يُكَفِّرَ عَنكُمْ سَيِّـَٔاتِكُمْ وَيُدْخِلَكُمْ جَنَّٰتٍ تَجْرِى مِن تَحْتِهَا ٱلْأَنْهَٰرُ ﴾

"O you who believe! Turn to Allâh in sincere repentance. It may be that your Lord will remit the evil effects of your deeds and admit you into Gardens through which streams flow" [At-Tahrîm: 8]

And His statement (ﷺ):

﴿ إِنَّ ٱللَّهَ يُحِبُّ ٱلتَّوَّٰبِينَ وَيُحِبُّ ٱلْمُتَطَهِّرِينَ ﴾ (٢٢٢)

"Allâh loves those who constantly repent to him and those who purify themselves" [Al-Baqarah: 222]

There are many verses about repenting. As for the Prophetic narrations regarding this subject, we will mention the following:

It is narrated by Al-Agharrî bin Yasâr Al-Muzanî (ﷺ). He said the Prophet (ﷺ) said:

يا أيها الناس توبُوا إلى الله واستغفروه فإني أتوبُ في اليوم مائة مرة

"O people, repent to Allâh and ask for His forgiveness. For verily I repent a hundred times in a day" [Collected by Muslim]

It is also narrated that Abû Hurayrah (ﷺ) said that the Prophet (ﷺ) said:

إني لأستغفر الله وأتوبُ إليه في اليوم أكثر من سبعين مرة

"Surely, I seek Allâh's forgiveness and I repent to Him more than seventy times a day" [Collected by Al-Bukhârî]

It is also narrated by Anas (ﷺ) who said, the Prophet (ﷺ) said:

لَلّهُ أشدُ فرَحاً بتوبةِ عبدِه حين يتوبُ إليهِ من أحدِكم كان على راحلتِه بأرضِ فلاةٍ فانفلتت منهُ وعليها طعامُه وشرابُه، فَأيسَ منها فأتى شجرةً فاضطجعَ في ظلِّها وقد أيسَ من راحلتِه، فبينما هُو كذَلِكَ إذْ هو بها قائمةً عندَه فأخذَ بِخِطامها ثم قالَ من شدَّةِ الفرحِ: اللهُمَّ أنتَ عبدي وأنا ربُّك، أخطأ من شدَّةِ الفرحِ

"Allâh is happier with His slave's repentance when He repents to Him, than one of you who is traveling on his riding animal in a desert land. And (then all of a sudden) the riding animal slips away, taking off with his provisions of food and drink (on its back). Having lost all hope to get it back, he comes to a tree and lays down under its shade, losing all hope about his ride. All of a sudden, while he is in that state, he finds his riding animal standing in front of him. So he grabbed the rein of the ride and then out of boundless joy he said: 'O Allâh you are my slave and I am your Lord.' He committed this error out of extreme joy." [Collected by Muslim]

Allâh the Glorified, the Most High, is happy with His slave's repentance only because He loves to be repented to. He loves to forgive and He loves the returning of His slave to Him after the slave has run away.

It is also narrated by Anas and Ibn Abbâs (؄) that the Prophet (ﷺ) said:

لو أن لابن آدم وادياً من ذهبٍ أحبَّ أن يكونَ له وادِيَانِ، ولن يملأ فَاه إلاَّ التراب، ويتوبُ الله على من تاب

"If the son of Ādam had a valley filled with gold, he would desire another one. Nothing will fill his mouth but the dirt. And Allâh accepts the repentance of whoever turns to Him in repentance" [Collected by Al-Bukhârî and Muslim]

The term repentance (i.e "التوبة") means: returning from (the state of) being disobedient to Allâh to (the state) of being obedient to Allâh. This is because He (ﷺ) is the only true deity who deserves to be worshipped. And the reality of worship is by showing (complete) humility and humbleness to the (one true) Deity, with love and veneration. If the slave rebelled against his Lord, then his repentance is by returning back to Him, standing at His door, like the one in need, expressing humility, fear, and humbleness before his Lord.

It is obligatory to hasten towards repenting to Allâh. It is not permissible to delay repentance. This is because Allâh and His Messenger (ﷺ) have commanded us to repent. And all the commands of Allâh and His messenger must not be delayed; rather they must be executed immediately. The slave does not know what will happen to him in the future. Perhaps death will overtake him, placing a barrier between him and repentance. This is also because persisting upon committing sin leads to stoneheartedness. It keeps the heart far away from Allâh and weakens the faith. Indeed, faith increases with obedience and decreases with disobedience. Also, persisting upon committing sins leads to getting used to it and clinging to (that sin). And if the soul is accustomed to something it will make it more difficult to give it up. It will be hard on him to desist from it. Then the devil will open for him other doors of evil that are worse and more major than the one he is already committing. For this reason, the people of knowledge and the psychologist said: **"Sin is the path to disbelief. A person moves on in it from one level to another until he will totally deviate from his religion."** We ask Allâh (ﷻ) to grant us security and protection.

The repentance which Allâh has commanded us with is the sincere repentance that must meet the five conditions of repentance. They are as follows:

The First Condition: It must be done sincerely for Allâh, which means that the motivation to repent is the love and veneration of Allâh, while hoping for His reward and fearing His punishment. (The repenting person) does not intend with it anything from this world, or to be close to the creatures. And if those are his intentions, his repentance will not be accepted because he did not repent to Allâh, rather he repented to (obtain) his worldly goals.

The Second Condition: He must regret and be sad about his previous sins, wishing that he did not commit them, in order that this regret will motivate him to turn to Allâh with humility while being angry at his soul for it commanding him with this evil, so that his repentance will be based on belief and insight.

The Third Condition: He must desist from committing the sin immediately. If the sin is committing an abomination then he must desist from it, and if it is abandoning one of the obligations, then he must establish the obligation immediately as long as the obligation that he abandoned is something that can be made up, such as alms-giving and pilgrimage. Repentance will not be accepted if a person is persisted upon a sin. If he said for example: "I repent from dealing in interest" while he continues to deal in it, his repentance is not valid and this repentance of his is nothing but mocking Allâh and His verses. It will only keep him far away from his Lord. Likewise if he repented from not praying in congregation, while he continues not to pray in the congregation, his repentance is invalid.

If the sin that he commits relates to the rights of the people, then he must return their rights back to them. Otherwise his repentance is invalid. If he took someone's wealth or denied (someone wealth which they were entitled to), his repentance from it will not be valid until he returns the wealth back to its owner if he is alive or back to his heirs if he is dead. And if he does not have any heirs then he should return the wealth to the treasure of the Muslims. If he does not know the owner of the wealth, then he should give it away for charity and Allâh is aware of it. If he spoke ill of someone in their absence, he should go and ask for his forgiveness if the individual is aware of it or if he is afraid that he may be aware of it. Otherwise he can ask forgiveness for that individual and praise him with his praiseworthy attributes in the gathering where he sat and spoke ill of him before. For indeed good deeds repel the evil ones.

Repenting from a sin while committing a sin different from the one you repented from is valid. This is because deeds vary, and faith also varies in its levels. However in order for repentance to be considered complete and for an individual to deserve the praiseworthy attributes of the repentant ones and their high ranks, one must repent to Allâh from all sins.

The Fourth Condition: Having firm resolve to never return back to the sin in the future. This is the fruit of repentance and the proof of the truthfulness of the repenting person. If the person has repented while having the determination to commit sin (again in the future) or is reluctant to commit sin, then his repentance will not be valid. This repentance is a temporary repentance in which the repenting person is looking for a suitable chance to recommit the sin. It does not indicate his dislike of that sin and nor does it indicate that he has fled away from it to the obedience of Allâh.

The Fifth Condition: The repentance must be done before the deadline for the acceptance of repentance. If he repents after the deadline, his repentance will not be accepted.

The deadline for the repentance being accepted is of two kinds: the first deadline is the one which is general for everyone, and the second deadline is the one which is specific for every individual.

As for the general deadline it is the rising of the sun from the west. If the sun rises from the west, repentance will not be beneficial. Allâh the Most High said:

﴿ يَوْمَ يَأْتِي بَعْضُ ءَايَٰتِ رَبِّكَ لَا يَنفَعُ نَفْسًا إِيمَٰنُهَا لَمْ تَكُنْ ءَامَنَتْ مِن قَبْلُ أَوْ كَسَبَتْ فِىٓ إِيمَٰنِهَا خَيْرًا ﴾

"The Day when some of the Signs of your Lord shall come, it shall not profit a soul to believe, which had not believed before, nor earned any good by its faith." [Al-An'âm: 158]

What is intended by "some" of His signs is the rising of the sun from the west. This is the explanation of the Prophet (ﷺ). It is narrated that 'Abdullâh bin 'Amr bin Al-'Âs (ﷺ) said that the Prophet (ﷺ) said:

لا تزال التَّوبةُ تُقْبَلُ حتَّى تطلعَ الشَّمسُ من مغربِها، فإذا طلعت طُبعَ على كلِّ قلبٍ بما فيهِ وكفَى الناسَ العمل

"Repentance will continue to be accepted until the sun rises from the west. When the sun rises from the west every heart will be sealed by whatever occupies it. There will be no more deeds to be accepted from the people" [Ibn Kathîr said its chains of narration are sound]

It is also narrated by Abû Hurayrah (ﷺ) who said that the Prophet (ﷺ) said:

مَنْ تابَ قبلَ أَن تطلُعَ الشمس مِنْ مغربها تاب الله عليه

"Whoever repented before the rising of the sun from the west, Allâh will accept his repentance" [Collected by Muslim]

But as for the specific deadline, it is when a person's appointed term has arrived. Whenever a person's appointed term arrives and he sees death, his repentance will not benefit him and it will not be accepted from him. Allâh said:

﴿ وَلَيْسَتِ ٱلتَّوْبَةُ لِلَّذِينَ يَعْمَلُونَ ٱلسَّيِّئَاتِ حَتَّىٰٓ إِذَا حَضَرَ أَحَدَهُمُ ٱلْمَوْتُ قَالَ إِنِّى تُبْتُ ٱلْـَٔنَ وَلَا ٱلَّذِينَ يَمُوتُونَ وَهُمْ كُفَّارٌ أُو۟لَٰٓئِكَ أَعْتَدْنَا لَهُمْ عَذَابًا أَلِيمًا ۝ ﴾

"There is no acceptance of repentance for those who continue to do evil until, when death faces one of them, he says,' I indeed, do repent now'; nor for those who die disbelievers. It is these for whom We have prepared a painful punishment" [An-Nisâ: 18]

It is narrated by 'Abdullâh bin 'Umar bin Al-Khattâb (ﷺ) that the Prophet (ﷺ) said: **"Indeed Allâh accepts the repentance of the one who repents to Him as long as his soul did not reach the throat."** [Collected by Ahmad and At-Tirmidhî. Al-Albânî graded it to be sound in Sahîh At-Tirmidhî]

Whenever the repentance is valid with all the conditions fulfilled, and Allâh has accepted the repentance, Allâh will wipe away, with his repentance, the sin which he has repented from. Allâh, the Most High, said:

﴿ ۞ قُلْ يَٰعِبَادِيَ ٱلَّذِينَ أَسْرَفُوا۟ عَلَىٰٓ أَنفُسِهِمْ لَا تَقْنَطُوا۟ مِن رَّحْمَةِ ٱللَّهِ ۚ إِنَّ ٱللَّهَ يَغْفِرُ ٱلذُّنُوبَ جَمِيعًا ۚ إِنَّهُۥ هُوَ ٱلْغَفُورُ ٱلرَّحِيمُ ۝ ﴾

"Say, 'O My slaves who have wronged themselves, despair not of the mercy of Allâh. Surely, Allâh forgives all sins. Verily, He is Most Forgiving, Ever Merciful.'" [Az-Zumar: 53]

This verse is referring to those who turn to their Lord in repentance submitting to His will. Allâh the Most High said:

﴿ وَمَن يَعْمَلْ سُوٓءًا أَوْ يَظْلِمْ نَفْسَهُۥ ثُمَّ يَسْتَغْفِرِ ٱللَّهَ يَجِدِ ٱللَّهَ غَفُورًا رَّحِيمًا ۝ ﴾

"And who so does evil or wrongs his soul, and then asks forgiveness of Allâh, will find Allâh Most Forgiving, Merciful" [An-Nisâ: 110]

Therefore, hasten with your lives towards repenting to your Lord, may Allâh have mercy on you, before death overtakes you and you will afterwards not be able to rescue yourselves.

O Allâh grant us success towards sincere repentance that will wipe away our previous sins. (O Allâh) ease on us the path of ease; forgive us, our parents, and all the Muslims of the former and the latter generations, with Your mercy. You are the Most Merciful. May Peace and Blessings of Allâh be upon our Prophet Muhammad, his family members, and all his Companions.

المجلس الثلاثون
The Thirtieth Sitting
Pertaining to the End of Ramadân

Praise be to Allâh the Encompassing, the Great, the Generous, the Most Kind, the Most Merciful. He created everything and measured it, and sent down the legislation and eases it. He is the All-Wise, the All-Knowing. He began the creation and will end it. He placed the planets in motion and set them running,

$$\text{﴿ وَالشَّمْسُ تَجْرِي لِمُسْتَقَرٍّ لَهَا ذَلِكَ تَقْدِيرُ الْعَزِيزِ الْعَلِيمِ ۝ وَالْقَمَرَ قَدَّرْنَاهُ مَنَازِلَ حَتَّى عَادَ كَالْعُرْجُونِ الْقَدِيمِ ۝ لَا الشَّمْسُ يَنْبَغِي لَهَا أَنْ تُدْرِكَ الْقَمَرَ وَلَا اللَّيْلُ سَابِقُ النَّهَارِ وَكُلٌّ فِي فَلَكٍ يَسْبَحُونَ ۝ ﴾}$$

"And the sun runs [on course] toward its stopping point. That is the determination of the Exalted in Might, the Knowing, and the moon, We have determined for it phases, until it returns [appearing] like the old date stalk. It is not allowable for the sun to reach the moon, nor does the night overtake the day, but each, in an orbit, is swimming" [Yâsîn: 38-40]

I praise Him for His protection and guidance. I thank Him for what He has bestowed and what He has given. I further bear witness that none has the right to be worshipped but Him alone, The King, the Most High, the First, there is nothing before Him, the Last there is nothing after Him, the Most High there is nothing above Him, the Most Near, there is nothing nearer than Him and He is the Knower of all things. I also bear witness that Muhammad (ﷺ) is His slave and His chosen Messenger over the creatures. May peace be upon him, Abû Bakr, his companion, the best of the truthful ones, 'Umar the one who is known with strength in religion, 'Uthmân the one who was killed wrongfully at the hands of the criminals, upon 'Alî the closest one of them in kinship, and upon all his family, his Companions, and whoever follows their footsteps till the Day of Judgment.

O My Brothers! Indeed the departure of the month of Ramadân has approached and soon it will be over. This month will surely be either a witness for you or against you based on what you have deposited in it of deeds. Whoever deposited righteous deeds in this month, he should be grateful to Allâh and rejoice with a good reward. For indeed Allâh does not waste the reward of the one who fulfills His command in the best manner. Whoever deposited evil deeds in this month, he should turn to Allâh with sincere repentance, for indeed Allâh forgives whoever repents to him. Allâh has already legislated for you in the ending of this month of yours some acts of worship that brings you closer to Him, strengthens your faith, and makes your scales of good deeds heavy. He legislated for us the giving of zakâtul-fitr, and we have already addressed this in details. Likewise He legislated for you to venerate Him upon the completion of the month of Ramadân, from sunset till the feast prayer. Allâh said:

﴿وَلِتُكْمِلُوا۟ ٱلْعِدَّةَ وَلِتُكَبِّرُوا۟ ٱللَّهَ عَلَىٰ مَا هَدَىٰكُمْ وَلَعَلَّكُمْ تَشْكُرُونَ ۝١٨٥﴾

"That you may complete your counting of the month, and glorify Allâh for guiding you, and that you may be grateful to Him" [Al-Baqarah: 184]

The manner of this glorification is to say: "**Allâhu Akbar, Allâhu Akbar, Lâ-Ilâha Illa-llah, Wallâhu Akbar Allâh Akbar, walillahil-Hamd**" which means "Allâh is the Greatest, Allâh is the Greatest, None has the right to be worshipped but Him Alone, Allâh is the Greatest, Allâh is the Greatest, to Allâh belongs all praise."

It is from the Sunnah for men to proclaim it in the Masjids, in the markets, and in their houses demonstrating their veneration of Allâh, their worship of Him, and their gratefulness to Him. The women say it in a very low tone of voice because they are commanded with concealment and speaking in a low tone while in the presence of men.⁶

How beautiful is the condition of the people when glorifying Allâh and venerating Him in all places at the conclusion of their fast? They fill the horizon with their voices, glorifying Allâh, praising Him, and singling Him out alone with worship, while hoping for His Mercy and fearing His punishment.

Likewise Allâh, the Glorified, has legislated for His slaves the Feast prayer on the Day of the Feast. It is one of the most complete forms of remembering Allâh (ﷻ). The Prophet (ﷺ) has commanded his nation, both men and women, to establish it and his command must be fulfilled due to Allâh's statement:

---

⁶**Editor's Note:** Ash-Sheikh 'Abdul 'Azîz bin 'Abdullâh bin Bâz said concerning the group takbîr, in which everyone collectively, with a single voice, says the takbîr before the 'Eîd prayer or even after the daily prayers: "**The Congregational Takbîr is a newly introduced matter in the religion, therefore it is an innovation. And if the people do an act which opposes the pure legislation, it is obligatory to prevent them from doing so and to refute them. Worship must be derived from revelation, only that which the Qur'ân and the Sunnah point to is considered legislation. As for the statements and opinions of men, there is no evidence in them if they oppose the legislative proofs…That which is legislated concerning the takbîr, is that each Muslim says the Takbîr in a manner that has been narrated, (and that they say it) individually.**" Source: [http://www.binbaz.org.sa/mat/8690]

Sittings During the Blessed Month of Ramaḍān رَمَضَانَ

﴿ ۞ يَٰٓأَيُّهَا ٱلَّذِينَ ءَامَنُوٓاْ أَطِيعُواْ ٱللَّهَ وَأَطِيعُواْ ٱلرَّسُولَ وَلَا تُبۡطِلُوٓاْ أَعۡمَٰلَكُمۡ ۝ ﴾

"O you who believe! Obey Allâh and obey the Messenger and make not your works vain" [Muhammad: 33]

The Prophet (ﷺ) has commanded the women to attend the 'Eîd prayer, even though the best place for women is their homes. This occasion is an exception. The proof which supports this is the narration of Umm 'Atiyyah, May Allâh be pleased with her, who said:

أَمَرَنَا رسولُ الله صَلَّى اللهُ عَلَيْهِ وَسَلَّمَ أن نُخرِجهن في الفِطر والأضحى، العَوَاتِق والحُيَّض وذوات الخُدور، فأمَّا الحُيَّض فيعتزلْنَ المُصَلَّى ويشهدْنَ الخيرَ ودعوةَ المسلمين. قلتُ: يا رسولَ الله إحدانا لا يكونُ لها جلباب، قال: لِتُلْبِسْها أختها من جلبابها

"The Messenger of Allâh (ﷺ) commanded us to bring out on 'Eîd -al-Fitr and 'Eîd-al-Adhâ, young women, hijâb-observing adult women, and the menstruating women. The menstruating women stayed out of actual prayer area but participated in good deeds and supplication. I (Umm 'Atiyyah) said to the Prophet (ﷺ): 'Oh! Messenger of Allâh, one does not have an outer garment.' He replied, 'Let her sister cover her with her garment.'" [Collected by Al-Bukhârî and Muslim]

From among the highly recommended deeds of 'Eîd Al-Fitr is to eat a few dates in odds: three, five, or more before leaving for the prayer. The proof for this is the statement of Anas bin Mâlik (ﷺ) who said:

كان النبيُّ صَلَّى اللهُ عَلَيْهِ وَسَلَّمَ لا يَغْدُو يومَ الفطر حتى يأكل تمرات ويأكلهن وترا

"The Prophet (ﷺ) did not leave out for the prayer on the Day of 'Eîd Al-Fitr until he ate an odd number of dates." [Collected by Ahmad and Al-Bukhârî]

One should leave out walking on foot, not on a ride except if there was an excuse such as: disability or the remoteness of the place. The proof for that is the statement of 'Ali bin Abî Tâlib (رضي الله عنه): "From the Sunnah is walking on foot to the 'Eîd prayer." [At-Tirmidhî narrated this report with a weak chain. However due to corroborating narrations, the report is strengthened to the level of Hasan. See <u>Irwâ Al-Ghalîl</u> 636 and <u>The Rulings of the Two 'Eîds</u> by Al-Faryâbî page 102, 103]

It is also from the Sunnah for the men to beautify themselves on that day, putting on their best garment. This is based on the narration of 'Abdullâh bin 'Umar (رضي الله عنه) who said:

أَخَذَ عُمَرُ جبةً من إِسْتَبْرِقٍ – أي: حرير – تباعُ في السوق، فأتى بها رسول الله صَلَّى اللَّهُ عَلَيْهِ وَسَلَّمَ فقال: يا رسول ابْتَعْ هذِهِ (يعني اشْتَرِها) تَجَمَّل بها للعيد والوفودِ، فقال له رسول الله صَلَّى اللَّهُ عَلَيْهِ وَسَلَّمَ: " إنما هذِهِ لباسُ مَنْ لا خلاقَ له

"'Umar (رضي الله عنه) bought a garment made of silk from the market and brought it to the Prophet (ﷺ) and said: 'O Messenger of Allâh! Buy this garment from the market and adorn yourself with it on the day of 'Eîd and for when delegates visit.' So the Prophet (ﷺ) said: 'This dress is only for those who do not have any portion of the hereafter.'" [Collected by Al-Bukhârî and Muslim]

The Prophet (ﷺ) said this to 'Umar only because it is forbidden on men to adorn themselves with silk and gold. As for the woman they must leave their home for the prayer with an adornment that is not eye-catching, without putting on perfume, and without unveiling her body, because she is commanded to veil herself and is prohibited from displaying her charms and from putting on perfume when going out.

(The Muslim) must perform the 'Eîd prayer with tranquility and with full attention. He should remember Allâh often, invoking Him, hoping for His Mercy, and fearing His punishment. One should also remember the greatest Sitting in front of Allâh on the Day of Judgment. (This should come to his mind while he is gathered) with the people in the prayer area. Also consider their difference in virtue amongst themselves in this Sitting, and the even greater difference there will be in virtue in The Hereafter. Allâh (ﷻ) said:

﴿ ٱنظُرۡ كَيۡفَ فَضَّلۡنَا بَعۡضَهُمۡ عَلَىٰ بَعۡضٖۚ وَلَلۡأٓخِرَةُ أَكۡبَرُ دَرَجَٰتٖ وَأَكۡبَرُ تَفۡضِيلٗا ۝ ﴾

"Behold, how We have exalted some of them over others in the present life; and surely the Hereafter shall be greater in degrees of rank and greater in excellence" [Al-Isrâ: 21]

(A Muslim) should be happy with Allâh's Bounty upon Him for allowing him to reach the month of Ramadân and for granting him success to keep up with the prayer, fasting, recitation of the Qur'ân, charity, and other than that from among the righteous deeds. For indeed it is better for him than the world and whatsoever is in it.

﴿ قُلۡ بِفَضۡلِ ٱللَّهِ وَبِرَحۡمَتِهِۦ فَبِذَٰلِكَ فَلۡيَفۡرَحُواْ هُوَ خَيۡرٞ مِّمَّا يَجۡمَعُونَ ۝ ﴾

"Say: '[All this is] through the grace of Allâh and through His mercy; therein, therefore, let them rejoice. That is better than what they hoard.'" [Yûnus: 58]

رَمَضَان Sittings During the Blessed Month of Ramaḍān

Indeed standing in prayer, during the nights of Ramaḍân, with faith and sincerity, is among the ways in which sins are forgiven, and (it is a means) of gaining salvation from them as well. Therefore the true believer is happy for completing his fast and his night prayer, in order for him to be purified from his sins.

As for the one who is weak in his faith, he is happy for the completion of Ramaḍân in order to be done with the fast which was a burden upon him and (a cause for) uneasiness and discomfort in his heart. The difference between these two groups is huge.

O my brothers! Know that, although the month of Ramaḍân is over, the believer's deeds must never end as long as he is alive. Allâh (ﷻ) said:

$$﴿ وَٱعْبُدْ رَبَّكَ حَتَّىٰ يَأْتِيَكَ ٱلْيَقِينُ ۝ ﴾$$

"Worship your Lord until certainty (i.e. death) overtakes you." [Al-Hijr: 99]

Also His statement, the Most High:

$$﴿ يَـٰٓأَيُّهَا ٱلَّذِينَ ءَامَنُوا۟ ٱتَّقُوا۟ ٱللَّهَ حَقَّ تُقَاتِهِۦ وَلَا تَمُوتُنَّ إِلَّا وَأَنتُم مُّسْلِمُونَ ۝ ﴾$$

"O you who believe fear Allâh as He deserves to be feared, and die not except in the state of Al-Islâm" [Āli 'Imrân: 101]

The Prophet (ﷺ) said:

$$إذا مات العبدُ انقطعَ عملُه$$

"When the slave dies, his deeds will be cut off." [Graded authentic by Al-Albânî in Saḥîḥ Al-Adab Al-Mufrad]

The Prophet (ﷺ) has not placed an end to deeds except with the arrival of death.

Even though fasting the month of Ramadân is over, the believer will not stop fasting due to that. This is because fasting remains legislated throughout the year and all praise is due to Allâh for that. It is narrated by Abû Ayyûb Al-Ansârî (﵁) who said that the Prophet (ﷺ) said:

من صامَ رمضانَ ثم أتْبعه ستاً من شوالٍ كان كصيام الدهر

"Whoever fasted the month of Ramadân and then follows it with six days of fasting in Shawwâl, it is as if he fasted the entire year." [Collected by Muslim]

It is also legislated for us to fast three days in every month. The Prophet (ﷺ) said:

ثلاث من كل شهر ورمضان إلى رمضان فهذا صيام الدهر كله

"Fasting three days in every month and fasting from one Ramadân to another, this is fasting the entire year." [Collected by Ahmad and Muslim]

Abû Hurayrah (﵁) said: "**My bosom friend (i.e. Prophet Muhammad (ﷺ)) has strongly advised me with three things.**" From amongst the three things which (the Prophet ﷺ) mentioned was to fast three days of every month. It is preferable for it to be on the thirteenth, the fourteenth, and the fifteenth of the lunar calendar. The proof for this preference is the narration of Abû Dharr (﵁) that the Prophet (ﷺ) said:

رَمَضَان Sittings During the Blessed Month of Ramaḍān

$$\text{يا أبا ذرٍّ إذا صمت من الشهر ثلاثةً فصُم ثلاثَ عشرةَ وأربعَ عشرة وخمسَ عشرة}$$

"O Abû Dharr! If you intend to fast three days of the month, then fast the thirteenth, the fourteenth and the fifteenth." [Collected by Ahmad, An-Nasâ'î and Ibn Hibbân. Al-Albânî graded it sound in Irwâ Al-Ghalîl]

In Saḥîḥ Muslim, it is also narrated that the Prophet (ﷺ) was asked about fasting the Day of 'Arafah, and he replied:

$$\text{يُكَفِّرُ السنةَ الماضيةَ والباقيةَ}$$

"It expiates the sins of the previous year and the future year." [Collected by Muslim]

Likewise he was asked about fasting the Day of 'Āshûrah and he replied: **"It expiates the sins of the previous year."** [Collected by Muslim]

He was also asked about fasting on Mondays and he replied: **"It is the day in which I was born, and the day the Qur'ân was revealed to me."** [Collected by Muslim]

Also in Saḥîḥ Muslim it is narrated by Abû Hurayrah (ﷺ) that the Prophet (ﷺ) was asked: "Which is the best fasting after the fasting of Ramaḍân?" He replied:

$$\text{أفضلُ الصيامِ بعد شهرِ رمضانَ صيامُ شهرِ اللهِ المحرم}$$

"The best fast after the fast of the Month of Ramaḍân is fasting in the month of Allâh Al-Muharram." [Collected by Muslim]

Sittings During the Blessed Month of Ramaḍān رَمَضَان

It is narrated in Al-Bukhârî and Muslim on the authority of 'Āîshah, may Allâh be pleased with her, that she said:

ما رأيتُ النبيَّ صَلَّى اللَّهُ عَلَيْهِ وَسَلَّمَ اسْتَكْمَلَ شهراً قطُّ إلاَّ شهرَ رمضانَ، وما رأيتُه في شهرٍ أكثرَ صياماً منه في شعبانَ، وفي لفظ: كان يصومُه إلاَّ قليلاً

"I have not seen the Prophet (ﷺ) completing an entire month with fasting except the month of Ramaḍân; and I have not seen him fasting in any months besides Ramaḍân more than he fasts in the month of Sha'bân." In another narration it says, "He used to fast the month of Sha'ban with the exception of a few (days)." [Collected by Al-Bukhârî and Muslim]

It is also narrated by 'Āîshah, may Allâh be pleased with her, that:

كانَ النَّبِيُّ صَلَّى اللَّهُ عليهِ وسلَّمَ يتحرَّى صومَ الاثنينِ والخَميسِ

"The Prophet (ﷺ) used to seek out fasting on Mondays and Thursdays" [Al-Albânî graded it to be authentic in Saḥîḥ At-Tirmidhî]

It is narrated by Abû Hurayrah (ﷺ) that the Prophet (ﷺ) said:

تُعْرَضُ الأعمالُ يومَ الاثنينِ والخَميسِ فأحبُّ أن يُعْرَضَ عملي وأنا صائم

"Deeds are presented to Allâh every Monday and Thursday. So I want my deeds to be presented while I am fasting" [Graded authentic by Al-Albânî in Saḥîḥ At-Tirmidhî and Saḥîḥ At-Targhîb]

Though the night prayer during the month of Ramadân is over, the night prayer remains legislated throughout the nights of the year and all praises are due to Allâh. This is a prophetic tradition that has been established both from the statements and actions of the Prophet (ﷺ). It is narrated in Sahîh Al-Bukhârî on the authority of Al-Mughirah bin Shu'bah (ﷺ) who said:

إن كانَ النبيُّ صلَّى اللَّهُ عَلَيْهِ وَسَلَّمَ لَيَقُومُ أَو لَيُصَلِّي حَتَّى تَرِمَ قَدَمَاه، فيقالُ لَهُ فيقولُ: " أَفَلاَ أَكونُ عبداً شكوراً؟

"The Prophet (ﷺ) would stand at night in prayer until his feet would swell up and it would be said to him '(Ease on yourself).' He would reply, 'Will I not be a grateful slave?'" [Collected by Al-Bukhârî]

It is also narrated by 'Abdullâh bin Salâm (ﷺ) that the Prophet (ﷺ) said:

أيُّها الناسُ أفشوا السلام وأطعموا الطعام وصِلُوا الأرحام وصَلُّوا بالليل والناس نيام تدخلوا الجنة بسلام

"O people! Spread the salâm, feed the poor, keep the ties, and pray in the night while the people are sleeping, you will enter the paradise of your Lord with peace" [Graded authentic by Al-Albânî in Sahîh At-Targhîb]

It is also narrated by Abû Hurayrah (ﷺ) that the Prophet (ﷺ) said:

أفضلُ الصلاةِ بعد الفريضة صلاة الليل

"The best Prayer after the obligatory prayers is the night prayer." [Collected by Muslim]

The night prayer includes all the supererogatory prayers (that are prayed at night) along with the witr prayer. (One should pray two units at a time), and if you fear the entering of the dawn prayer then you should pray one unit, making odd the total of number of units prayed (that night). And if one wills he can pray according to what was previously explained in the fourth sitting.

It is narrated by Abû Hurayrah (ﷺ) that the Prophet (ﷺ) said:

يَنْزِلُ رَبُّنا تباركَ وتعالى كلَّ ليلةٍ إلى السماءِ الدنيا حينَ يبقى ثلثُ الليلِ الآخِرِ فيَقولُ: مَنْ يدعوني فأَسْتجيبَ له؟ مَن يسأَلُني فأعطيه؟ من يستغفرُني فأغفرَ له؟

"Our Lord, the Glorified, the Most High descends every night to the lower heaven when only one third of the night remains, and He says: 'Who will invoke Me so I can answer his invocation? Who will ask Me so that I will give him what he asks? Who will seek My forgiveness so that I will forgive him?'" [Collected by Al-Bukhârî and Muslim]

The voluntary prayers that follow the obligatory prayers are twelve units. Four before the Midday prayer, two after the midday prayer, two after Sunset Prayer, two after the Evening Prayer, and two before the morning prayer.

It is narrated by Umm Habîbah, May Allâh be pleased with her, who said, "I heard the Prophet (ﷺ) saying:

رَمَضَان Sittings During the Blessed Month of Ramaḍān

ما من عبد مسلم يصلِّي لله تعالى كلَّ يومٍ ثِنْتَيْ عشرة ركعة تطوعا غير فريضة إلا بنى الله له بيتاً في الجنة "، وفي لفظ: " من صلَّى ثِنْتَي عشرةَ ركعةً في يومٍ وليلة بُنِيَ له بِهن بيتٌ في الجنة

"There is no slave who will pray twelve units voluntarily every day, for the sake of Allâh, except that Allâh will build for him a house in Paradise." [Collected by Muslim]

Also Allâh has commanded (the believers), in His Book, to remember and glorify Him after the five daily prayers. The Messenger of Allâh (ﷺ) has encouraged to do the same. Allâh, the Most High, said:

﴿ فَإِذَا قَضَيْتُمُ ٱلصَّلَوٰةَ فَٱذْكُرُوا۟ ٱللَّهَ قِيَٰمًا وَقُعُودًا وَعَلَىٰ جُنُوبِكُمْ فَإِذَا ٱطْمَأْنَنتُمْ فَأَقِيمُوا۟ ٱلصَّلَوٰةَ إِنَّ ٱلصَّلَوٰةَ كَانَتْ عَلَى ٱلْمُؤْمِنِينَ كِتَٰبًا مَّوْقُوتًا ﴿١٠٣﴾ ﴾

"And when you have finished the Prayer, remember Allâh, standing and sitting, and laying on your sides. And when you are secure from danger, then observe Prayer in the prescribe form; verily Prayer is enjoined on the believers to be performed at fixed hours" [An-Nisâ: 103]

Whenever the Prophet (ﷺ) used to finish his prayer, he would ask (Allâh) for forgiveness three times and would say: "O **Allâh** You are Salâm (i.e. free from any deficiency) wa minkas-salâm (i.e. security is obtained from You) Glorified You are 'from all that they attributed to You' O Owner of Might and Bounty." [Collected by Muslim]

Sittings During the Blessed Month of Ramaḍān رَمَضَانْ

Likewise the Prophet (ﷺ) said:

من سبَّح الله في دُبُرِ كلِّ صلاةٍ ثلاثاً وثلاثين، وحمد الله ثلاثا وثلاثين، وكبَّر الله ثلاثاً وثلاثين فتلك تِسْعةٌ وتسعون، ثم قالَ تمام المائة: لا إله إلا الله وحده لا شريك له، له الملك وله الحمد وهو على كلِّ شيء قدير غُفِرَت خطاياه وإن كانت مثل زَبَدِ البحر

"Whoever glorified Allâh (i.e. saying subhânAllâh) at the ending of every prayer thirty three times and praised Allâh (i.e. saying Alhamdulillah) thirty three times and venerated (i.e saying Allâh Allâhu Akbar) thirty three times, and then said at the completion of a hundred 'none has the right to be worshipped but Allâh Alone without a partner, to Him belongs the kingdom, and to Him belongs the praise and He is able to do all things,' (the person who says this) his sins will be forgiven even if they are like the foam of the ocean." [Collected by Muslim]

O My brothers! Strive earnestly in doing good deeds. And stay away from sins and shortcomings in order that you will be successful with a pleasant life in this world and with a great reward in the hereafter. Allâh (ﷻ) said:

﴿ مَنْ عَمِلَ صَٰلِحًا مِّن ذَكَرٍ أَوْ أُنثَىٰ وَهُوَ مُؤْمِنٌ فَلَنُحْيِيَنَّهُۥ حَيَوٰةً طَيِّبَةً ۖ وَلَنَجْزِيَنَّهُمْ أَجْرَهُم بِأَحْسَنِ مَا كَانُوا۟ يَعْمَلُونَ ۝ ﴾

"Whoso acts righteously, whether male or female and is a believer, We will surely grant him a pure life; and We will surely bestow on such their reward according to the best of their works" [An-Nahl: 97]

O Allâh! Keep us firm upon faith, righteous deeds, grant us a pleasant life, and join us with the righteous. All praise belongs to Allâh, the Lord of the Worlds. (May the) peace and blessings be upon our Prophet Muhammad, his family, and all his companions.

To here we have arrived at the end of what we intended to write. We ask Allâh (ﷻ) to make our deeds sincerely for His sake, bringing us closer to Him. (Likewise we ask Allâh to make our work) beneficial for the slaves, to protect us in this world and in the hereafter, and to guide us to the truth of which the people have differed by His will. Indeed He guides whom He wills to the straight path.

The writing of this book was completed on Friday the 29th of Muharram in the year 1396, at the hands of its author, Muhammad bin Sâlih bin Al-Uthaymîn, the one who is in need of his Protector. All praises belong to Allâh, The Lord of the worlds. And may peace be upon our Prophet Muhammad, his family, and all his companions.

Other Books from Riwayah Publishing......

The Explanation of Al-Hâiyah

By Dr. Sâlih Al-Fawzân

The Disappearance of Knowledge

By Muhammad Al-Imām

20 Pieces of Advice to My Sister before Her Marriage

by Badr bin Ai Al-Utaybī

The Correct Creed that Every Muslim Must Believe

by Abdus Salām Burjis

The Explanation of the Foundations of the Sunnah

by Dr. Rabī' bin Hadī Al-Madkalī

Expl. of the Hadīth of the Man Who killed 99 Men

by An-Nawawī, Al-Uthaymīn, and Salīm Al-Hilālī

NOTES

NOTES

NOTES